Frederic Harrison

Twayne's English Authors Series

Herbert Sussman, Editor

Northeastern University

TEAS 341

FREDERIC HARRISON
(1831–1923)
Reproduction of frontispiece photograph
from Frederic Harrison's Autobiographic
Memoirs, Vol. I, authorized by Macmillan
and Company, Limited, London.

Frederic Harrison

By Harry R. Sullivan

University of South Carolina

Twayne Publishers · Boston

To Ramona

Frederic Harrison

Harry R. Sullivan

Copyright © 1983 by G. K. Hall & Company
All Rights Reserved
Published by Twayne Publishers
A Division of G. K. Hall & Company
70 Lincoln Street
Boston, Massachusetts 02111

Book Production by Marne B. Sultz
Book Design by Barbara Anderson

Printed on permanent/durable acid-free
paper and bound in the United States of
America.

Library of Congress Cataloging in Publication Data

Sullivan, Harry R., 1916–
    Frederic Harrison.

    (Twayne's English authors series ;
    TEAS 341)
    Bibliography: p. 198
    Includes index.
    1. Harrison, Frederic, 1831–1923
—Criticism and interpretation. 2. Positivism.
I. Title. II. Series.
PR4759.H4Z87   1983   192   82-15621
ISBN 0-8057-6827-0

Contents

About the Author

Harry Richards Sullivan received the B.A. degree in English from Louisiana State University, the M.A. degree from Stanford University, and the Ph.D. from the University of Georgia. He has done graduate study at the University of Toronto. His publications include articles and reviews in the related fields of literature and history, mainly in the nineteenth century in England and America, as well as a book on Walter Bagehot for Twayne's English Authors Series. Of particular interest to him over the years have been the works of John Cowper Powys, with whom he privately corresponded for about five years before Powys's death.

Preface

The name of Frederic Harrison is usually associated with the Positivist movement in England during the latter half of the nineteenth century, and quite rightly so. It is hard for us today to realize how seriously this intellectual movement was taken then, for it was perhaps as vital an issue as Marxism. Harrison, by no means the only important defender of Positivist principles, was perpetually involved in controversy with many Victorian intellectuals whose names have become legendary. This nineteenth-century French ideology very likely thrived in England simply because it fortunately found there, in addition to Harrison, such able advocates as Harriet Martineau, George Henry Lewes, George Eliot, and John Stuart Mill (for a considerable period of time). And there were those who, like Harrison, actually became members of the Positivist Society, such as Professor Richard Congreve, Professor E. S. Beesly, Dr. John Bridges, Vernon Lushington, and J. Cotter Morrison. Perhaps as important for the continued vitality of the movement were the distinguished opponents it aroused, such as John Stuart Mill (who later quarreled with Comte), Thomas Henry Huxley, Herbert Spencer, R. H. Hutton, Fitzjames Stephen, Mark Pattison, John Ruskin, and Matthew Arnold, not to mention many another just below the level of general recognition today.

As shall be seen in the following pages, Harrison was no mean antagonist for his rather formidable critics, many of whom have been well established as adept at controversy and debate. Oddly enough, nearly all his opponents were either friends or friendly acquaintances, many of whom served on committees with him, joined in various other causes with him, or were simply personal friends. And even though they might be ideological combatants, they were virtually never personally antagonistic.

I have devoted three chapters to clarify those ideas forming the basis of Harrison's thoughts and beliefs on virtually all important matters, public or private, be they scientific, political, social, educational, literary, or religious. But I shall investigate no aspect of Positivism that is not relevant to Harrison's very active involvement in Victorian life. I shall devote less space to his many contributions to public affairs in England than they deserve in order to spend as much time as possible on his important literary activities. But not to clarify sufficiently the elaborate and all-encompassing philosophy of Positivism would be like writing a study of St. Paul without investigating the tenets of Christianity or considering the central role of Christ. We allude to and quote from Auguste Comte, the founder of Positivism in France, just enough to illustrate the impact of his thought on Harrison and to make the reader conscious of parallels and divergencies between them.

Perhaps honoring Harrison's request that no biography be written on him, his son Austin wrote a valuable volume on his impressions of his father but not a systematic study and certainly not a biography. I begin with a biographical chapter to give a general idea of the varied activities of his life, including his travels, his involvement in public affairs, his friendships and associations, his role in the Positivist Society, and, of course, his constant writing on a variety of subjects. In addition to the chapters on the scientific, religious, and social philosophy of Positivism, I devote the final chapters to his specifically literary activities. His literary estimates are by no means beneath notice even today. As with much of his Positivist thought, many of his literary judgments have become common staple in our century and have lost the identity of their origin. It may seem that I have given his own creative literary efforts more attention than they merit, but they serve better to acquaint the reader with his intense preoccupation with the human side of the important culture of the Byzantine Empire that, until his own century, had been largely ignored by historians. He thought that a treatment of it in terms of tragic human drama would serve his purpose better than the historical monograph he had originally planned.

Harrison tilted with such Victorian giants as Huxley, Arnold, Spencer, Ruskin, Mark Pattison, and R. H. Hutton on even terms. His style becomes especially witty and ironic, but never sardonic, when he jousts with an opponent, be it on a literary, philosophical, political, or religious problem, and insofar as space has allowed, I have tried to illustrate his very distinctive, albeit quite Victorian, personality. He felt much akin intellectually to the great Victorian Agnostics, but he found his faith and repose in a philosophy, a religion, made possible, for the first time, in the nineteenth century. Here was a true Victorian Compromise between Science and Religion, a union of the spiritual and the rational. These were two very strong sides of his own nature, which Positivism seemed to satisfy. Positivism was, for him, the ultimate triumph of Humanism.

Harry R. Sullivan

University of South Carolina

Chronology

1831   Frederic Harrison born in London on October 18, 1831, the eldest living son (the first having died in infancy); five boys and no girls.

1837   Saw coronation of Queen Victoria, his first impression of public life.

1841   Placed for two years in day school of Joseph King, whom he always treasured as the ideal teacher.

1843   Enrolled in King's College School, where he remained until 1849 and where he met friends who would later become prominent in the life of the country.

1849   Entered Wadham College, Oxford, where his favorite tutor was Richard Congreve, later founder of the Positivist movement in England, and where Mumbo-Jumbo was formed with friends who would later join him in the movement.

1853   Received the B.A. degree and remained at Oxford two more years, postponing his study of law; became librarian of the Union Society and tutor.

1855   Met Auguste Comte in Paris for the first and only time, the most important interview of his life. Declined to take Holy Orders and began the study of law at Lincoln's Inn, where he remained until 1858.

1857   Visited Richard Congreve constantly, read Comte's *Positivist Catechism*, and began teaching at the Workingmen's College with Ruskin and others.

1858   Called to the bar.

1859   Formed committee for Italian independence.

1860   Visited the English Lakes, the Yorkshire moors, and architectural monuments.

1861   Became intensely interested and involved in labor problems.

1862   First visited Ruskin. *The Meaning of History* published (enlarged in 1894).

1865   Wrote article for the first issue of the new *Fortnightly Review* (and at least one article for each succeeding year); joined the Alpine Club and ascended Mount Blanc and many other formidable mountains; began his friendship with John Stuart Mill (which lasted until Mill's death in 1873).

1867   His *Six Letters on Martial Law* published by the Jamaica Committee during agitation over Governor Eyre. Put on the Royal Commission for Trades-Unions.

1868   Adopted the Positivist faith; attended lectures by Huxley.

1870   Married his cousin, Jane Harrison, having long planned to marry her when she should become old enough. The Chapel Street group of Positivists founded by Richard Congreve.

1871   Became one of the original members of the Metaphysical Society (introduced by Lord Alfred Russell), where he debated for years with the leading intellectuals of Great Britain.

1875   Completed and published his translation of *Social Statics*, the second volume of Comte's *Positive Polity*.

1877   Became correspondent for the *Times* in France and became heavily involved in French politics.

1878   Elected to the Athenaeum Club, having been proposed by John Morley.

1881   Visited Greece, Egypt, and Turkey, often being reminded of Byron and Homer. The Newton Hall group of Positivists founded, of which Harrison was made president.

1882   Published his *National and Social Problems*, the principles from which Gladstone said he would be guided by.

1886   Published *The Choice of Books*.

1892   Edited and partly wrote *The New Calendar of Great Men*.

1893   The *Positivist Review* was founded.

1895   Published *Studies in Early Victorian Literature*.

1898 Represented England at the Congress of Historians at the Hague and was made an honorary president there.

1899 Published *Tennyson, Ruskin, Mill.*

1900 Delivered and later published the Rede Lecture at Cambridge, entitled *Byzantine History of the Early Middle Ages*; here he was invited by the American ambassador to give the address on Washington's birthday at the Union Club at Chicago.

1901 Attended funeral of Queen Victoria and visited America, where he was lionized; met famous Americans in many fields. Published *George Washington and Other Addresses.*

1902 Moved to Hawkhurst, Kent, where he lived until 1912. Published *John Ruskin* in the *English Men of Letters Series.*

1904 Published *Theophano: The Crusade of the Tenth Century. A Romantic Monograph.*

1906 Published *Nicephorus—A Tragedy of New Rome* and *Memories and Thoughts.*

1907 Published *The Creed of a Layman* and *The Philosophy of Common Sense.*

1908 Published *My Alpine Jubilee* and *Realities and Ideals.*

1910 Made president of the Eastern Questions Association, which expressed the policy Harrison had advocated for fifty-five years on the Ottoman Empire.

1911 Published *Autobiographic Memoirs* in two volumes.

1912 Moved from Kent to Bath, where he spent the remaining years of his life.

1923 Died on January 13 of a sudden failure of the heart as he was correcting proofs of his *De Senectute*, which was published posthumously.

List of Abbreviations

Chapter One
Biography of an Active Victorian

Introduction

If anyone knows anything at all about Frederic Harrison, it would probably be that he was the leading British Positivist during the latter years of the nineteenth and the early years of the twentieth centuries. He is as closely associated with Positivism as Thomas Henry Huxley with Darwinian evolution. However, although much modified, Darwinian evolution has persisted to the present time, whereas Positivism has passed into other streams of thought and thus has lost its specific identity. Its fate has been rather like that of third-party movements in the United States, which generally become absorbed into the programs of the two larger parties. The contributions of Norman Thomas, the Socialist, and Frederic Harrison, respectively, have undoubtedly been considerable, but their fame has faded with the disintegration of the specific identity of their respective creeds.

But, unlike Norman Thomas, Harrison is noteworthy for many other reasons than his reputation as the leading British Positivist, or Comtist, important though he was in this capacity. It is not sufficiently realized how instrumental he was in the attainment of legal recognition for labor unions in Britain and in the passage of legislation for the working classes, in general. Never just the theoretician, he knew intimately most of the leading workmen and economists in the England of the middle and latter nineteenth century. Despising mere pedantry, he was convinced that political economy is worth very little if it be not based on personal knowledge and experience. A thousand blue-books would not have taught him what he learned from the Rochedale Pioneers, trades-union congresses, union committees, and international congresses. Rather like the think-tank men of Laputa devising methods of extracting sunbeams from cucumbers, those economists and bureaucrats, who do not scruple to regulate the lives of countless human beings, have themselves, all too often, scant personal knowledge of a single workman or a single fact in a workman's life, as Harrison explains in *Memories and Thoughts*.[1]

Not content merely to read about the great issues of the day, Harrison actually traveled to Italy to study firsthand the crisis there in the period of 1860, meeting and conversing with Mazzini, Garibaldi, Farini, and Pepoli. In the same way, he studied the communal insurrection of 1871 in France, conversing with Gambetta and most of the leaders of the republican and socialist parties in that country. Nothing could take the place of his personal intercourse with such leading men of the latter half of the nineteenth century as, for example, Renan, Michelet, Louis Blanc, and Comte in France; Francis Newman, G. H. Lewes and George Eliot, John Bright, John Stuart Mill, Carlyle, John Ruskin, Cardinal Manning, Herbert Spencer, John Morley, and Gladstone in England. His relation with these men was by no means merely a random interview, the sort of thing that he terms "a silly and odious habit of our day" (*M&T*, 13).

As a prodigious contributor to the leading periodicals of the age, he frequently debated timely issues of education, religion, science, politics, and philosophy with leaders in those respective fields. Although he admits to having a dash of the Jacobin in himself that may not be amenable to pure literature, he nevertheless tried his hand as an amateur at writing both a tragedy and an historical romance.[2] And his writing on political and historical subjects was seriously read and debated then, and has not been entirely forgotten today. Acutely conscious of his ungovernable urge to teach his fellow men, he perhaps too modestly concedes that he took slight care for style and that never for an hour was he seriously concerned with literary success. He indulged in his attempts at creative writing very much "as a man turns to a game of billiards or to gardening after his day's work" (*M&T*, 15–16).

Living to 1923, Harrison could look back to the coronation of Queen Victoria in 1837, an experience which was his first distinct impression of public life. He was able to recall Wellington and other heroes of Waterloo as he saw them on that "most wonder-stirring day" (*M&T*, 2). He was told how the Abbey and the Hall at West-minster had been built by the men of the Crusades and had been the scene of the coronation of many kings and queens over the centuries. For the first time, as a child in 1837, he became aware of the enchantment of the development of history, which would become one of the principal preoccupations of his life as a heart-and-soul Posi-tivist. Unlike the American people, whose civilization is the work of only several generations, the British, as Harrison is fully cognizant, grow up in their small, densely populated island with the sense of an old order surrounding them from early childhood.

As one of the last of the eminent Victorians, Harrison recalls the days of the rotten boroughs, when omnibuses, cabs, and policemen were seen for the first time and were considered to be new-fangled—the era of Pickwick, as Harrison says. It was a world without railways, the telegraph, fire brigades, central water supplies, or main sewers. Slavery still existed in the colonies, India was governed by a private company, and innumerable men were still hanged for a variety of reasons, including forgery. Southey was the poet-laureate, and Cole-ridge and Scott still lived. Macaulay, Carlyle, Dickens, Thackeray, and Darwin were yet unknown. Many men still alive could remember Washington and Jefferson, and his own father could recall the ex-ploits of Lord Nelson. These were the days of Metternich, Czar Nicholas I, and Louis Philippe (*M&T*, 2−3).

Harrison lived through the era of technological progress that followed the dissolution of the old absolutism in Europe after 1830, with the development of railways, steam navigation across the oceans, great megapolises, the telegraph, the dominions and colonies throughout the world, and popular literature and journalism. Also, he was contemporaneous with the succession of the three great Re-form Bills, so fundamental to the political and social history of nineteenth-century England. Few Victorians played a more active role in the vital controversies of the latter half of the century than Harrison—so little known now, so deeply involved and prominent then. Nevertheless, the present-day world is clearly discernible in the Victorian, when the modes of contemporary life first became clearly recognizable, for the Victorians were undoubtedly the first moderns. The impingement of science, technology, and industry had already affected every aspect of life: practical, intellectual, and religious. And Harrison lived through the transition from the old world into the first quarter of our century.

John Stuart Mill, after first reading Bentham, discovered an object in life: namely, "to be a reformer of the world."[3] Similarly, Harrison came to believe that the entire purpose of his life was to espouse the cause of Positivism as a solution of the world's problems. He was too deadly in earnest to be either a man of letters or an active politician: "But the demon soon rises, and I find myself in earnest trying to bring men over to our side" (*M&T*, 15–16). Like Ruskin, Carlyle, and Mill, Harrison could well be called a "Victorian lay-prophet." If moral earnestness was one of the most identifiable Victorian characteristics, Harrison qualified as much as any other contemporary.

The Victorians combined the sense of duty and moral earnestness with faith in the freedom of thought; they had high hopes that society could be reconstituted on the basis of reason. In Positivism, Harrison saw the possibility of a new affirmation, a synthesis of those virtues that he thought were the foundations of civilization and the huge possibilities that the rapid development of science was bringing into view. As passionately as Marx, he believed in the inevitability of historical evolution. He defended his beliefs against the most formidable thinkers of the age, confident that he understood the drift of the modern world and the necessary change in viewpoint toward its problems. As forceful and positive as Carlyle, yet as reasonable and conscientious as Mill, he courageously advanced his own beliefs openly and honestly.

His son Austin Harrison writes in *Frederic Harrison*[4] that he was a completely normal man, with no secrets and nothing in the past to be ashamed of. "He said he never smoked a pipe or got drunk, and had nothing to retract or to regret" (*FH*, 31). Gertrude Himmelfarb writes that the Victorians, both believers and unbelievers, intensified a dependence on moral zeal. She quotes Mill to the effect that the best of the unbelievers were actually more religious, in the best sense of the word, than those who so called themselves. She then concludes that no wonder such people felt a need to turn to a Religion of Humanity.[5] In this pursuit, none was more ardent than Harrison. After slowly but surely having assimilated the philosophy of Auguste Comte, he remained as dedicated to his newly adopted religion as John Henry Newman did to his. The study of no other Victorian reveals the crisis-of-faith dilemma more thoroughly: his moral ardor is the more intense for having moved from High-Church Anglicanism to Humanism. Man must still have a religion, but it will now be the Religion of Humanity.

Harrison might be better known today as one of the eminent Victorians had the cause to which he was wedded remained viable into the twentieth century. Like the Nile, it was dissipated in many other channels and ceased to exist, as one broad stream, in its own right and identity. Perhaps for this very reason, its essence was more genuinely passed on into history, for nothing so alters the nature of a movement than its triumph under its own banner in the world of affairs. The huge success of Marxism in the twentieth century and the enthronement of Christianity by Constantine in the fourth wrought incontestable transformation in oftentimes scarcely recognizable original motivations. But the names of their founders are glorified by followers who might have difficulty accepting them on their own terms. The spirit of Positivism still lives, although, as a movement, it has not persisted. Its leaders have consequently been, for the most part, forgotten.

Austin Harrison refers to his childhood impression of his father as a "large, fiercely-whiskered man with his massive head and boisterous voice, his keen, steady eagle-eyes . . ." (*FH*, 51). He was "father," not "daddy," for in those days the attitude of children was one of respect, a code that was taken entirely for granted. The sons in the family never referred to their father by a nickname, such as "Guvner" (*FH*, 52, 53). On the other hand, Austin has memories of his father's breeziness, jollity, and a "pantomimic ebullition." But he was no more a bully than he was a buddy; the whip was never an accoutrement of household training. Nor was he ever too busy to see his children: they could burst into his room at any time without importuning him, busy though he might be.

Harrison was probably never ill a single day in his life of ninety-two years, being neither delicate nor nervously constituted. Austin says that he was neither a fanatic nor an ascetic but rather a passionate moral enthusiast. Two contrary natures strove for mastery within him: religious emotion and cold reason. Austin says that as one who wished above all things to act, to do, he may be most properly characterized as "Victorian." Everything mattered to him, especially all public affairs. For a man who was normally notable for his self-control, geniality, and healthy sociability, Harrison possessed that peculiar kind of Victorian irritability, indulging in passionate outbursts several times daily. Austin recalls that many people were intimidated by his emphatic, plain-dealing, no-holds-barred manner. But he detested cruelty to animals as well as to men. His passion was channeled into the cause of Humanity. Ruskin wrote to him, "You are the strangest mystery of all the men I know in the world" (*FH*, 123). Few eminent Victorians had less *amour propre* and more sincere passion to wed action to thought in order to find some new evangel for modern man, already embarked on an experience heretofore unknown in history.

Austin described his father's faith as "splendidly Western," independent of prayer, ecstasy, and mortification. "He had no sin and he had no God" (*FH*, 131). This humanism was the key to his father's whole life, to which he dedicated himself without any expectation of material reward. Interestingly, he never really personally believed that Positivism should be just one more new cult among the many striving for preeminence. On the contrary, his own idea was that Positivists should, for the present, pursue an educational aim, although simply to accommodate the zealousness of others did he consent to help form a Positivist society. Unlike his prophet, the idealistic theoretician Comte, Harrison was eminently a practical man, distrustful of mere speculation and airy utopias. Austin never found his father "on his knees in the lonely hours of the night" (*FH*, 136). He had learned from Comte that the modern intellectual man should concentrate his attention exclusively on the how's and should firmly ignore the why's, which are quite beyond human ken. Bacon's distinction between the philosophy of fruit and that of thorns was never more seriously adopted.

Early Years

Having been born in London on October 18, 1831, Harrison would later jokingly tell his children that Frederick, the late German emperor, had been born on the same day of the same year. But, of course, his father could not have had this coincidence in mind, not having heard of the royal birth across the Channel. Since his father was also named Frederick, he named his son after himself, dropping the final *k* to distinguish his son's name from his own, as Harrison reveals in *Autobiographic Memoirs*.[6]

Because Harrison considers the family the fundamental social unit of a Positivist society, toward which the whole world is inevitably evolving, his own family life becomes all the more significant. Although born in the metropolis, his early life was spent in the peaceful countryside amid the avid discussion in his home about the First Reform Bill. His earliest political recollection—indeed, the first time in his life that he had to suffer for his political position—involves the time some Whig children, wearing their buff colors, attempted to tear from his hat the blue rosette of the Tories. Despite his subsequent radical positions and associations, Harrison remained throughout his life a staunch conservative to the core, although in no stereotyped sense of the word. To the end of his life, he had no sympathy for change simply for the sake of change, without any improvement in moral quality. Of course, he would learn only later from books about the momentous events of the period of his early boyhood.

His father, having trained as an architect and worked in the office of his older brothers, retained a passion throughout his long life for art and gardening.[7] While the father spent the day at his later occupation as stockbroker in Threadneedle Street in London, the mother taught her sons history, French, and Latin.[8] The father in the evenings and on weekends would tell the children intriguing stories of men and events that thrilled them during these idyllic days spent in a rural village outside London, during an age in which a Londoner could easily take a morning walk into the country. It was an era in which the railway, steamboat, telegraph, and penny post were either unknown or in an inchoate state. It was the era of the stagecoach. He could recall having seen the first steam road-engine along the present Marylebone Road.

Harrison deplores the lost art of the woodcut engravings that flourished in his childhood, making vivid his early ideas of art, history, literature, and geography. Woodcut engravings of scenes from the Bible and of famous Italian paintings, along with the inevitable *Sandford and Merton*, the tales of Maria Edgeworth, and the varied writings of Mrs. Barbauld, fired the imagination of his childhood. And pictures of the history of Greece, Rome, and England, which he pored over in childhood, would form the basic ideas of history that remained with him throughout his adult life. He avidly believed in the tales of Alfred's cakes, Mucius Scaevola's heroism, Horatius, and Cincinnatus. His father, passionately interested in art, took the boy to the National Gallery and the Royal Academy, where the paintings of Wilkie and J. M. W. Turner especially impressed him. When the young Harrison was taken to London for the extraction of a double tooth, his father made it up to him by taking him to the Royal Academy Show where a new Turner was being exhibited.

From the *Penny Magazine*, the boy obtained his first understanding and feeling for the great styles of painting, architecture, and sculpture, especially the latter art. Not least important, there was the reading aloud by his parents from the great works of literature. Harrison deplores the disappearance from the land of this accomplishment during his later years, insisting that no one that he has heard could read so well as his wife. And he has never heard anyone who could surpass his father in reading aloud. Even his mother read and sang beautifully, although she never made any attempt to train her sons in music or singing on the premise that it would be unmanly for them to engage in them. But when Harrison later heard performances of Mozart and Beethoven, in particular, he found that he was extremely susceptible to the musical art. In the middle part of the century, he would hear such fabled singers as Grisi, Mario, and Jenny Lind; and he attended the debut of Adelina Patti.

Strangely, Harrison's reading as a child contained very little poetry or fiction and omitted all familiarity with fairy tales. He met the Three Bears, Bluebeard, and Jack the Giant-Killer when he taught them to his own children. But when he was around ten years old, he read both Cowper's and Pope's translations of Homer, *Robinson Crusoe*, and *Pilgrim's Progress*. Reflecting on the reading of his youth, he considers it superior to that of later times because boys then could obtain a more thorough grasp of the fundamental lessons of life. Life in those days for this middle-class family with adequate means was passed in a more leisurely manner, with yearly trips to the seaside and some summers in France. Despite the vast material changes in life during the course of the century, however, Harrison insists that the difference is mainly quantitative.

He attributes his vigorous health and customary happiness to his experience in the country as a child, memories of which were never lost as long as he lived. Although he supported to the end of his life a cause that seemed to be ebbing away, he never lost his confidence and bounding optimism. Even the death of one of his sons in World War I, a tragedy which must have affected him profoundly, was accepted stoically. Indeed, no ancient figure ever aroused more admiration in him than the Stoic emperor Marcus Aurelius.

In 1925, Bertrand Russell writes that the "Victorian age, for all its humbug, was a period of rapid progress, because men were dominated by hope rather than fear. If we are again to have progress, we must again be dominated by hope."[9] Belief in progress dominated the Victorian mind. In this respect, Harrison was almost the archetypal Victorian. His son Austin writes that no man was ever more remote from sackcloth and ashes. And there was no trace of gloom or conscientious pedantry in him. Though intensely and severely moral, he was joyous, unlike the father of John Stuart Mill, who "saw life with the severe, relentless sorrow of a Scottish Covenanter" and unlike George Eliot, with "her Sibylline cry of 'Duty.'" Harrison was ever prompted by a Puritan conscience but never suffered from any sense of self-recrimination. In short, he was a Puritan-Humanist (*FH*, 180).

He dates his infancy from the last years of the revolutionary age in literature of Shelley, Byron, Cobbett, and Leigh Hunt. Southey was the luminary of the time when Tennyson, Dickens, and Thackeray were scarcely known. As a child, he was as naturally unimpressed by the passing of Coleridge, Sir Walter Scott, or Goethe as by the abolition of slavery. But the penny postage of 1840, as well as the marriage of Victoria to Prince Albert and the attempt in 1840 on the queen's life by would-be assassins, remains a vivid memory. He recalls the excitement over the birth of Edward VII, whose funeral he would witness sixty-nine years later. Of the foreign celebrities he would not forget, Czar Nicholas in 1844 seemed the most magnificent when Harrison saw him at the Ascot races.

At five and a half years of age, Harrison for the first time experienced the great world outside the quiet country life he had known when he was taken up to the city to witness the coronation of Queen Victoria. In the procession there were leaders who had been opponents in the great war of the first years of the century, heroes like Marshal Soult, who had fought Wellington in Spain, and the Iron Duke himself, who had become a living myth. Many a time Harrison would see Wellington riding along the streets, very much resembling the famous picture on horseback by Landseer. The huge spectacle of the coronation—the pageantry and glamour of the scene and its overwhelming vastness—overcame his repugnance at this early age at the thought that the king was to be succeeded by a mere girl.

School

In 1840, the Harrisons moved to Oxford Square, Hyde Park, where they would live for twenty years. Before Frederic was sent at the age of ten to the day school of Joseph King, his mother had educated him with patience and care in geography, history, and the elements of Latin. Grounded in King's highly individual training, he was, after two years, quite able to read Homer, Virgil, Herodotus, and Livy without ever having to study the ordinary rules of grammar. The spontaneous methods of King bore little resemblance to practices in the schools of Dickens, Thackeray, or Charlotte Brontë or in the Rugby that Dr. Thomas Arnold found.

Although King perpetually delighted the boys in both their work and their play, he was by no means a soft master and would not hesitate to thrash the idle and the incorrigible. His students included a son of his friend Macready the actor, a son of Charles Dickens, a nephew of Sir Edwin Landseer, and a son of Lane, the eminent engraver. When King later wrote to Frederic's father, upon hearing of his son's place in the Oxford Class List, he attested to the pride he felt in his own contribution to this success and in the elder Harrison's recognition of it. Frederic's memorial to the old man deserves recording: "Dear, large-souled, wise old Master!" (*AM*, 2:32n.).

At the age of eleven, Harrison entered the sixth form of King's College School, which he attended from 1843 to 1849. Here again he seems to have been fortunate in his teacher, and he soon reached the top of the Lower Sixth. What he especially liked, however, was his freedom to do rather much as he wished. Even his verse resembled more the style of Swinburne than that of Ovid or Tibullus. But he was later unable to gain a place in the Oxford scholarships, for he could never look upon composition as a trick of mimicry, which, he is convinced, suppresses one's spontaneous expression. He has nothing but contempt for many ignorant and mindless men who have become known as brilliant scholars. Harrison at the age of twelve studied with students from two to six years older than himself, an honor he attributes to King. In fact, he won first prize in the school for Latin verses in alcaics on the song in *Marmion*. But he never really became a classical scholar and probably never learned much more Greek or Latin after this time.

Because of his youth, he received the nickname "Fan," although he was very active in nearly all sports. Try though he might, he was unable to avoid being favored and treated like a girl by the older students. Consequently, he resolved never to put a boy of his own into a form with boys considerably older. Here again he was acquainted with students who would later become prominent men in English life, such as the future Canon Liddon, who, even in those early days, was as much a High Churchman as he would ever be, talking eternally of Dr. Pusey and the *Tracts for the Times* rather than attending to Greek. Even then Liddon regarded himself as a priest among boys, and he always treated Frederic with affectionate condescension as both a child and a worldling. Another friend was the only son of Edward Irving, whose home Frederic visited. Perhaps his most intimate friend at the school was Charles Cookson, later to become longtime consul at Alexandria, where he would be murdered in the riots of 1882. Three years older than Frederic, Cookson, with his great knowledge and many connections, opened up a world of politics and literature that had been heretofore comparatively unknown to the younger boy. And it was Cookson who freed Frederic from the onerous nickname. Cookson virtually knew the prose and poetry of Wordsworth (with whose family he was connected) by heart. Along with John Rolfe, a lad who later died at the age of eighteen, they formed a literary and philosophical fraternity for discussion of poetry, drama, morals, religion, architecture, and politics, all of which aroused in Frederic a new sense of the meaning of life.

Cookson was a divine-right Tory and a fervent advocate of the High-Church persuasion; Rolfe, a radical and a skeptic; and Frederic, a high-and-dry conservative and a moderate churchman of the Paley sort. Cookson endeavored to fire Frederic with his own passion for Shakespeare and Wordsworth, for the High Church of the Pusey kind, and for his own ideal of the gentleman. Rolfe disagreed with Cookson on nearly everything but Shakespeare. In their magazine, they debated a variety of subjects. Frederic's father felt some misgiving when he learned that his son attended the Puseyite service at St. Andrew's. Ironically, Frederic's later religious convictions would lie quite elsewhere, although throughout his entire life he would read the Bible, and in his own writing he would draw from it copiously.

During these school years, Frederic was intensely religious, praying earnestly throughout the day and feeling the presence of Almighty God, to Whom he often confessed his sins. Only gradually did he lose this implicit faith, perhaps coming to feel that his habit of prayer was motivated by egotism and a desire for personal advantage. Gradually, he began to believe that confession to a perfect Being very likely weakens the moral fiber and energy of character, even leading to spiritual vanity and pride. The answering of prayers too much resembles the awarding of a bonus by a Mutual Benefit Club (*AM*, 1:42n.). Somehow one's personal deeds lose their essentially human and social meaning when they become exclusively a matter between the self and God. It is really the working of humanity all about us that redeems the essential goodness of the heart, which excessive prayer would otherwise negate.

Although he had once believed in the future life as dogma, the idea of it never really penetrated his inner life or affected his outer significantly. He never feared Hell or the Devil. And he was never subjected to the darker Calvinistic side of religion, which he had already come to regard as harmful and degrading, especially when used to intimidate the young. The sense of God's personal intervention, which he thinks reaches its highest form in the Moslem and the Puritan soldier, unfortunately fosters in them hardness and pride. But he was consoled by the thought that this unlovely trait is softened by both the essential goodness of the human heart and the incessant working of humanity all around us, abetting a social purpose amid our very weaknesses and vices.

It is especially interesting to note that although during his adult life he was the very image of health and virility, as a lad he was liable to aimless reverie and to inexplicable depression, culminating often in a vague sense of despair. He thinks the cause might have been largely physical, the remedy for which would probably have been systematic work and exercise at the age when a boy easily becomes prey to idleness and chance. Nevertheless, he had the boyish dreams of raising armies and conquering Africa and Asia, firmly believing up to the age of fourteen that glory is the natural aim of man. After that age, however, he felt his first zest for moral and social problems, becoming aware of the antithesis between the utilitarian Christian morality of Paley and pagan heroism, the latter now seeming rather childish. His lust for fame and power receded before his new interest in duty and moral character.

An extremely important trait now became evident for the first time: he had no interest in trying to win for the sake of winning, a characteristic that made him indifferent to success and fame. Success of others no longer aroused envy, nor did it seem to do so in future years. At that early age, he felt an aversion to prizes and place. And toward the end of his life, he would reject the offer of knighthood. In none of his rather copious writings can I detect any invidious note, although he would have had ample opportunity to entertain such a feeling. In the large purposes of life, he never indulged in ambition, as it is usually understood. At the university he never sought the prizes that must be won through very serious competition.

By the age of sixteen, he could read and speak French, having already spent three summers in France. He had also learned to swim, row, and ride. He believes that very few Englishmen of his period had the opportunity that he had had in learning firsthand about the provincial and family life in France during the first half of the nineteenth century. Before the age of the railroads, Normandy, where he lived for long periods at a time, was genuinely a province, and it was here that he learned to value the great importance Positivism places on the family as the basic institution of social life. He was especially impressed by the Norman simplicity and lack of pretence, the equality between social ranks, and the passion for saving. While in France, he studied the Bayeux tapestry, from which occupation he first obtained his lifelong interest in history. At this time, he began to read French history by the hour. At Caen, he met the Rev. W. Hayes, in charge of the Lower Sixth at King's College, who, as a competent antiquarian in architecture, taught Frederic much about the cathedrals of France and so imbued him with another lifelong passion. Ruskin condescendingly referred to Harrison's "chattering about traceries" (in *Fors Clavigera*, letter 67, 1876) thirty years after Harrison had seriously begun the study of medieval architecture, in which he was not unworthy of being compared to the great master himself.

The year 1848 was a memorable one for Frederic, with the erection of barricades in Paris, Vienna, Berlin, and Rome; the toppling of dynasties; and the activities of the Chartist movement in England. At first, he watched it all as he might have done a tragedy on the stage, but gradually he began to lose his monarchial and aristocratic prejudices and to sense a just fate in the dissolution of absolute dynasties. It was also this year that he went up to Wadham College, Oxford, where he came in third for the scholarship, although he postponed matriculation until Easter 1849. For over sixty years thereafter he would have some definite connection with Wadham.

During the summer of 1848, before matriculation, Frederic often went boating in a seventeen-foot yawl and on one occasion swam for a mile with the tide off Southsea beach. He recalls having seen the oldtime sailing ships of the navy at Portsmouth, and he reflects on the changes that have since occurred, "the most amazing transformation in naval armoury that has ever taken place in the history of war" (*AM*, 1:57). [10] From Southsea, he made a walking tour of three days around the Isle of Wight, thereby beginning one of the real joys of his life, observing and studying, on foot, mountains, downs, and rocky seashores. In later years, the epitome of this pleasure would be reached in his passion for mountain-climbing, especially in the Alps. It was on the long vacation of 1849 in Scotland that he took what proved to be one of the most important tours of his life in a countryside that then was reminiscent of *Rob Roy*. It was on this tour that he climbed Ben Nevis, reaching the top at sunset and not coming down until three o'clock in the morning. His love for the vast solitudes of Nature had now become a passion, one that remained throughout his life and about which he wrote the last of his spontaneous rhymes.

Harrison believes that he learned more at his private day school than he would have done in five years at one of the public boarding schools. Above all, he objects to the cramming of students for the purpose of winning prizes, a process that does not inform or train the mind but only forces it to conform to a given pattern. Also, he thinks it sheer folly to force all boys to study ancient languages, although for a few, such training may be valuable. He wrote immense quantities of Latin verse and prose with considerable ease, but he thought no hours of his entire life were more uselessly employed. And the committing to memory of endless lines of Latin poetry, often with no real sense of their meaning, was quite as worthless.

But even a more serious criticism is the inculcation of the rigid caste system that dominated the social life of Britain during the century. The more original boys were packed off as "undesirables." Harrison also opposes forced athletics, although all through his life he was an active outdoorsman and was given to boating, swimming, riding, tennis, and mountain-climbing. However, the rabid addiction to sports would become a national disease, brutalizing the manners and degrading the true standard of manly excellence. Above all, he loathes what is called "sport"—that is, the killing of vertebrate animals in fox-hunting, shooting, stalking, fishing, and the like. If anything illustrates Harrison's independent spirit, it is this conviction in nineteenth-century England, by virtue of which he admitted to standing with the Indian Jains. Although he never adopted the practice of vegetarianism, he was as sensitive to cruelty as were Bernard Shaw and Henry S. Salt, who did so.[11]

University

Frederic actually began his college career at the age of eighteen in the fall of 1849 as a scholar of Wadham College, Oxford. Already divested of the political and theological traditions that Oxford represented, he felt such a distaste for it that he wrote home about his state of depression. He felt only contempt for its honors and prizes, for its pomposity and narrowness, its barracks-style life, its boring and formal lectures, its timid and noncommital professors, its hostility to anyone with original taste.

There was one exception among the tutors. Richard Congreve taught history with breadth of mind and with taste for culture and thought. His grasp of history was "wide, systematic, and full of life, in the best traditions of Dr. T. Arnold" (*AM*, 1:84). Although Congreve would later also become one of the leading British Positivists, Harrison is at some pains to disavow having ever heard Congreve at Oxford mention the name of Comte. Although he admits to having been significantly influenced by the character and ideals of Congreve and to having learned from his tutor in every possible way, he insists that he never lost his own power of judgment and never became Congreve's disciple. Harrison confesses he was appalled at the transformation in Congreve over nearly forty years, wrought by ambition and fanaticism. "I could not have believed that human nature could undergo such a transformation in the same man, if I had not been a close witness of the whole process" (*AM*, 1:84).

In an article in the *Wadham College Gazette* on the occasion of Congreve's death in 1899, Harrison pays warm tribute to his former tutor. He had had the singular ability to inspire students to teach themselves, to cultivate right judgment and high thinking. His point of view was always basically historical, political, and moral, always free from technicalities and specialism. At that time, such an approach was rare at Oxford. Inspired by Dr. Thomas Arnold and Grote, Congreve's teaching of Thucydides, Tacitus, and Aristotle was sound and thorough, always avoiding the cant and cloudy thinking of the academician. Above all, he was not concerned with teaching to the examinations. Although the impression was given that Wadham College was thereby indifferent to honors, never had its students been more successful on the examinations. Even Mark Pattison was once supposed to have told Congreve that his students were unusual in that they wrote down "no nonsense" (*AM*, 1:86).

In 1851, Harrison saw the building of the Crystal Palace in Hyde Park, the first of the great iron-and-glass houses in Europe. So often was he in attendance at the Great Exhibition that he felt that he was familiar with every object and every stall in it. Although impressed with the scientific inventions on display, he was disgusted with the so-called art objects, which so exhibited the tastelessness of the era that he exclaims that he was by birth a "Georgian," but not in the least an "Early Victorian."

In the same year, he had an experience of a different sort. With several Wadham classmates, he traveled to Germany and Switzerland for the first time. The Rhine was glorious then since there were no railroads, factories, or even bridges at Cologne. And then he proceeded through Baden and the Black Forest until finally coming upon his first sight of the Alps at the very place that John Ruskin had also first seen them. Immediately, he became intoxicated with the wonder of the experience and felt a passion for mountaineering that never left him the rest of his life. Later, his four days in Paris filled him with a craving for foreign travel that also never left him.

Harrison had been brought up as a high churchman and had even leaned a bit toward transubstantiation, but at the university he began to consider the whole problem of theology more carefully. Both Newmans, John Henry and Francis William, interested him equally.[12] He hardly ever missed either a university sermon or a copy of the *Westminster Review*, the rationalist journal. But very gradually he came to regard the whole system of theology as an open question, and when he left the university at the age of twenty-four, belief in the supernatural had entirely disappeared from his mind. The change was so gradual that he could never say at what point it had taken place. At any rate, he had never experienced any loss of peace or felt any spiritual perturbation. Nor did he ever feel any resentment toward his former convictions, for he looked on his earlier belief in theology as part of a process of moral evolution and even enjoyed reading the Bible and other religious writings with more pleasure than when he had believed in them. He read what he enjoyed and enjoyed what he read, never having been put through the mill by his tutors. Not only religion, but also poetry, history, and art afforded him and his fellow students endless hours of discussion and debate as they spent much of their time rather "like the Athenians in the days of St. Paul" (M&T, 10).

In 1853, two of his examiners for the degree were Mark Pattison and Benjamin Jowett, who, operating under the new system that had just been adopted, put more emphasis on thought, good sense, and general grasp of subject that on technicalities. [13] It was this emphasis that doubtless enabled Harrison to place among the five who took First Class that year. After his examinations, he continued to reside at Oxford, reading literature and later being elected Librarian of the Union and, still later, tutor. This brief period of his life he considered the most valuable for the cultivation of his mind. Perhaps his fondest memory was of the Essay Society, where papers were avidly read and discussed.

In 1855, he left Oxford, where he had been for six years. It was in this year that he wrote Auguste Comte in Paris, saying that he had been a pupil of Congreve's and that he requested an interview, a request that was granted. Among the many interviews with celebrities during the course of his life, this one was surely the most crucial. Comte received him with great courtesy and, over a period of several hours, inquired what his studies had been and how much he knew of Comte's own writings. Harrison replied that he had read several of Comte's volumes translated by Harriet Martineau but admitted that he had studied very little mathematics or science. Comte spoke freely and at some length on topics that he had invited Harrison to bring up, impressing the younger man with the clarity and cogency of his thought. When Harrison admitted that he called himself a Christian, Comte said that he did not expect one to abandon theism altogether, although he thought that interest in problems of the universe would gradually give way to hopes for humble good on this earth. All in all, Harrison was more impressed with Comte than with any other man he was ever to meet, unless it was Mazzini.

Harrison made three close friends during his Oxford years: Edward Spencer Beesly, later professor of history at University College, London; John Henry Bridges, later M.D.; and George Earlam Thorley, later Warden of Wadham. Their group was nicknamed "Mumbo-Jumbo" by those who gloried in boat racing, the exploits of the playing field, and other such convivialities. This appellation refers to what outsiders took to be the group's meaningless activities and obscure rituals, its hankering after and worship of strange gods. After Sunday sermons, the four friends would take walks into the countryside lasting into the early hours of Monday morning. Frederic was a bit shocked that his friends had already rejected all bibliolatry and even the creeds, for, as he had told Comte, he still regarded himself as a Christian. But since his friends had been brought up in the strictness of the Evangelicals with their gloomy predestinarianism, he could understand how they might well have revolted against their background. At the age of twenty-one, however, under the influence of his friends and of Congreve, he passed from an ardent Christian faith to a liberal latitudinarianism which would ultimately evolve into scientific Positivism. Actually, he had become a disciple of Cobden and Bright while still a believer in the Established Church.[14]

Frederic succeeded in reconciling his father to his explanation why he would not take Orders for a career in the Church; and although his father was opposed to his tutorship, he acquiesced in Frederic's remaining two more years at the university before going to Lincoln's Inn in London to study law in 1855. Although he had ceased living in Oxford by 1855, he continued his active association with the university as Fellow of the College for fifteen more years, attending meetings, elections, examinations, and various commemorations.

In 1910, Harrison reflected on the changes at Oxford since 1853. His attitude had now become divided in sympathy between the old and the new. Having been in touch in those early days with Congreve, Jowett, Stanley, and Pattison—men who led the reform movement at Oxford—he welcomed their efforts, only partially successful, to dispel clerical domination and archaic obscurantism. One particularly unfortunate consequence of change, however, has been the mania for specialization, the breaking up of subjects into periods and separate

categories.[15] Throughout his life, Harrison emphasized the importance of learning in terms of organic wholes. Important as specialization is for modern civilization, it is not suited to Oxford, where not
one in a hundred young men will become specialists. At twenty-one,
a student needs to have his mind vivified, clarified, and organized; he
needs to become a sensible young man with a mind braced to face the
problems of life. The addition of modern history was a step of genuine
importance, but it was broken up into disparate segments known as
"periods" and thereby has become a collection of dried historical
specimens. The old system, he admitted, did produce such men as
Peel, Gladstone, the two Arnolds, the two Newmans, Keble, Goldwin Smith, Congreve, Pattison, and Jowett. The new system, in
effect since 1853, has been changed each year rather like the fashions
of Paris hats.

But Harrison would remain an Oxford man to the marrow of his
bones, convinced that it is the best school in the British Isles. He
would continue to believe that the sense of hallowed tradition remains
with the Oxford graduate, enabling him to feel that life has a purpose
and that education is invaluable. Having outgrown his first unfavorable impression of the institution, he treasures, in retrospect, his
six years there as the most satisfactory part of his life, realizing that
one seldom values such experiences until much later on.

Early Adult Years

Frederic was the eldest of five surviving sons, the first-born,
Frederic Robert, having died within four months of birth (AM,
1:68). He could not speak too highly of his father's intense devotion
to wife and children. Both parents seemed to have lived for the
children, nearly always preferring the children's happiness to their
own. The father personally took Frederic to each new school that he
attended, including Oxford, lavishing every possible attention on his
son. Whenever they traveled, the parents always did so with their
boys.

The parents do seem to have been surprisingly indulgent on one of
the crucial issues of the intensely family-conscious Victorian age: the
matter of what their eldest son was going to do for a living. Remark-

ably, the father did acquiesce in Frederic's request to remain a few more years at Oxford before commencing his study of law in London. Actually, the young man had little taste to remain as tutor of undergraduates, but he wished to devote his thoughts and energies to those turbulent intellectual discoveries he had made only quite recently, so far removed from the technicalities involved in the study of law. Also, he wanted to take part in the reforms at Oxford that Congreve and others were fostering at that very time.

But the shock he had to administer to his mother was more serious still. In a long letter to her, he explained his present ideas on the Church of England, an exposition which could only pain her deeply. In it, he roundly denounced the worldliness of the bishops and curates, saying that most thinking people were dissatisfied with the Church as it then existed. The best students shrank from taking Orders any longer, and those who did so were scarcely fit to impart spiritual counsel to others. He denounced the jobbing of clerical appointments, the good assignments going to men who were rich and who perpetuated the prejudices of their class. Frederic told his mother that he dreamed of a true Church that honestly represents the interests and feelings of all classes of society and one that does not merely surrender to mediocrity.

He wrote this letter from London at a time when he was closely associated with those Oxford friends who would later become dedicated Positivists and while he was hearing F. D. Maurice and others connected with the Working Men's College, with which he himself would soon become involved. He even paraphrased Auguste Comte by saying that he did not find in the clergy of the Church a firm or clear conviction in religious matters which is needed to clear up human perplexities and to teach and regulate society. There was lacking in the clergy any high purpose, driving energy, or horror at social miseries which beg for correction. The only answer he ever got from them was a reference to the ambiguous Thirty-nine Articles. This communication must have been rather strong stuff for a gentle Victorian lady of the 1850s, who had for so many years personally trained her eldest surviving son.

At last, young Harrison did commence the study of law at Lincoln's Inn as a pupil of Joshua Williams, an eminent conveyancer, together with a brother of Sir John Seeley.[16] But he had little relish for the conveyancing trade, which he considered to be sheer antiquated nonsense by which lawyers filled their pockets. Consequently, he soon found himself reading more history and philosophy than law; after a year, he felt hardly qualified to settle so much as a common mortgage. He was now reading Comte, Mill, Gibbon, Dante, and Milton. And soon he was joining F. D. Maurice, Ruskin, Kingsley, Thomas Hughes, Vernon Lushington, and Ford Madox Brown at the Working Men's College.

Harrison soon incurred the opposition of F. D. Maurice at the Working Men's College by drawing up a plan to systematize the study of history. Maurice even threatened to resign as President of the College if such a systematization were adopted over the current method of following the reigns of the kings of England, accusing Harrison of being a disciple of Comte (*AM*, 1:159).[17] Ironically, it was the writings of Maurice that had largely emancipated Harrison from theological creeds. However, dear man that he thought Maurice to be, he had never known anyone more muddleheaded. After the kindly old gentleman had eloquently and logically exposed what he conceived to be the moral weakness of the Mosaic Law, the doctrine of Hell, and the Christian doctrine of Atonement, he would thereupon justify them on the strength of the beauty of Christ's mission. This attempt by the Broad Church to keep the Church going while rejecting its creed and its Bible was repellent to Harrison.[18] Although he got along quite well enough personally with Maurice, the latter always rather feared him as an emissary of Congreve, whom he equated with the Devil.

The only way that Harrison could tolerate the study of law was to become, at the same time, a pupil of Henry S. Maine in Roman law and historical jurisprudence. Fortunately, it was just this extracurricular pursuit that led to Harrison's succeeding later to the professorship held by Maine at the Inns of Court, in conjunction with James (later Lord) Bryce, future author of the monumental *The American Commonwealth*. As a matter of fact, this was the only professional work with which Harrison was ever seriously occupied. All the while he was studying law, he was busily engaged in working with young radicals on schemes of various types of reform, one of which was to limit the power of the heads of Oxford colleges and to put the government into the hands of the tutors; another was to free the university from religious tests. Many committees of agitation met in Harrison's chambers to formulate such plans, often in collaboration with Jowett, James Bryce, and John Bright.

Two other members of Mumbo-Jumbo, Beesly and Bridges, now also lived in London, and the three of them continued their earlier Oxford plans to shape public opinion on a variety of current controversies along the lines of John Bright radicalism. They vehemently attacked Austrian oppression in Italy, the Crimean War against Russia, and imperialism in general. Most of all, they hated defending the remaining decadent despots of Europe, and they ridiculed the doctrine of balance of power that England already was depending on. Even so, Mumbo-Jumbo, although going so far as to propose a true People's party to attack the real social problems and to avoid merely tedious slogans, wanted a gradual approach that would steer clear of wild and extravagant programs. In 1856, Harrison seriously hoped to found a periodical to be named the *Republican* that would express the views of the reformers. These hopes would later materialize in the Positivist Society in England in 1870 and in the *Positivist Review* in 1893.

Harrison was prophetic when he predicted in 1857 that English rule in India would come to an end, although he expected the demise to occur at the close of the nineteenth century. As the English worked to improve the Indians, they were only hastening the day of their own overthrow. Anyway, the loss of India, he argued, would not really incur financial loss for England, whereas maintaining a huge army there would. The English are a great and courageous people, but their politics were rotten, especially when they trusted to a sickening reliance on Christian platitudes and "hypocritical garbage." After 1857, Harrison would remain antiimperialist.

But no cause so engaged Harrison's attention in the 1850s as that of Italian independence. Aurelio Saffi, friend of Mazzini's and one of his colleagues in the Triumvirate at Rome in 1849, had at Oxford become Harrison's teacher of Italian and also his close personal friend, who introduced him to many other Italian exiles. Because of Saffi, and later Francis Newman, Harrison obtained his deep interest in the causes of nations struggling to regain their independence (*M&T*, 6). Harrison admired John Bright as a home reformer but felt he was far too neutral on foreign matters. In 1859, he had written Bright to take up the cause of Italy. He had gotten the active support of the *Daily News* and had an arrangement to submit letters to its columns several days a week. And he had written Francis Newman and contemplated writing Harriet Martineau for their respective support. Very soon thereafter, he arranged a meeting in his private quarters, attended by Francis Newman and by various important Hungarian and Polish exiles as well. Harrison and Newman planned to enlist twenty volunteers to write letters in all the newspapers to support the Italian cause in line with a very specific program that Harrison and Newman had drawn up. These letters, Harrison thinks, formed the policies of Palmerston and Russell in their ministries from 1859 to 1866.

The phrase "suiting actions to words" certainly applies to Harrison during this intensely active period of his life. With the approval of Palmerston and Russell, though he declined their active help, Harrison set out for Italy to determine the state of affairs firsthand, which he communicated by telegraph to the *Daily News* and the *Morning Post*. These despatches, Harrison thinks, had much to do with winning the British public over to the Italian cause. He also wrote for the *Westminster Review*, but from none of these journals did he accept payment for his expenses, preferring to remain a volunteer. His "Garibaldi and Cavour" in the *Westminster* brought him a letter in English from Cavour, thanking him for his invaluable contribution to the cause of Italian freedom.

Middle Adult Years

Joining Mill, Bright, Goldwin Smith, and many other intellectuals of the age, Harrison actively participated on the Jamaica Committee in 1866, formed to attack the use of martial law in Jamaica by Governor John Eyre to suppress Negro riots there. This *cause célèbre* split England in two, with Thomas Carlyle heading the committee for the defense of Eyre and Mill the committee that hoped to punish him. This trial in many ways resembled that of Warren Hastings and was fraught with as great significance for the future course of the Empire itself. The partisans on both sides made up a sort of *Who's Who* of Victorian England. Harrison, drawing on his legal training, wrote a series of letters to the *Daily Mail*, establishing the legal precedent that would henceforth be used in the field of martial law in England. Mill, Bright, and Goldwin Smith were elated with Harrison's careful reasoning. Virtually the same issue arose during the Boer War, when the legal principles in these letters were revived by the South African Committee in 1901 concerning the legality of martial law; Harrison very willingly repeated these very principles in speeches and articles, which were published by the committee.

No work of his life was more important than that on the Royal Commission on Trades Unions from 1867 to 1869. When the trades unions insisted that the Home Secretary put a workman on the commission, he finally agreed to accept, instead, a lawyer of their choice. They chose Harrison, although he knew nothing about the appointment until he read about it in the *Times*. He had also known nothing about the objection by the Permanent Secretary of the Home Office to the appointment because of some "revolutionary" articles in the *Beehive* which Harrison had contributed. Certain members of Parliament had to guarantee Harrison's good character before he was accepted on behalf of the workmen. Fearing that would injure his legal career were he to accept the appointment, his father was opposed to his getting involved; but Harrison had no sincere desire to succeed as a lawyer, and he did discern an opportunity to proceed toward a seat in the Commons.

His role on the commission has been fully discussed by Sidney and Beatrice Webb in their monumental *The History of Trade-Unionism*. [19] The Webbs cite the important contributions of the Positivists to the labor movement. They say that Harrison, in the late 1860s, had a big hand in laying "down in general terms the principles upon which all future legislation [in re: Labor] should proceed."[20] "The complete charter of Trade Union liberty, which Harrison and his friends had elaborated, became for seven years the political programme of the Trade Unionists."[21] There had been an attempt to implicate the entire union movement with inherent criminality. Harrison signed a minority report and contributed an elaborate appendix in which he examined the entire evidence and argued each legal point of the proposed legislation. This appendix laid the foundation for all trades-union laws passed between 1868 and 1906, and it was very likely Harrison's most nearly permanent work in the political field. He also, in an open letter, defended his old friend Professor Beesly, formerly of Mumbo-Jumbo and later an active fellow-Positivist, because he was about to be dismissed as head of University College, London, for a speech he had made to the workmen at Exeter Hall.

Harrison, in the late 1860s, also became deeply involved in the perennial Irish problem, a petition to the House of Commons having been drawn up in his chambers favoring palliation of punishment of the offenses of Fenian rebels in that troubled land. Harrison, Beesly, Bridges, Cookson, and others signed the petition as "citizens of England," a phrase that then suggested republicanism of a subversive nature. Their "Irish Society" anticipated by several decades the reforms that would be implemented by Gladstone.

Harrison was prominent in the formation in 1865 of the *Fortnightly Review*, modeled on the Parisian *Revue des Deux Mondes*, in which writers signed their own articles. Asked by G. H. Lewes and George Eliot to write an article for the first number of the *Review*, he boldly chose for his subject the strike and lock-out in the iron trade in the Midlands. For about ten years, he would continue to contribute about two or three articles a year, and during the forty years after 1865 he contributed close to ninety articles to the *Fortnightly*, the *Contemporary Review*, and the *Nineteenth Century*. After writing for G. H. Lewes, he continued producing articles in the *Fortnightly* for John Morley, who became a permanent friend.

The most intensely busy period of his life was the decade of the 1860s. Very sensibly, he was careful of his health. He owned a horse and rode almost daily. Half the year he would live in his father's home at Eden Park in Kent, and each year he would take four to six weeks in autumn to climb in the Alps or to walk in the English Lake country or through the Yorkshire moors. During these ten years, he wrote some twenty articles, edited *International Policy*, and lectured at the Working Men's College as well as at Chapel Street, the first Positivist Hall. As if all that and much more were not enough, he was occupied with legal work in the equity courts and with drafting legislation for the Houses of Lords and Commons. During all this time, his professional income never exceeded £600 in any given year and usually was no more than half that.[22] In the latter 1860s he was busily engaged in long and serious litigations both at common law and in chancery, although this professional work was so distasteful to him that he wrote a friend, "A life like this would make me cut my throat" (*AM*, 1:329). After this period, he was busy as examiner in jurisprudence, Roman law, and constitutional history for the Council of Legal Education, work that he found much more congenial during the next twenty years.

In addition to these commitments, Harrison was appointed secretary to the Royal Commission for Digesting the Law, with the ambition of compiling all the English case law during the past several centuries. Much of his effort was devoted to trying to cover the indiscretions of retired Lord Chancellor Bethell, whom Harrison considered totally unsuited to direct a project of this sort, especially during the last years of his life. Sir Henry Maine proposed Harrison to Sir Henry Lytton Bulwer, ambassador to Constantinople, for promulgating a legal code for the Khedive of Egypt, a task Harrison would have willingly taken on for about three years, "to be a new Joseph," as he jokingly wrote a friend. The khedive probably never seriously meant to have such a code drawn up in the first place. If Harrison had shocked the permanent secretary with his *Beehive* articles, I wonder what impression he would have made on the khedive as his English Daniel.

It was during this general period that Harrison joined many eminent Victorian clubs and societies. Soon after coming to London, he was elected to the Reform Club. In 1865, a close friend of Cobden and Bright got him membership in the Cobden Club. In 1864, he joined the Alpine Club in anticipation of his climb of Mount Blanc, an exploit on which he was later joined by Leslie Stephen and his guides; this sport they both held to be the most delightful of all sports. In his eightieth year, Harrison attributes his persistent health to his walking at every opportunity in the mountains or along the coasts.

In 1869, he became a life-member of the London Library, later becoming a vice-president. With Leslie Stephen as president, he worked on the authors' catalogue of 1903 and the subject-index of

1909.[23] This circulating library was first formed in 1841 by well-known literary scholars and scientists, with books chosen by such literary men as Thomas Carlyle and Sir Leslie Stephen. The new subject index for some 250,000 volumes includes, in a single volume, literature of all ages and countries under 18,000 subject headings. A landmark in the history of English bibliography, it was planned by a committee headed by Sir Leslie Stephen and including Harrison, Sidney Lee, Edmund Gosse, and Austin Dobson.

In 1871, he was proposed by Lord Houghton as a member of the Cosmopolitan Club, where he met many politicians, military men, artists, dramatists, and novelists, including Millais, Anthony Trollope, Fitzjames Stephen, and Tom Hughes. Of its perpetual president, Lord Houghton, he cannot speak highly enough as unequaled in the fine social art.

The most interesting and important organization that Harrison joined was the Metaphysical Society, where serious matters of religion and philosophy were discussed by the leading men of the age. It was a kind of Victorian equivalent of Dr. Johnson's Literary Club, with such distinguished members as Tennyson, Gladstone, Dean Stanley, Ruskin, Froude, Tyndall, Huxley, Cardinal Manning, Walter Bagehot, R. H. Hutton, Mark Pattison, James Martineau, W. G. Ward, Dean Church, and Prof. W. K. Clifford. Many of the papers read and discussed at the Metaphysical Society, including some of Harrison's own, were later published. It was at these meetings that Harrison formed one of his strangest acquaintanceships with none other than Cardinal Manning, with whom he often privately discussed Positivism at the cardinal's own table. It was also at the society that Harrison made other such lifelong friendships as the one with Mark Pattison, although the latter had written an article in which he had tried to cover Comte with ridicule.

John Morley proposed Harrison as a member of the Political Economy Club in 1876, and in 1878 he proposed Harrison as a member of the Athenaeum Club. So many knighted individuals had received membership there at that time that Harrison remonstrated with a waiter for addressing him as "Sir Frederick," whereupon the man replied, ". . . But I did think you were in the last batch." Harrison agreed with Herbert Spencer that in these days it was a mark of distinction to have neither order nor star. It was a club that was especially suitable to a quiet family man of more advanced years and a cultivated taste.

But the especially significant event of this period of his life was his engagement to his cousin Ethel Harrison in 1869 and their marriage in 1870. As Austin puts it, "He subsequently converted his cousin (my mother) and married her . . ." (*FH*, 33). According to Austin, a more ideal marriage is scarcely conceivable. Ethel's influence on Frederic was so profound for forty-six years (she died in 1916) that they both lived as one, always able to reconcile their rather different temperaments and certain somewhat different abilities and qualities. He consulted her on nearly all occasions, having her read his manuscripts as both counselor and friend. Austin thought few have exceeded his parents in the romance of living: "Today such a marriage would be styled Victorian, old-fashioned, yet man and woman can reach no higher" (*FH*, 196). She shared her husband's life on every level with genuine enthusiasm.

When Harrison traveled to America in 1901, he made the trip without his wife, who had been forbidden by her physicians to travel, especially by sea. He published some of the letters which he regularly wrote her at great length all along the way, explaining that he, through forty years of marriage, had never kept back a thought or incident of his life from her. Oftentimes he would write her late at night or in the early hours of the morning, after having spent a busy day with his American friends sightseeing, attending parties, or sometimes lecturing to audiences. The reader is as nearly impressed with his unflagging devotion to his beloved wife as with his boundless energy. He explains his hesitation in mentioning "the one constant and undiminished passion" which has absorbed his entire heart: "a passion of the sort which cannot be made manifest in any words or explained to those to whom it is unknown" (*AM*, 2:193).

One gets a picture of Harrison's habits from his son Austin. His interests lay in the works and the spirit of man: ancient city walls, towers and temples, statues and pictures, the silence and huge space of vast cathedrals. But he was equally at home in snow and forests, on the sea, or in great and open expanses of land. At home, he functioned with regularity. Arising early, he worked in his room until luncheon, after which activity he walked. In the evenings he read. He disliked small talk, and he had the Victorian requirement of respect for the head of the family. But the children did not feel oppressed by this "master in my own house" disciplinarian; on the contrary, when Austin after some years returned home from the Continent and its bohemianism, he found the "orderliness, intensity, and routine calmness" of his father's life quite comforting and welcome. A happy man is a heartening spectacle, and his father was always that, Austin observes. Above all, he fairly thrived on restless energy (*FH*, 195–97).

His Life from 1870 On

Because the remaining chapters will deal primarily with this especially significant period of Harrison's eventful life, the present section will be limited to a brief survey of the main direction of his career henceforth to its conclusion. The year 1870 is a watershed that divides his life in two. It is the year of his marriage. With his wife at his side, hardly ever again would he feel weariness or disappointment. It was at this time that he ceased living in his father's home and set up his own establishment. Now, for the first time, he felt completely enfranchised as an adult citizen, with a clear course before him, with a new faith that had at long last completely supplanted the former one. He was no longer without a systematic religion, for Positivism now filled all his spiritual needs.

This was the period of the Prussian victory over France, which prompted Harrison to write a series of letters to the *Pall Mall Gazette*, affording him an opportunity to denounce Bismarckian imperialism. During the turbulent 1870s, Harrison traveled to France as a correspondent for the *Times* of London, where he familiarized himself with every part of France, rural as well as urban, and met the important personages of every political persuasion. Not only did he meet such eminent Frenchmen in political life as Louis Blanc, Gambetta, and Clemenceau, but also such literary figures as Renan, Michelet, and Hugo.

Harrison also was intimately acquainted with the luminaries of the literary world of Victorian England, including such celebrities as

Tennyson, Carlyle, Mill, Ruskin, Browning, George Eliot and G. H. Lewes, Arnold, Huxley, Spencer, Leslie and Fitzjames Stephen, and Meredith. At George Eliot's Sunday-afternoon receptions, he met Trollope, Turgenev, Richard Wagner and his beautiful wife, Cosima, Longfellow, Lowell, Emerson, Motley, Tyndall, Darwin, Lord Acton, and Lecky, to mention but a few. From an early age, he seemed to enjoy easy access to anyone he wished to meet, regardless of rank or reputation.

One usually has the impression that the eminent Victorians, for the most part, were intense and energetic, but Harrison impresses one as being quite indefatigable. Having originated the idea of a committee to continue the Reports on State Trials from the date they had been discontinued, 1820, he was appointed by the lord chancellor to a post on it, which he held from 1885 to 1898. When he moved into the countryside in nearby Kent, he was appointed justice of the peace for that county, an assignment he undertook with the utmost seriousness, as was usual with him.

Harrison was always convinced that his one certain advantage over many of his colleagues—John Stuart Mill, for instance—in the field of labor problems was his practical, firsthand knowledge. He actually belonged to several unions. But for party politics he felt altogether unsuited because his private opinions were heartfelt and uncompromising. Against his better judgment he did permit a number of graduates of the University of London to persuade him to run for a seat in the Commons against Sir John Lubbock in July 1886, to whom most influential groups had already pledged their support. No doubt, Harrison was lured also by a chance to support Gladstone's Home Rule policy for Ireland, a policy he himself had long advocated. With Coriolanian contempt for canvassing or appearing on the public platform, Harrison was defeated two to one by Sir John, but he was proud that he had gotten the vote of 516 graduates who had approved his principles on Home Rule. This attempt was his only foray into the arena of active party politics.

To his surprise, Harrison received late one night in 1889 a telegram to the effect that the next morning he would be nominated as an alderman for the first County Council of London. He felt it was his duty to serve the city in which he had been born and in which he had lived for nearly half a century; his brother Charles, having been trained in the law like Frederic, was also nominated. As architects and builders, his father, grandfather, and uncles had been much involved in building the newer city, and Frederic had nearly always felt a keen interest in such matters. When in 1892 he was made chairman of the Improvements Committee of the council, he helped plan some of the important avenues of the present city of London. And many of his accounts of his travels abroad reflect this interest in city planning. After five years of very active service, he resigned from the County Council, praising it for being as high-minded and capable a group as has ever governed a city.

But the principal preoccupation of his life was the Positivist movement in England. In 1910, he writes that he was very likely the only living Englishman who had ever met Comte in the flesh, an experience he deems the chief honor of his life. From that meeting in 1855 he became convinced that he needed to study the physical sciences, realizing that his education had been almost catastrophically deficient in this area. With characteristic determination, he set about remedying this lack, avidly studying on his own and attending lectures by such authorities as Owen, Huxley, and Tyndall in their respective fields. Still not a disciple of Comte, he studied the Frenchman's works with an open mind, finding himself increasingly in sympathy with his entire scheme of historical evolution. He found that every page of Gibbon, Hallam, Carlyle, Ranke, and Dr. Thomas Arnold gained new meaning in the light of the Positivist explanation of progressive civilization.

He joined with Congreve, Beesly, and Bridges—those friends from his Oxford days—in a plan to translate the four volumes of Comte's *Politique Positive*, undertaking to do the second volume, the *Statique Sociale*, himself. In 1867, Congreve founded the first English Positive Society, modeled on Comte's first such organization (Paris, 1850), the preliminary meetings having been conducted in Harrison's chambers. Uninterrupted meetings of the society were continued for over half a century. From this nucleus sprang the Chapel St. group in 1870, the Newton Hall group in 1881, and the *Positivist Review* in 1896. Although Harrison had opposed the formation of both the Chapel St. and the Newton Hall groups, out of loyalty he participated in their respective foundings. He thought it was unwise to risk the danger of remaining a small cult when adherents were so few, and he advocated that their main effort should at first be public education.

By 1878, many of the group thought that Congreve planned to make himself head of a religious and philosophical society, divorced from the French movement headed by Pierre Laffitte, who had inherited the mantle from Comte himself. The schism was caused entirely by personal and not at all by doctrinal considerations. When in 1879 the Newton Hall group was founded, Harrison was forthwith made president, rather much against his private inclination. The hall was appropriately named after Sir Isaac Newton. The editor of the *Pall Mall Gazette* invited Harrison to submit a paper describing the aim and methods of the new society to an article in that periodical on centers of spiritual activity. Dean Church had contributed the first paper on St. Paul's Cathedral. Harrison obliged with the second paper, which was published in 1883. In it, he emphasized that the purpose of the courses conducted at Newton Hall was to promulgate one gospel: the perfecting of man's life on earth by a genuinely scientific understanding "of man's powers, limits, and wants." And the primary function of the society would be to educate. There would be no priest, no ritual, no adoration, and no ceremony in this new religion. The society was to be operated without profit and without charge, and its ideal was that of complete freedom. Harrison lectured there on Sunday afternoons for several months of the year over a period of about twenty-five years.

During the mid-1870s, he worked closely with Joseph Chamberlain, John Bright, and John Morley for the Disestablishment of the Church of England. He even joined forces with the Liberation Society, which reprinted as a pamphlet his article "Church and State" in the *Fortnightly Review* (May 1877) and for which he sketched a bill advocating Disestablishment and Disendowment. Although this bill was never introduced into Parliament, it became the platform, as it were, of the liberation group, which had done much to bring about the abolition of the religious tests that remained in the English universities until passage of the University Tests Act of 1871. Harrison suspected the failure to achieve Disestablishment was due to the narrowing of the contest to a struggle between Nonconformity and the Church Establishment. Unlike his temporary allies, Harrison opposed the privileges of the Church because of its connection with the upper classes. He had no particular sympathy for Protestant Dissent.

In 1877, he was appointed professor of Jurisprudence, International and Constitutional Law by the Council of Legal Education, and lectured on jurisprudence in conjunction with James (later Lord) Bryce at Middle Temple Hall for twelve years from 1877 to 1889, and published widely on legal subjects in a number of leading periodicals. Meantime, in 1884, he was invited by the distinguished Philosophical Institution of Edinburgh to give two lectures, in which he examined the theories of Henry George in *Progress and Poverty* (1879) and *Social Problems* (1884) at a time when those theories were provoking intense interest in the liberal and radical circles of Britain. In 1885, he addressed the Conference on Industrial Problems on the same general subject at Newcastle. In 1885, he participated, together with Sir Charles Dilke and A. J. Balfour, among others, in a National Conference to consider the problem of Capital and Labor.

When Harrison gave the Rede Lecture at Cambridge in 1900, he met the American ambassador, who received the LL.D. degree on that occasion. This gentleman invited Harrison to deliver the Annual Address on the birthday of Washington at the Union League Club of Chicago, the first time that an Englishman would ever have done so. In due time, a formal invitation arrived from Theodore Roosevelt. After attending the funeral of Queen Victoria, Harrison set sail on the *Majestic* in 1901. Already he foresaw that America would overshadow Europe, but he was equally prescient in realizing she had some great problems of race, of democratic government, of social economy, of education, of art, of family. But, most of all, he was impressed with the American energy and ambition. The van of human progress, he was convinced, must point to the West.

He was completely overwhelmed by the "inexhaustible friendliness" with which he was greeted wherever he went. Everywhere he was treated as though, as he said, he were Dickens, Spencer, and the Prince of Wales all in one person, and he was introduced to and entertained by the president, the vice-president, members of the Cabinet, congressional leaders, and literary and cultural celebrities.

Next to the president, he thought he might well be the most hand-shaken man in the United States. He lectured at Harvard, the University of Chicago, Johns Hopkins, at innumerable clubs and societies, feeling all the while like a dreadful imposter who was really no more than an average magazine writer. No subject so excited his audiences as his recollections of the famous men and women he had personally known over the past fifty years. He found more interest in Comte in America than he ever did in England. Quite surprising were the American women, who freely said what they thought and felt. He dined with Mark Twain, was made a member of seven New York clubs, lectured at Princeton, Bryn Mawr, the University of Pennsylvania, Columbia, and Carnegie Hall. He heard Theodore Roosevelt at Yonkers, N.Y., tell camp stories of the Rough Riders, visited in the home of Charles Eliot Norton at Cambridge, and got to know on his return trip J. P. Morgan, who had just made a $6 billion deal.

He succeeded James Bryce in 1910 as president of the Eastern Questions Association. Earlier he had represented Britain at the Congress of Historians at the Hague, where he had attended the installation of Queen Wilhelmina. In 1899 he was elected honorary fellow of Wadham College. Having lived at Hawkhurst, Kent, from 1902 to 1912, he moved to Bath, where he spent the remaining years of his life. He was made vice-president of the Royal Historical Society and of the London Library, and he received honorary degrees from Oxford, Cambridge, and Aberdeen.

In 1908, Harrison agreed to collect for the Alpine Club some earlier pieces he had written about mountaineering, which, together with six letters he had written his wife from Lake Leman only the year before, he published *My Alpine Jubilee*[24] in memory of Sir Leslie Stephen, the arch-Alpinist of them all (*MAJ*, 106). He recalls how he had joined Stephen in October 1864 in his ascent of Mount Blanc. Harrison compares mountaineering to the thrill of the ocean, except for the fact that the Alpine solitudes are more lonely and terrible than those of the sea, with forms and shapes "stupendous beyond all comparison." In order to find an even more compelling analogy for his English readers, Harrison relates how much the English love the "throb of the gallop, the bounding leap, the stately tread" they feel in the "first of all animals," the horse (*MAJ*, 107—108). But no gallop warms the blood so much as the mad whirl down a snow slope, for mountain-climbing exceeds horsemanship as completely as does the mystery of Alpine solitudes the pleasant landscape of English downs.

He had no interest in setting records or in competition of any sort. Never does he write with more poetic passion than when describing his Alpine experiences. When he first witnessed the Alps, he was almost carried out of his mind by the fascination he immediately felt for this new transcendent world, behaving "like a youth in delirium." He recalls that only Byron ever felt all the glory, humanity, and terror of the Alps, with their "pastoral simplicity, the love-lorn memories, the flashing storms, thundering avalanches, stupendous cataracts of the higher Alps, the awful solitudes of the Upper Snowfields, where Man stands fearless and even masterful face to face with the very Spirit of the Earth" (*MAJ*, 14). Who could have written *Manfred* but Byron? For him, only two other men knew the charm of the Alps better than Byron, but not their awe and majesty—Ruskin and Turner. Harrison's sensation there is "as fresh as Adam's" when he first awoke and beheld the world and wondered what it was (*MAJ*, 130).

Harrison died on January 13, 1923, on the same day that he was correcting proofs for *De Senectute*.[25] His mental strength and vivacity of manner had seemed more lively than during the previous summer. It is suitable that his final volume should open with the dialogue "De Senectute," for his old age was a living example of what he preached. Austin Harrison says that his father died of a sudden failure of the heart, the very way he had hoped he might pass away. His ashes were mingled with those of his wife's and were deposited in an urn in the chapel of Wadham College (*FH*, 221).

Chapter Two

The Scientific Foundation of Positivism

Harrison stated his views on the scientific basis of Positivism in various articles appearing in several periodicals, many of which he collected and published in *The Positive Evolution of Religion*,[1] *The Creed of a Layman*,[2] *De Senectute: More Last Words*,[3] and *The Philosophy of Common Sense*.[4] Because Harrison is indebted to Auguste Comte for virtually his entire philosophy of Positivism, I have emphasized the French philosopher's contributions throughout my discussion, especially those on science. It is my intention to indicate the consistent correlation between their ideas, and where there is any deviation or difference, I shall make it clear. However, on the subject of science, there is virtually no difference at all.

It is important to make clear that Comte had no thought of writing manuals on the sciences or proposing new scientific theories. His intention was to articulate a philosophy of science, something which he thought had not been done before and which had now, in the nineteenth century, become possible for the first time. He developed his theories of the Law of the Three States and of the Classification of the Sciences, which would become the basis of his Religion of Humanity. Harrison fully agreed with Comte that an understanding of the sciences is necessary before one can understand man's evolution to the positive state when religion can be placed on a rational basis, purged of the supernatural, and applied to all human activities in this life. Harrison became convinced that the Positive synthesis uniquely makes possible the reciprocal relationships among thought, activity, and feeling. He finds a harmony, a balance, that contrasted sharply with the disruptive and divisive development occurring in the nineteenth century, beginning as it did in the throes of the French Revolution and its aftermath. No problem more seriously preoccupies both nineteenth- and twentieth-century intellectuals than this revolutionary loss of synthesis, which he believes only Positivism can supply.

Auguste Comte: Father of Positivism

I say it advisedly—the whole story of human thought contains no example of powers so vast—powers of intellect, powers of will—even by the grudging testimony of those who oppose him—powers so vast, I say, exerted incessantly to a great end and yet from birth to the grave so completely unrecognised by men, so utterly without a ray of sympathy or respect by the world around, so all but utterly buried in systematic neglect and obloquy. (*PER*, 260)[5]

Frederic Harrison pays this tribute to the founder of Positivism, Auguste Comte, who, for the last thirty-five years of his life, applied himself with intense philosophic absorption. In his zealous preoccupation, Comte, in Harrison's opinion, was probably surpassed by few others, not even by Kant or Hegel in modern times or by Jerome, Aquinas, or Thomas à Kempis of an earlier age. After he met Comte in Paris two years before the philosopher's death in 1857, Harrison believes that he has never been quite so overwhelmed as he was by this interview, a conviction he would maintain until the end of his life. This opinion is all the more important when one considers the acquaintance Harrison had with many of the illustrious figures of the latter half of the nineteenth century, especially in England.

Comte was the last great thinker who wrote before Darwinism began to permeate the philosophic thinking of Europe. Although he did not affect the theory of cosmic organic evolution, he was important in conceiving of human history as a natural developmental process deriving from human nature and from the accumulation of past human experience.[6] Comte believed that the occurrence of the French Revolution demonstrated the failure of the Enlightenment and that consequently the salvation of society would depend on the ascendancy of scientific knowledge. The basis of the new social order would be inconceivable until Comte advanced his theory of the ordered system of the positive sciences, only made possible by their level of development in the mid-nineteenth century. Pushing Hume's and Condillac's epistemological theories to the limit, Comte not only confined human knowledge to the reciprocal relations of phenomena but also did not recognize as demonstrable anything absolute at the foundation of phenomena: that is to say, all is relative.[7] As the founder of the science of sociology, Comte's dream was to transform society with a new system that would sweep away the last vestiges of theological and metaphysical dreaming. And Harrison adds that he courageously attempted to bring order and stability to "one of the most anarchical ages in human history" (*PER*, 252).

Comte was born in 1798 during the most tempestuous decade of French history. In 1818, he made the acquaintance of Saint-Simon, whom he early admired and later loathed. It was the contrast between the dreamer and the systematizer, but the influence of the former on the latter was indubitable in the philosophic direction he was to take. From Saint-Simon, Comte learned to look for laws of social and political phenomena in the same way that he did in other areas and to realize that the purpose of philosophy is to reorganize our social, moral, and political life. Comte early saw that in a world characterized mainly by disintegration the answer must be some form of synthesis and reintegration. After six years, Comte, having long chafed because of Saint-Simon's presumptuousness and condescension, broke with his master. In 1825, he married Caroline Massin, with whom he was unable to get along even from the beginning.[8] He attempted to begin a school, which proved to be unsuccessful. Then he gave a course of public lectures which anticipated the works by which he was to become famous.

In 1828, after recovering from an attack of cerebral derangement, he returned to his lectures, which he published in 1830 as the first volume in his *Course of Positive Philosophy*, the sixth and last volume of which he published in 1842. This was the first of his two important works, conceived to be the foundation for the second, the *System of Positive Polity*, published in four volumes from 1851 to 1854.[9] Although by profession Comte was a teacher of mathematics, his only genuine devotion was given to work on his philosophy. Throughout his life he suffered the direst penury. Although he separated from his wife in 1842, he loyally sent her an allowance as long as she lived. For many years, he lived as a hermit, subsisting on just as little food as possible, divorcing himself from virtually all the social, political, literary, and scientific activities of his time, intently putting into practice his *hygiène cérébrale*, as he called it. Virtually his only reading had become Dante and Thomas à Kempis.

It was during this ascetic period that he evolved his elaborate system of philosophy and religion, divesting himself of every other interest, as he worked along hour after hour, year after year. It was during the last few years of his life that Harrison saw the philosopher for the first and only time, observing "the severe simplicity of his material existence, the intense conviction which gave him fire within, his personal courteousness and dignity, and the pure and noble spirit which he threw into all that he touched" (*PER*, 257). Never did he show a single hour of weakness or any vestige of compromise with the outside world during "this terrible martyrdom in the cause of truth" (*PER*, 258). Here Harrison is obviously anxious to lay to rest the frequent charge that Comte was motivated by an egotistical obsession.

But far from being a mere adulator of Comte, Harrison was by no means lacking in the rugged individualism that especially characterized such great Victorians as Mill, Ruskin, Leslie Stephen, Herbert Spencer, and T. H. Huxley. Perhaps his wholehearted devotion to Positivism, including the Religion of Humanity (which some Victorians sympathetic to Comte were simply unable to tolerate), could be likened to John Henry Newman's embrace of Roman Catholicism (to the disbelief of Charles Kingsley). Perhaps the reason for their respective religious devotedness is rather much the same: Harrison, in his early years, was also drawn to Puseyism, or the Oxford Movement. He notes that some of the great thinkers of the nineteenth century who became agnostic had not been brought up in the Anglican communion, a sacerdotal church, and so never understood the power of its spiritual associations. But Harrison recalls that he had been reared in such an environment, and at Oxford he had been taught by men whose roots were there.

At King's College School, when Tractarianism was at its height in the religious world, several of Harrison's closest friends, such as Charles Cookson and H. Parry Liddon, had become enamored of the movement (see *AM*, I, 36–38). As a child, he felt that he had literally received the actual body and blood of the Saviour (*CL*, 8). In Scotland, he had felt chilled to the bone by the bareness and austerity of the Presbyterian form of worship. And even in his latter years, he continued to prize the Evening Service in an Episcopal cathedral as "the most moving form of Art ever devised by man" (*CL*, 9). Were he a wealthy man, he would build a splendid temple like his favorite St. Sophia in Byzantium or the original Pantheon in Rome, where a beautiful choral service would be chanted at least three times a day so that he could rest for hours outside and let the music fairly float through his soul (*CL*, 9). Obviously, the form and the ceremony of Roman Catholicism that Comte, to some extent, retained for his own Religion of Humanity found a more receptive attitude in Harrison than it could possibly have done in such a Victorian agnostic as John Stuart Mill, who was otherwise quite favorable to Positivism, in general.

Harrison was no more an idolator, however, than his intensely independent fellow-Victorians Mill and Leslie Stephen. Much as he admired Comte as the founder of Positivism and as the profoundest thinker of modern times, he did not consider Comte an ideal type for imitation, nor did he "claim for his teaching any abstract authority or universal supremacy" (*PER*, 260). Imitation of Comte's life is scarcely a rational idea and would therefore be unworthy of the rationality which Harrison so venerates and would be nothing short of theological extravagance. Further, Harrison categorically asserts that no system of science whatever, not even if it be the result of the sum total of the intellect of the whole human race (much less of one man, even of the highest genius), could ever achieve finality. The very suggestion of such an idea fills him with loathing and disgust. The genius of Comte for Harrison is that he was the first to sketch the broad outlines of a synthesis of knowledge so soon as such an undertaking had become possible. So long as human thought was largely theological and metaphysical, it was not possible to conceive of such a synthesis until the social science of sociology had made its appearance. Comte, then, is to be doubly honored for having founded sociology and for having sketched the scientific synthesis. Harrison compares Comte as an important innovator to Sir Isaac Newton as the founder of celestial physics and to Aristotle as the encyclopedic genius of the ancient world (*PER*, 263).

In 1845, Comte made the acquaintance of Madame Clotilde de

Vaux, whose husband had been sent to the galleys for misdeeds as tax collector but who was prevented by law from obtaining a divorce. While vainly attempting to earn her living by the pen, she made the acquaintance of Comte. He fell instantly in love with her, and the experience entirely changed his mode of thought. Their relation, for less than a year (she died in 1846), never went beyond a kiss and was conducted mainly through letters. She was probably a rather ordinary woman, who was very likely never in love with him. The armchair in which she sat while on a visit to borrow some money was later converted into a private altar where he worshiped her as a Roman Catholic might pray to the Virgin Mary.[10] From 1846 on, she became, in some respects, the Virgin's equivalent in the Religion of Humanity.[11] This woman held some of the same ascendancy over Comte's mind that Mrs. Taylor held over Mill's. Every Wednesday afternoon, he made a regular pilgrimage to her tomb, and three times each day he paid devotions to her memory. Perhaps he had Dante's Beatrice in mind, for he continued to read that poet during periods when he read hardly anything else at all.

Comte planned a Positivist Church, for which he wrote the *Positive Calendar*, containing the lives of great men who had advanced civilization and whose names he substituted for those of the Christian saints.[12] For his *Calendar*, Comte devised a method by which he counted 364 days, with an extra day which he called the Year Day. There would be thirteen months with twenty-eight days each, thus eliminating uneven months. Harrison used this calendar in his private correspondence with friends. However, two considerations militated against its use: it ran counter to immemorial tradition and it aroused fear of the number thirteen.

Comte also devised a plan for a priesthood, whose role will be more fully described later, as will the role of women, his idea of which was determined by his memory of Madame de Vaux. John Morley, a lifelong friend of Harrison's, marvels that Comte's stress on the observation of real facts ever culminated in a system "so retrograde." Nevertheless, Morley pays tribute to Comte's highly original encyclopedic system that touches life, society, and knowledge at every point, and to his invaluable contribution to modern thought.[13]

On September 5, 1857, Comte died of cancer. He provided in his will for the preservation of his rooms at 10 rue Monsieur-le-Prince as the headquarters of the Religion of Humanity, which he was convinced would inevitably prevail.[14] Positivism remained a live issue during the latter half of the nineteenth century and was heatedly debated by such intellectuals as Mill, Huxley, Spencer, George Eliot, G. H. Lewes, Harriet Martineau, Leslie and Fitzjames Stephen, Mark Pattison, and Harrison himself, to mention but a few.[15] Harrison thought that the most insidious deterioration in the twentieth century, which underlies all our other problems, is the decline in religious faith. The Religion of Humanity, which he was convinced was the only sound synthesis adapted to modern civilization, brought him a quiet life of both peace and hope, and he spent most of his life in serving its cause. Of course, to Auguste Comte he would remain forever indebted.

The Law of the Three States and Evolution[16]

Comte thought that until the point of development science had reached in the nineteenth century, theology and metaphysics had been the only ways the human mind had to conceive of the world. It was his theory that the natural law of the history of society may be found in his own principle of the Three States. Man must intellectually progress through, first, the theological phase and, later, the metaphysical phase before reaching the positive. The first two states are essential to the subsequent development of the positive, or scientific, method. Importantly, at the present time, the three states coexist, but the positive encroaches more and more on the other two.

The Three States do not refer to the religious evolution of humanity but rather to the stages of the progress of the human intellect in history, the successive interpretations of natural phenomena, with each stage developing naturally and logically from the preceding one. This law of the intellectual evolution of humanity is really the foundation of the social sciences, for it assumes that every branch of our knowledge depends on this passage through the three states. Comte's proposal of the Law of the Three States, or the law of social dynamics, made possible, for the first time, the study of man's characteristics from both the historical and the sociological point of view.[17]

All forms of the first stage, the theological, have this in common: the conviction that there is a supreme Will intelligible to, and in contact with, man, a force which has ordained and has continued to order all things—physical, mental, and moral. This theory assigns supernatural and arbitrary causes to the origin of natural phenomena, that is, to will rather than to laws. At the beginning, the human mind could not do otherwise than resort to the theological method of interpretation of nature. Man understood the workings of nature in the same way he had his own volitions and actions. Comte believed that man first anthropomorphized his concept of the gods, who were discovered to be remarkably like himself. Now man needed to propitiate these deities, whose will was law, for he thought that he himself had very little direct power over nature.

Comte especially valued this early stage of thought as essential to the formation and development of human society. In addition to a certain mutual sympathy of feeling, there must also be an intellectual commitment to common beliefs that are closely associated with hopes and fears concerning both this world and the next, which are now bound together. Furthermore, there is the formation of a new specialized class—the priests—which, being devoted to intellectual activity, is distinguished from the rest of society. Its appearance initiates a division of labor, which is essential to a complex society. Comte supposed that our engineers, scholars, and philosophers descend from those early priests and sorcerers.

But the theological viewpoint contains the seeds of its own destruction. As man uses his mind, he begins to wonder whether his earlier ideas were not antiquated and rather ridiculous as his first realization of laws forces him to question those acts of capricious beings all too much like himself. For one thing, he perceives there are many operations that do not seem to be controlled by the will of these deities he has imagined, for these activities seem to be invariable in their function. The mind of man, though, does not move right away into the positive stage but rather into an intermediate, transitional stage. Comte thought that the second, or metaphysical, state, represents the modifications that physics makes on the theological, an early manifestation of the positive, actually. Before this early incursion of the positive, the theological state is relatively self-contained, as the metaphysical state, by its very nature, can never be. However, the positive at this stage lies concealed behind metaphysical entities and thereby does not alarm the theological-minded unduly, for the first two stages are equally reliant on the absolute rather than on the relative.

Comte thought that the substitution of Nature for God in the eighteenth century is a good example of the resort to entities of the metaphysical stage, amalgamating the divine element of religion with the idea of natural laws. Since the metaphysical stage is basically a compromise, it is more negative than positive and so can scarcely furnish a foundation for morality and religion. The positive stage replaces the use of imagination with that of observation, the idea of the absolute with that of the relative. But Comte concedes that the three modes of thought coexist at the present time, even in the most educated individuals. All our ideas evolve through this pattern of the three states, and even in the most developed positive sciences there are discernible traces of the earlier stages. Therefore, Comte devised a method by which it is possible to determine the degree of the positive any given science has reached. It is called the Classification of the Sciences.

Comte thought that the various branches of science have not proceeded along the three states at the same pace. He concluded that the conditions had to mature in a given branch in order that progress in another could become possible. And, importantly, he classified only the so-called theoretical sciences, leaving out the so-called applied and practical (or technical) sciences; he wished to deal with those sciences that concern altogether the knowledge of laws, exclusive of concrete phenomena. The practical sciences such as zoology and geography derive their principles from the abstract, or theoretical, sciences. It is from the theoretical sciences that Comte expected to find the progess of the human mind through the three states.

Harrison points out that Positivism as a system of thought refers not only to science but also to philosophy and religion as well, with each one aiding the other two and completing them. He regards Positivism as a synthesis. The important thing is that the purported facts of Positivism must be subject to demonstration and verification. Religion in the Positivist sense does not refer to the supernatural and thereby the undemonstrable. There are certain ultimate problems in metaphysics and theology that defy human solution, the preoccupation with which has no appreciable advantageous effect on man's human condition on the earth here and now. It is the knowledge that is slowly won by man over nature and her laws that is progressive. Such problems that yield no fruit are abandoned. "There is no single instance," writes Harrison, "of this filiation of truth in the whole theological department of metaphysics. There is here no torch handed on" (*PCS*, 103).[18] Metaphysical theories are like so many bubbles that pop and are superseded by countless others that go and do likewise. The discussion of them never really advances as virtually every thinker starts *de novo*, building according to his own personal fancy. The creation of the planet and the origin of the Universe are problems as insoluble as when they were first essayed. Man's intellect, Harrison is persuaded, can find rest only in realities, not in dreams. Man craves a synthesis of intellect, feeling, and activity to be realized in a larger sense of Humanity and in a perpetual development of its earthly life (*PCS*, xxxvii).

At the Metaphysical Society (*PCS*, 131−63), a follower of Hegel delivered a paper on the Absolute, which Harrison answers, evidencing considerable skill in philosophical argumentation, subjecting his opponent to the kind of analysis that Hegelians themselves like to use.[19] Defining the Absolute as an entity without either conditions or categories, Harrison argues that it cannot be a cause, or The Cause, or the First Cause; if it were, one would have to assume that something else is as necessary as itself which is not itself. If it becomes a Cause, it must then change from Absolute existence to Causal existence and so become either more or less. But the Absolute is held to be Perfect in itself, Eternal, and Infinite. Is the Absolute more the Absolute when it becomes a Cause or less the Absolute? One must always remember that it can admit of neither degree nor change.

Harrison quotes his ontological-minded opponent as contending, "When we say we cannot know the Absolute, we affirm that there is an Absolute." Harrison bluntly comments that this may be Hegelianism, but it is also a "contradiction in words." And he continues: "When we say we cannot know the Sea-serpent, do we affirm that the Sea-serpent exists?" When the metaphysicians allude to "an indefi-

nite, undefinable, subliminal consciousness, which is wholly independent of logic . . . ," Harrison jokingly says that "there is a sort of
something" which makes us conscious "in a kind of way" of a
Transcendental Absolute, Real, Unknowable. He thinks that the
lowly man in the street oftentimes has hold of the subject, whereas the
metaphysician grasps at the shadow of his brain "cast on the clouds of
Non-Entity." If this transcendentalism disposes of all logic and
reveals alogical dogmas of its own, it would descend to the vulgar
level of superstitious faith-healing. All this talk about "universal
consciousness" is mere verbiage (*PCS*, 134–37).

If the Absolute is everything, everything, by the same token, is the
Absolute. Therefore, thought becomes impossible because nothing
remains to be distinguished. It is better, he concludes, to rely more on
the common sense of sensible men, for we can understand nothing
about the Absolute, the Unconditioned, and the like. The very ideas
they denote are "unmeaning, cobwebs, spun industriously out of
infinite subtleties and non-entities—which rest upon nothing, and
can lead to nothing" (*PCS*, 141). If the Absolute should do anything,
or become anything, the idea of change is involved and there is the
emergence of a new mode of existence. That is to say, it ceases to be
the Absolute and becomes the Relative.

In *Novissima Verba: Last Words—1920*,[20] Harrison comments on
the theories of Albert Einstein. He notes that mystics and obscurant-
ists have gleefully contended that since Einstein has superseded
Euclid and Newton, they can now return to their "sublime and
antique fancies." However, he rejects their supposition that science is
thereby unreliable and therefore useless, arguing that scientists have
never thought their knowledge to be either complete or final but
rather have always been open to new improvements and corrections.
Neither Euclid nor Newton ever thought they were demonstrating
ultimate or absolute laws of the Universe. As a matter of fact,
Harrison is pleased that Einstein has only corroborated Harrison's
own belief that there is no limit to relativity, for nothing is true any
further than human powers or conditions permit. He has always
thought that Time and Space are no more than "mere working forms
of the human understanding." Even so, Einstein's theories should not
be considered as absolute verities, for no one can prove that "the

objective order of the Universe" is not different from our own conception of it, for even Time, Space, the Aether, and Gravitation are nothing but our human conception of them and possibly no more than dreams (NV, 165−68).

The transition from the first two stages of thought to the third, the positive, representing the shift from the Absolute to the Relative, parallels the shift from ancient thought to modern. Ancient thought traced an eternal outline in every object and classified the varieties of life by kinds. In contrast, nothing can be known, on modern terms, except relatively and under certain conditions. The latter viewpoint has naturally developed under the influence of the sciences of observation, which discover a gradation of the types of life through minute refinements of change. The modern mind wishes no longer to seek eternal, immutable forms but rather seeks to discover gradations and connections in the world that change as we ourselves also do.[21]

Although Comte brought the idea of evolution just up to that of the transmutation of species, he still clung to the Aristotelian *eidos*, or form. For two thousand years it had been thought that change and transiency are sure signs of defect and unreality. True knowledge consisted of comprehending the permanent end that realizes itself through changes. There were but two alternative courses open: (1) to find reality in changing things or (2) to find reality in some transcendent, supernal region. In 1860, Harrison found no difficulty in hailing the *Origin of Species* (1859), for upon it the ark of absolute permanency was wrecked. Darwin completely vindicated, for him, the reality of change and relativity. The evolutionary theories of the nineteenth century dealt the death blow to Transcendentalism and Deism, both which Comte had attributed to the Metaphysical stage and therefore destined to be replaced. The argument for Design had depended on the idea of fixed and final Causes.

Comte disposed of the problem of evil in the history of Humanity in a way not dissimilar to Darwin's treatment of the problem of harmful variations in the struggle of existence. Natural Selection abolishes the antecedent intelligent force that predetermines organic adaptations, which are in fact caused by constant variation and elimination of elements that are detrimental in the struggle of existence. Darwin thought there are useless as well as useful variations.

But the useful ones are sifted out through the arduous conditions of the struggle of existence. Thus the argument for Design seemed untenable. Although Comte had even rejected Lamarck, Harrison had no trouble embracing the main features of the *Origin*, for it seemed to vindicate the movement from the Metaphysical state to the Positive.

When Helmholtz discovered the principle of the Conservation of Energy and when Darwin published his theory of Natural Selection, Comtean Statics and Dynamics in a self-contained universe seemed to have been corroborated. Matter and energy were never destroyed but were forever changing form. In the Law of the Three States, Comte had thought in terms of the evolution of social forms and of human thought, if not of biological forms. Evolutionary thought permeated the *Zeitgeist* of the middle and latter nineteenth century. Comte contributed the scientific conception of human history as a process of natural development through general laws governing human nature.[22]

Comte would not have found displeasing Darwin's belief that there is a grandeur in the scientific view of man, because he is actually ennobled by it. Since man has risen to the very top of the organic scale, rather than having been, at his creation, simply put there for no particular merit of his own, he has hope that he may, on his own, gain a still higher destiny in the distant future. And, very much like Comte, Darwin sacrifices the furtherance of individual happiness to the promotion of the general good of the species as a whole. As with Comte, man's good actions are those requiring self-sacrifice, self-command, and the power of endurance to attain the ends of the tribe rather than the happiness of the individual.

Of course, the principal theological objection to Darwin's theory of the transmutation of species has always been that it treats man as though he were simply the summit of the animal kingdom rather than a unique creature made in the image of God. It has not been much palliation for the Darwinian to explain that man has descended not from the ape but from a creature very much like him. Harrison, not unlike Comte, believes that a sound view of man's relations to the lower animals contributes to his gaining a correct understanding of Humanity itself. This relation must rest on a healthy, scientific, social, and even religious basis. Human duty includes not only sympathy toward the animal kingdom, of which we ourselves are a definite part, but also religious reverence, as well. Like Darwin, Harrison insists that there is no fundamental distinction between man and animal, because man is essentially an animal; he is the first among animals, though in no absolute sense (*M & T*, 401–2).

The higher animals, for Harrison, share with us the various qualities of feeling, action, and intelligence, and even the lower animals show some rudiments of these qualities. The essential instincts of man are nutrition, sex, parenthood, destruction, construction, love of power, love of praise, attachment, reverence, and kindness (or love). All these instincts may be found in the animals, some in greater degree than in man. Most of the nobler animals show germs of all the aspects of our moral character.

Harrison always felt a strong abomination for field sports, and having tramped in the woods for over sixty years, he could not ever be induced to carry a gun or anything but a good stick or possibly a map and field glass (*M & T*, 401–2). Darwin, similarly shocked by wanton cruelty, was horrified by the idea that a First Cause, or the Christian God, might have sent afflictions just to afford man an opportunity to win moral and spiritual improvement. Even so, Darwin wondered what moral advantage there could be in the sufferings of untold millions of the lower animals throughout time. The chief evil of religion, he thought, would then be that pain and misery come from on High rather than merely occurring at random. That God works through Natural Selection is no exculpation. However, Darwin, like Comte, assumes no such directing force or intelligence. And Thomas Henry Huxley in *Evolution and Ethics* sees no implicit relationship between evolution and ethics.

Harrison, as a Positivist, also refuses to try to reconcile Divine Mercy with a world of misery and death or to have faith in the suspension of laws that clearly operate throughout nature. He frankly concedes that Humanity, through no fault of its own, finds itself in such a condition. But he realizes that it has the tools and the opportunity to improve life in this world, however gradually, so that amelioration will accrue progressively from generation to generation. In this way, we may become a "part of that very Providence which nourishes the infant, strengthens and informs the man, and lays our weary bones to rest in tender memory of whatever good we may have left to our fellow beings who will follow us on earth" (*PER*, 231—32).

The historical consummation of the Three States, then, is reached in the third and last one, the Metaphysical being no more than a bridge between the first and the third. The metaphysical state takes from the Theological the Absolute of reality, explicable as a First Principle, and it derives from the Positive in that it attempts to demonstrate through explanations. It originates in theology and ends in science. Positivism is the triumph of the Relative and of the law of social dynamics. The Positivist must accept nothing less than scientific evidence for anything that he believes. The Three States refer to the development of the way the human being sees and understands phenomena, only that and nothing more. It is perhaps Comte's most important contribution to philosophy.

The Classification of the Sciences

Comte establishes a classification, or hierarchy, of the fundamental sciences in order to trace the development of the positive spirit through the various kinds of phenomena.[23] It is in the development of these sciences that we can find the intellectual evolution of the human spirit. Some of these sciences, of course, have reached the positive state, whereas others still partially remain in either the theological or metaphysical states. But it must be understood that our own conceptions have all, for the first time, reached the positive form because Comte has discovered sociology and the Law of Three States. Now the sense of the hierarchy is perceived, and it becomes possible to classify the theoretical sciences in a rational order. Further, the study of the Absolute has been replaced by that of the Relative. Importantly, Comte is different from other systematizers in that he repudiates any identity of governing principles, any attempt to explain the sciences by general principles that rule in the Universe.

The first science in the series, mathematics, is the most general and abstract and therefore farthest removed from humanity. But Comte does not mean that the sciences are chronologically formed one after the other. On the contrary, the classification has to do with the sequence of their reaching the positive state, each one paralleling our own intellectual evolution. In other words, this classification relates not to the universe objectively but to the intellectual development of man. Each science becomes the preliminary to that which succeeds it, each one remains homogeneous and irreducible, and each one has its own methodology. Yet the ascent of the sciences is a progressive order toward the unity that sociology makes possible. For the first time, Comte believed, a philosophy of science becomes possible (see *DeS*, 172–76, and *PCS*, 66–101).

The progress of the scientific mind has evolved with the rational extension of plain common sense to all subjects amenable to human reason (*PCS*, 42). The foundation is observation of constant relationships among simple phenomena. The purpose of science is to confirm the existence of laws in place of the unsupported imagination. These laws are really no more or less than the constant relationships among given phenomena. Although practical science leads to the theoretical, ironically the theoretical, in turn, leads to the practical. A good case in point is the modern space program, wherein many theoretical discoveries that had earlier seemed devoid of practical application made possible the exploration of our solar system. And there have been innumerable practical spin-offs from that program back into the realm of our daily life.

Comte conceives of science as the collective work of humanity, which should rightly be accessible to all mankind. Its proper function is to rise above mere empirical recognition to a real knowledge of the laws of science. The State owes scientific instruction to its citizens, but, in general, they should not be required to receive a deep knowledge of the fundamental sciences, which on no account should be simplified. It is important that all men should be taught the habit of understanding that all phenomena are equally controlled by constant laws. They should be taught a summary of each fundamental science from mathematics to sociology. Of course, the scientists are the first to pass from a traditional to a new positivist attitude.

Positive science avoids the two extremities of mysticism and empiricism. It avoids attempting to ascertain cause and substance, on the one hand, and sheer simple fact on the other. Emphasizing the relativity of science, Comte scrupulously avoids developing a theory of knowledge. The very laws we can determine are never true except under certain conditions. Absolute notions are impossible, and new laws may always be discovered. Even so, all our laws and facts are no more than approximations. Actually, our science is relative to our own organization; were it different, so would our data be. Further, our conceptions, religions, and philosophies are social as well as individual phenomena—moments in a continuous and collective life. With the founding of sociology, science can be conceived only as relative, for the concept of social progression eliminates the absolute fixity of metaphysicians (see *PCS*, chap. 5).

Human science, in effect, is not a state but rather a progress. And truth, at any given period, is the logical correspondence between our conceptions and our observations. Traditional frames ultimately disintegrate, only to be redeveloped and then again to disintegrate. Therefore, positive philosophy recognizes no immutable, absolute truth. Paradoxically, understood from the sociological point of view, science is both true and relative. Comte completely abandons the idea of an ultimate law from which all other laws may be deduced. But all phenomena are subject to laws, a principle that ironically becomes virtually an essential dogma of positive science and philosophy. But a belief in a final cause, as understood in the metaphysical stage as the order of Nature instead of the Christian God, gradually disappears.

The exclusive cultivation of a single science is dangerous. Under the aegis of sociology, scientific anarchy is eliminated and the relationships among the sciences are recognized. In mathematics, we have the art of reasoning. In astronomy, we must resort to the art of observation as well as of forming hypotheses. In physics, we make use of experimentation. In chemistry, we develop the art of nomenclature and classification. In biology, we work with the comparative method of science. And, at last, in sociology, we come to the historical method. Each fundamental science requires the use of methods peculiar to itself. But methods developed in particular sciences may then be utilized in the other ones, whether earlier or later. And ultimately the scientist must also be the philosopher, thus utilizing all the resources of the positive method. The reader may recall Harrison's disagreement with F. D. Maurice over breaking history up into narrow compartments instead of seeing it as total development.

One crucial problem for Positivism is the reconciliation of the objective method with the subjective, the one reaching out from knowledge of the world on up to that of man, and the other reaching from the consideration of man out to that of the world. They would appear to be contradictory. As early as the third volume of the *Course in Positive Philosophy*, Comte had recognized this problem and its seeming impasse and had explained that the laws of nature of the special sciences can be examined only by the means of the objective method, whereas the universal view of philosophy can be attained only by the subjective method. The individual sciences are but parts of the whole; therefore, an objective synthesis is impossible. But a subjective synthesis is able to furnish a synthesis of the whole. Ironically, the many laws of nature that we can never get to know reach outwardly indefinitely; it would be impossible to unify all knowledge with the objective viewpoint that would give us a single idea. But if we change our viewpoint to man as the center, i.e., the sociological viewpoint, we shall be able to subordinate the entire series of the sciences to the final one, that of sociology. Actually, the positive philosophy assumes the role that theology had always attempted to perform, but the positive philosophy utilizes observation instead of the imagination. The new sociology, for the first time, accurately unifies and systematizes the laws found in the separate sciences of the hierarchy. The individual has been made universal (*PCS*, 34–37).

The subjective and the objective methods are complementary to each other. Harrison explains that, as in man himself, there is a dualism of observations and conceptions. Knowledge is necessarily an equipoise between the two. Similarly, a purely speculative philosophy develops conceptions at the expense of observations and so is unable to produce true verification. It ends in nothing more than a dream. A purely objective science emphasizes observations at the expense of conceptions and so ends in chaos. The whole system of man's observations should correspond with the entire system of human nature. Since all ideas are relative, knowledge is inescapably subjective. Science is no more than "the systematic form of spontaneous good sense," for there is no single and final test of reality (*PCS*, 42). It is this subjective synthesis, establishing a harmony among thought, feeling, and action, that shall remedy the present failure and anarchy that results from the separation of religion, morality, and science. The central idea of Positivism is that until the human heart, intellect, and energy are unified, human life can never be either healthy or sound. Once we accept the relativity of all knowledge, the subjective nature of all our thoughts about the external world follows. And all we know is a process of inference from the impressions of the senses. In short, the only true synthesis has to be subjective (*PCS*, 42).

Harrison takes pains to dismiss the natural theology so often relied on in the eighteenth century with its theory of divine adaptation. Paley is famous for having instanced the human eye as proof of the existence of the Divine Architect, Whose work is perfect. As wonderful as the eye is, though, it has often been shown that its defects are numerous, of the kind that man has easily eliminated in his own optical instruments. Harrison observes that the human eye is more easily seen as a witness to the adaptation and use of evolution than to the omniscience of God. He notes that scientific study has revealed a world of anything but a benevolent Deity, with its incredible waste, destruction, and mutual antagonism, as though it were created for no other purpose. He obviously believes that science does not reveal the universe as the work of Omnipotent Goodness, a fond theory of the metaphysical stage. Rather he believes that the world of Humanity will be revealed neither by divine inspiration nor by metaphysical intuition but by positive science (*PCS*, 96−97).

Comte does not classify psychology as a fundamental science, fearing that its reliance on introspection, or internal observation, is likely to encourage a return to the metaphysical retention of the theological idea of the soul. Also, Comte fears any tendency to exalt interest in, or consideration of, the individual as opposed to society. Thus sociology, not psychology, is the science that follows biology in the scale. He wonders how the observing organ and the observed could be identical at any given instant. Sociology is alone capable of analyzing affective, intellectual, and moral functions, for it has to do not with just the individual but with society as a whole: to know himself, the individual must know history (*PCS*, xxviii−xxx).

Harrison believes that both Mill and Huxley mistakenly thought that Comte had repudiated psychology, whereas he had merely dismissed intuitional introspection as unreliable and not positivistic

(*PCS*, xxviii—xxix). Further, psychology relies on both biology and sociology and is therefore a mixed and concrete rather than an abstract, fundamental science. In the same way, geology relies on astronomy, physics, and biology: it is mixed, concrete, not a pure, theoretical science. There are only six distinct, fundamental, theoretical sciences in Comte's hierarchy. And, importantly, Comte does not attempt any unification of the sciences under one principle or any resort to monism (*PCS*, xxvii). Harrison believes that Mill mistook the French word *l'unité*, which Comte uses to mean harmony. He charges that Mill had not read the *Politique Positive* with care and that Huxley had not read it at all (*PCS*, xxviii).

Nor, he insists, is the Positivistic system materialistic. Its conceptions about nature depend on collaboration between the world without and the mind within man, although he deems it quite impossible to apportion the relative amount of subjective and objective elements involved. Nor is there any Hegelian attempt to equate the objective world without with the subjective mind within. Man is a compound of intelligence, feeling, and activity. And philosophy cannot be separated from morality, sociology, or activity. A purely subjective philosophy ends in dreaming; a purely objective philosophy ends in anarchy and chaos. Knowledge must be the equipoise between observations and conceptions. The deficiency of metaphysical speculation is that conceptions are divorced from observations, making true verification impossible (*PCS*, xxx—xxxii).

Comte closely associates his philosophy of the sciences with that of his philosophy of history and of progress. And this philosophy of the sciences has no truck with cloudy speculations on the nature of reality or the vain attempt to explain what the sciences themselves do not attempt to explain. But a philosophy is necessary to a viewpoint of the whole, one that must be positive and relative, like the sciences themselves, and very unlike the a priori knowledge that metaphysicians use to account for knowledge beyond the bounds of experience. Comte wants a synthesis of the whole of our actual knowledge of invariable relationships rather than of causes and substance. Until Comte, a philosophy of the sciences had been only a metaphysical conception.

Positivist philosophy recognizes two complementary aspects of reality, the static and the dynamic. From the static point of view, the unity of the sciences is seen in their hierarchy, or classification. From the dynamic point of view, the Law of the Three States is seen in the progressive movement of human intelligence through its understanding of the fundamental sciences which culminate in sociology. Comte's guiding principle throughout is to eliminate from consideration that which man has no way of knowing and that which he does not need to know. Also, no longer should he attempt to know for the mere sake of knowing (*PCS*, 46).

Although this philosophy seems limited in one sense, Harrison contends that it is the metaphysical philosophy, like that of either Kant or Hegel, that is not a philosophy of the sciences at all but rather one that is limited to ontological and psychological enigmas. At least, the theological philosophy does have the advantage of supporting the great primary truth that religion is the dominant principle of man's social life. But it omits the consideration of the development of modern science as well as of the statics and dynamics that underlie our modern world. Four-fifths of life lies outside both metaphysics and theology (*PCS*, 67). Neither one provides a synthesis of human knowledge and experience (*PCS*, 68).

There must be, maintains Harrison, a true human synthesis that is coextensive with human nature, susceptible to logical verification, and able to appeal to the whole range of human thought, affection, and energy. This is the meaning of the Religion of Humanity: a true synthesis of thought and life. Man's intellectual, moral, and active life must be made one by the presence of one great unifying principle—Humanity—which he should believe in and adore and which is integrated with every activity and thought of his life. To attempt to attain an understanding of absolute existences, or even absolute relations, is futile. No absolute synthesis, therefore, is possible. The relative synthesis is the corolary of the relativity of knowledge, with man as the central point, with the entire life of the race, as well as its highest ideals and hopes, composing this synthesis. This has nothing to do with some ecstatic contemplation or imaginary vision that is essentially irrelevant either to the logic of modern thought or to the complex accumulations of the masses of modern knowledge (*PCS*, 78−79).

Harrison compares and contrasts the two famous syntheses of knowledge in the nineteenth century that purport to be based on scientific principles: those of Comte and Herbert Spencer, respectively (*DeS*, 192−93). He contends that Spencer, who gives very little credit to Comte, must have learned a great deal about the Frenchman's theories from his intimate friends, George Henry Lewes and George Eliot, with whom he was closely associated for three or four years. He charges that Spencer's Synthetic Philosophy was largely an imitation of Comte's theories, utilizing Comte's ideas on the universal reign of laws, the law of evolution, the relativity of knowledge, the repudiation of nonverifiable hypotheses, the idea of a synthesis of science, and the purpose of philosophy being the improvement of the human organism (*DeS*, 193).

But the differences between the two philosophies are considerable, also, Harrison concedes (*DeS*, 192−93). First, Spencer, like the nonscientific philosophers, also attempts an objective synthesis of the entire Universe. Comte rejects any idea of accounting for cosmic realms quite beyond our actual understanding or experience as "a pretentious dream," as hypothetical as the cosmogony of Moses or as the "sonorities of the *Welt-idee.*" Second, Spencer omits discussion of mathematics, geometry, astronomy, physics, and chemistry, as well as the whole world of numbers, space, mechanics, and inorganic science. Comte, on the other hand, devotes innumerable chapters to all the sciences precedent to biology. In Spencer's Synthetic Philosophy, "this mighty ocean of thought is a vast *Mare ignotum*" (*DeS*, 195). The third important difference is that whereas Spencer limits himself to the static principles of sociology and ethics, Comte devotes much space to social dynamics, or a philosophy of history. Whereas Comte describes major epochs and events of history down to the Revolution of 1848, Spencer has nothing to say about them. How, Harrison asks, could such a philosophy be properly termed "synthetic"? Harrison believes that Comte's is the first true philosophic synthesis in history (*DeS*, 195−96).

Chapter Three

Positivism: Religion for Modern Man

Harrison believes that no other religion has ever depended so much on a scientific background or a concern with sociological principles as has Positivism. Fearing that other religions, which have relied too much on the supernatural, have abandoned a great number of man's vital concerns, he thinks a modern religion should be rooted both in human nature and in human history. Affected by the rise in the nineteenth century of biblical criticism and by the development of theories of biological evolution, many Christian intellectuals, Harrison is convinced, have attempted to graft vague theories of what he calls Neo-Christianity and of theism onto the old stock of traditional Christianity. This resort has led to nothing more than attenuated ideals and barren formulae. Attacking the new cult of Neo-Christianity, Harrison insists that Positivism is not an assault on traditional Christianity but rather a rational extension of it, enabling religion to become an essential part of man's daily life. He has no patience, however, with either agnosticism or atheism: man's religious feelings are valid and normal when rational and fruitful.

In such works as *Autobiographic Memoirs*, *The Creed of a Layman: Apologia pro Fide Mea*, *De Senectute*, *The Positive Evolution of Religion*, and his contribution to *Great Religions of the World*,[1] Harrison discusses the Religion of Humanity, which is the culmination of Positivist beliefs and the most controversial of Comte's philosophical contributions. Unlike John Stuart Mill, George Henry Lewes, and other English intellectuals, Harrison was able to go all the way with Comte by embracing the new religion. In public debate and in print, Harrison faithfully resisted all attacks by friend and foe on what he thought to be the one theory that treats human nature as an organic whole in an age that exalts specialism and ignores synthesis. He never wavered in his assertion that the Religion of Humanity affords modern man all the necessary elements of a genuine religion, minus beatific visions and transcendent mysteries. Comte, he believes, translated religious fairy tales into sensible, adult reality.

Essays and Reviews and Harrison's "Neo-Christianity"

It is precisely the Religion of Humanity, which the leading English agnostics (otherwise sympathetic with Comte's Positivism) especially abhorred, that Harrison embraced wholeheartedly. He agrees with Comte that one should never take away anything that he does not replace with something else. It is true that agnostics like Mill, Huxley, Spencer, and Leslie Stephen thought a vigorous, honest, forthright sense of morality was immensely to be preferred to any supernatural religion. The Victorians differed from us in the form of belief which they adopted in place of unbelief: in a word, morality. If anything, the loss of faith resulted in an increase in their moral earnestness and led to a need to create a kind of Religion of Humanity. This replacement of religion by morality is evident in the crisis-of-faith novels of the period. (Mrs. Humphrey Ward's *Robert Elsmere* was one of the best-selling novels of all time.) This new "atheistic" morality completes the process already begun by Protestantism.[2]

One of Leslie Stephen's strongest criticisms of Christianity is that it promotes an intense selfishness. He pictures the cringing Christian who is too fearful of his own hide to care about the interests of his fellow-sufferers. Although he criticizes the third Earl of Shaftesbury's philosophical Optimism, he does prefer that philosopher's reliance on inward virtues to the Christian's morbid fear of the intervention of an external power.[3] How long, he wonders, will the shadow of Christianity survive the substance of reality? The modern Socialist, he continues, unlike the early Christian, aspires to conquer the world instead of withdrawing from it, to abolish poverty rather than idealize it, and to enter utopia rather than heaven. He envisions not a promised land of eternal happiness without labor but an indefinite vista of material and social progress. And he would never think of consigning his oppressors to an everlasting hell. The Christian criterion of virtue, continues Stephen, ignores improving this life and, on the contrary, encourages indifference to temporal interests.[4]

Harrison's constant admonition is that we must learn to live for others; it was Comte who invented the very word *altruism*. Harrison and Stephen speak rather much the same language except for the Religion of Humanity. However, the nineteenth-century British liberal's love of freedom remains a bar to Stephen's reverting to a medievalism that high-church Anglicans themselves would abhor. Stephen, in his *Science of Ethics*, hopes to make evolutionary ethics do the work of religion and take the place of God. Evolution is an Immanent God, or Process, at work within the world, and society is an organism which, like the species, evolves by laws that are analogous to scientific laws.[5] In background and character, then, Stephen and Harrison are much alike, but Harrison, so much less insular, falls under the influence of the Frenchman Comte.

Two books of remarkable importance were published at about the same time: Darwin's *The Origin of Species* (1859) and *Essays and Reviews* (1860), a manifesto by seven important representatives of the Broad Church movement.[6] Publication of the latter work was the most important event in the history of English rationalism during the nineteenth century. The Broad Church wished to advance two main ideas within the Establishment: (1) to defend the right to free inquiry on theological matters and (2) to reconcile the growing differences between traditional religious beliefs and the recent influence of science and of the Higher Criticism. The Broad Church had been increasing in prestige since the collapse of the Tractarian movement.[7] When this work was published, intellectual attention was being focused at the moment on Darwin's *Origin*, Gladstone's important budget, Garibaldi's Sicilian expedition, and Eliot's *The Mill on the Floss*.[8] It was not until Harrison published an essay on the book in the *Westminster Review* in the same year, his first serious piece, that the manifesto was catapulted into immediate prominence. The serious attention these seven Anglican liberals had vainly tried in *Essays and Reviews* to get for their viewpoint was ironically obtained by Harrison's article in the rationalists' journal entitled "Neo-Christianity," a term invented by Harrison. The title suggests a comparison between the attempt of the Broad Church to put new wine into old bottles with that of the Neo-Platonists to revive the old pagan religion of Rome and Greece by imbuing the old myths with sublime spiritual and metaphysical truths. A. W. Benn suggests that Harrison jealously hoped that the Religion of Humanity would replace the old effete Christianity and feared the likelihood that this Neo-Christianity might serve the purpose instead. However, Benn continues, Neo-Christianity has actually become the religion of the educated classes in England and has indeed swallowed up the sum and substance of the Religion of Humanity.[9]

Harrison's article proved to be such a bombshell that now the book had to be faced by the clergy and the bishops of the Church.[10] Although the contributors suffered persecution and some temporary disadvantages, in the long run three or four of them were promoted to some of the highest positions in the Church, including, in one instance, the archbishopric of Canterbury. Harrison, quite inadvertently, aided their success. At Oxford, he had been urged by several disciples of Benjamin Jowett, one of the well-known contributors, to write something about the book in order to get it better known; up to that time, it had fallen rather flat. But when Harrison read it carefully, he became convinced of what he deemed to be its "cynical insincerity, shallowness, and muddle-headedness." After proposing to John Chapman, editor of the *Westminster Review*, that he write the article, he set about the assignment with vigor, taking no longer than a fortnight as he produced nearly five or six pages of print per day. Realizing that this article might mean his expulsion from Oxford, he nevertheless wrote with the excited conviction that it was his public duty to write it. Right away, after its publication, he received letters of congratulation from Huxley, Tyndall, and various writers for the *Westminster*. And then a veritable storm broke, with shock waves that spread throughout the rest of the century and beyond. In 1861, Bishop Colenso, himself a mathematician, published his work in which he revealed many arithmetical errors in the Pentateuch. The conservatives were really now on the defensive.

The Reviewers had questioned many of the doctrinal foundations of Christianity, which, they argued, out of all honesty should be analyzed and investigated within the Church itself, but they by no means suggested the dismantling of the Church or their own departure from it. It was simply necessary for the Church to abandon untenable positions that were no longer defensible. Harrison points out that the message of the book is incompatible with the religious beliefs held by the mass of the British public as well as with the broad principles of English Protestantism, in general. He fears that it would do no good to try to graft the principles of rationalism onto popular Christianity. And he asks whether it is reasonable to expect the Christian world to reconsider its cardinal doctrines and to accept recent improvements. Can the public be brought to believe that the Bible is full of errors and even untruths? If the public should be expected to read the Bible in that spirit, they would not read it at all. What becomes of the Christian scheme of things if the origin of man now is explained by Darwin and if Adam and Eve are classed with Deucalion and Pyrrha (*CL*, 99)?

Justification by faith, Harrison maintains, now simply means "peace of mind" (*CL*, 105). The fires of hell have become no more than images of tortured remorse of spirit. The very Incarnation becomes spiritual rather than literal. The Messianic predictions have been dismissed. Indeed, the whole supernatural system has been eliminated from belief (*CL*, 106). The Old Testament is put on the same level with the historical writings of Livy. The serpent-tempter may be taken as allegorical. But Harrison notes that Dr. Temple, headmaster of Rugby and future archbishop of Canterbury, actually adopts the idea of the organic development of history, which is the Positivist conception of mankind, each age collecting within itself the results of the preceding one; but Temple reaches quite different conclusions. For one thing, Harrison cannot concur with Temple that any one race has been given the preeminent position. Further, Temple omits many important peoples and nations from the civilizational development of mankind, not to mention important world religions other than Christianity. It is clear, Harrison concludes, that the Neo-Christians have little idea of the development of Humanity by invariable laws (*CL*, 111−12).

The Reviewers step by step surrender the Hebrew cosmogony as they do the scripture itself, explaining and modifying the very doctrine of inspiration. Asking what is driving them to do this, Harrison answers his own question by asserting that it is the advance of the idea of development and of the evolution by law, which Comte was the first to understand. But the Reviewers are forced to conclusions not found in their Holy Book and which are vigorously contradicted by its tone and spirit. They do, it is true, reject facts contrary to science, such as the miracles, but they still retain theories contrary to history. Like the Neo-Platonists, the later Buddhists, and the Sufis, the Quietists had spiritualized Catholicism into a kind of moral perfection, and the Wesleyans had spiritualized Protestantism into an ecstasy of soul (*CL*, 145). Invariably, reformers cast off the dead frame of their tenets and seek to revitalize the essence. But every religion that ever flourished has relied on the strength of a body of doctrines and a system of definite axioms. Without these, a religion could give no sense of unity or permanence. Thus Harrison would answer Leslie Stephen as much as he did the Neo-Christians, contending that endless attempts have been made to attain a moral union in an ideal life, yet they have inevitably ended in chimera and confusion. No collection of rules of life or moral principles, he continues, can endure for long "when deprived of dogmatic basis and common intellectual assent" (*CL*, 146). The influence of every religion has depended ultimately on cardinal propositions universally accepted as true. St. Bernard, Harrison instances, knew how much his moral power rested on the doctrine of Transubstantiation (*CL*, 146).

The contemporary Protestant theologian Francis A. Schaeffer attacks somewhat similar attempts by Neo-Christians and Christian Existentialists since Kierkegaard. Dr. Schaeffer contends that the modernist theologians make the "great leap" from the rational and logical up into the nonlogical and nonrational, no longer believing that Christianity may be based on propositional truths found in Scripture. Although arguing for the inerrancy of the Scriptures, Schaeffer is making essentially the objections to Neo-Christianity that Harrison did more than a century ago. Religious truth becomes detached from the historical truth of the Scriptures, leaving no place for reason and no place for verification. There is usually the necessity for the Kierkegaardian "final leap," without any verification in the rational. All hope is removed from the realm of rationality by the modern Existentialist, Christian or non-Christian, whether it be in Sartre's "existential experience," Jaspers's "final experience," or Heidegger's

"*Angst.*" These modern theologians and philosophers are mystics with Nobody (i.e., God) there. For them, faith is the important thing, which is actually no more than faith in faith. The leap is the thing and not the terms in which the leap is expressed, for content is immaterial and mysticism is without categories. The new theologian, Schaeffer continues, uses connotation words rather than defined ones—words as symbols without any definition or referent. Therefore, since the experience is the important thing, faith is unchallengeable because it could be anything.[11]

Harrison says that Jowett, like the Moravians, Fox, Fenelon, Thomas à Kempis, and Wesley, proposes as a religion the following of the Christian life, the imitation of one great ideal. Creeds are dismissed as accidental and variable, whereas principles are valued as essential and eternal. But, Harrison warns, the moment that one cardinal dogma is surrendered as either uncertain or provisional, the whole intellectual framework dissolves. The unguided feelings and the resultant variety of moral conceptions, losing their rational moorings, pitch and toss in endless agitation and discord. Once doubt the story or the reality of the vicarious sacrifice of Christ, and to what will the preacher appeal? Even St. Paul would be left with the truism, "To be good, for it is good to be good" (*CL*, 147). The facile preachment of a body of beautiful maxims of humility and love could never bring order out of the intellectual anarchy all around us. And, like Schaeffer, Harrison holds little hope for this Neo-Christian severance of reason from religion, resulting in a gulf between the highest thinking and the deepest feeling. Neither loose accommodation nor sonorous principles will endure. For religion to regain the world, Harrison contends, it must be in harmony with science, philosophy, morals, and politics. It must have a doctrine that embodies the growth of human thought, flowing from and summing up the whole. The Reviewers by no means achieve this goal, as they attempt to sublimate religion into an emotion and to effect an armistice with science. Their adaptation is able and earnest, but false and even suicidal.

In 1876, Harrison wrote a "Socratic dialogue" in the May issue (vol. 27) of the *Contemporary Review* in answer to an article in the March issue by Mark Pattison (one of the seven Reviewers) that was unfavorable to Comtism. The scene is laid amid the "studious groves" around Magdalen College in May, as Sophistes, a college don (an admirer of Pattison), and Phaedrus, a barrister from town (obviously Harrison himself), converse on the respective merits of the Religion of Humanity and the extremely rationalistic Christianity espoused by Pattison. Harrison is very much at his best in a controversial situation of this sort, perhaps because of his legal training. Doubtless here he had in mind the form of the dialogues between Bishop Berkeley's Hylas and Philonus, with the thrust and parry of dialectical discussion—in form, but scarcely in conclusion. Or, nearer at hand, he might have had in mind Comte's *The Catechism of Positive Religion*, in which there is a colloquy between a priest (Comte himself) and a woman (Clothilde de Vaux, doubtless), but here there is no debate or parody.

Sophistes incredulously observes that he has heard that, in addition to being a student of Comte, Phaedrus has embraced the Religion of Humanity. Through the mouth of Phaedrus, Harrison explains that some twenty years ago he had accepted Comte's philosophy of history and society; however, although the Higher Criticism had shaken his faith in the Church, he had at least retained a sense of some inscrutable Power behind the appearances of life that (like the Neo-Christians) he had felt no particular need to define. However, since that which cannot be defined is more than likely to disappear, he began to believe that the religious life and a devotion to human welfare were synonymous. And Phaedrus adds: " . . . and this I take to be the real religion of many honest men around us" (*CL*, 154). After long study and very serious hesitation, however, Phaedrus has at last come to feel that Humanity is the most real and the most ennobling object of reverence, for it is the true disposer of our lives and our thoughts. Unlike a vague faith in the Infinite, the human religion can always explain its faith.

To the surprise of Sophistes, Phaedrus explains that the human, relative, and rational spirit of Positivism does not depend on revivalism, asceticism, or extravagance of any kind to spread its message. When Sophistes wonders at his loss of a sense of religion of the kind holy men have practiced for centuries, Phaedrus replies that it is he that is appalled at the sight of contemporary theologians busily tearing into shreds nearly every remnant of the old, hallowed revelation, whereas he himself reposes in the security of the strength of a real religion. He will neither rely on a phantasmagoria of dissolving creeds nor abandon the spirit of true religion. He retains some faith, reverence, and love that need the satisfaction that only religion can afford one. But he finds no solace in a faith like that of the Byzantine Homoiousian (the fourth-century Arian), which in time becomes only wire-drawn skepticism. He needs some real, demonstrable Power to revere, a system of belief in plain relation with life and conduct. He requires a faith that connects his religious and his active life, that avoids all paroxysms of emotion and appeals to all honest and reasonable men.

Sophistes says that Mark Pattison and he himself retain their hold on the idea of God without letting it collide with other admitted truths. But, asks Phaedrus, does not your attitude divest God of all of His own attributes? Oh, replies Sophistes, we retain the philosophic, not the vulgar, idea of God. This idea, so purely transcendental, may be found outside the realm of nature, of science, of the knowable. Is this idea not rather ethereal, asks Phaedrus, for the business of life? Really, your idea of God seems seriously close to the idea that there is no God. Should you not call your philosophy Atheosophy rather than Theosophy? You make of your philosophic God an inscrutable and negative Essence, Who never shows His personality and Who remains neutral in human affairs.

When Sophistes accuses Phaedrus of materialism and even atheism, Phaedrus replies that there is more atheism in these philosophical theisms than in all the writings of Comte. He then accuses the philosophical theists of so whittling down their God to a philosophical nullity that they are destroying the very body and bones of religion, which cannot be defined merely as a hypothetical solution of a logical dilemma. At least the orthodox faiths, even that superstition (as Sophistes terms it) Roman Catholicism, do preserve a belief in a real Providence, which governs all our acts and thoughts. Well, replies Sophistes, now that you have dispersed our metaphysical deities, prove to me that your Religion of Humanity is anything but a phrase.

Do you not think, replies Phaedrus, that the collective power of man's life is not a majestic phenomenon in its immensity, its heroism, and its sufferings? Every artist, inventor, monarch, mother, worker— all have vitally contributed to the history and development of Humanity. Even the history of every religion is but an episode in the history of Humanity. Sophistes wonders whether this idea is not like that of Matthew Arnold's stream of tendency. Possibly, responds Phaedrus, if only we had a clearer idea of what Arnold means (CL, 169). Our idea of Humanity, on the contrary, is capable of exact analysis and of description by history. But, replies Sophistes, when you talk about reverencing and adoring it, is this not a kind of Pantheism or, better, a Pantanthropotheism? And by Pantheism, Sophistes means the worship of the sum total of existence, of the things that we know. Phaedrus agrees with him that Pantheism consecrates everything, good and bad alike, and eliminates thereby all possible moral discipline. The Religion of Humanity, however, considers the vicious energies of man to have been largely abortive and to have been absorbed in the way that a healthy man can restore the balance of his body after a disease. The good energies alone find permanent absorption in the course of the development of civilization. But importantly this reverence of Humanity has nothing to do with the Divine. Rational science has eliminated any ideas of absolute perfection and so has confirmed that in order to be real, Humanity must be relatively great and good. A son or daughter may reverence the father and mother, although they are naturally not absolutely perfect beings. And it is the business of sociology, which Comte has founded, to make clear the great and good part of civilization as it has developed historically.

Sophistes exclaims that all this is nothing more than plain common sense, to which Phaedrus answers: "Of course." But, Sophistes objects, it is this Humanity with a capital "H" that the Rector (i.e., Mark Pattison) says is the crazy part of your doctrine, the bee in your bonnet. A man may often speak rationally until you hit upon his special craze. The Rector calls you antiintellectual. He calls your Humanity a "new idol," "a metaphysical simulacrum," "the hypocrisy of materialism," and "a helpless absurdity" (CL, 173). You spoke just as harshly, you must admit, of his Essays and Reviews, to which he contributed the next-to-last essay. But, come now, why do you call Humanity a Being?

Phaedrus then proceeds to explain the Positivist contention that Humanity is a living organism, an aggregate of living parts in which all have mutual dependence and reaction. Humanity and its many parts have both organ and function. An inorganic crystal is symmetrical, but its units are unable to exchange effects or modify each other. Similarly, the Gulf Stream lacks organ and function as well as a reciprocal action of parts. There is no internal growth, modification, or adjustment. But a human being does have all this. And the same functions of the individual organism are found in the social. In addition, the social organism is far more permanent and also the more real because it is the most complete of all beings.

But, asks Sophistes, does this explanation prove that Humanity is a deity? No, replies Phaedrus, it is neither a deity nor even a person. And you may use a capital B for Being only if you wish. This Being is the source of all immediate human improvement; it is a power that is as real as you or I and more permanent than either of us. Sophistes, having objected that Humanity is too abstract, now proceeds to accuse it of being too material. Phaedrus amusedly replies that Sophistes' true objection is that Humanity does not suggest the Milky Way, does not have anything of the Absolute about it. Humanity is real, purely human, sympathetic, and omnipresent. Sophistes then makes the most crucial objection to the Religion of Humanity: namely, that it has no consciousness of its own existence, no thought, no love. First, Phaedrus forces Sophistes to admit that as a theosophist he is unable to fathom the consciousness of his own transcendent Deity, nor His personality, heart, or soul. Well, then, Phaedrus says, neither can we. Further, were we not an organic part of Humanity, we would find ourselves face to face with grim nature; but, being an organic part, we feel all the effects of love and mind. However, we spin no cobwebs of metaphysics about the self-consciousness of Humanity. It rose out of relative thought and perhaps cannot satisfy anyone who remains in the absolute frame of mind.

Sophistes then wonders whether Humanity does not remain an abstraction which we can conceive only in thought. Noting that his opponent is now complaining that Humanity is too abstract rather than too material, Phaedrus explains that he is able to feel the energy of Humanity throbbing in every human thought and act and feeling of daily life. Compared to this patent reality, the essence of all other religions seems rather abstract and ideal. And when Sophistes doubts that man can feel reverence and devotion toward such an abstract Being, Phaedrus answers that if men can reverence an abstract hypothesis, how much more likely it is that they can reverence an abstract reality. For example, patriotism, which can become quite fanatical, is based on that aggregate of vital energies, one's country; and he instances the heroism exhibited in the loyalty many Romans felt for their city. Even the Church is a real and living thing, although recognizable only in thought. Both of these entities are incomplete when compared to the all-encompassing reality of Humanity as a whole.

Sophistes argues that Humanity falls far short of the mysterious infinitude of the Absolute. But Phaedrus is ready again for him by asserting that to sensible men it is not which is more gigantic but which is more real. It might be more fascinating were men able to fly into space like the bird, but it would be a foolish thought to act upon this aspiration in terms of actual fact. If an idea has no practical relation to human life, it is useless to speak of its being grand. Then Sophistes, quoting Mark Pattison, plays his trump card. Religion is entirely an affair of the individual conscience and its private relation to God. Comte seems more interested in social regulation than individual. Phaedrus asks Sophistes whether the Buddha, then, had no religion since he did not subscribe to the idea of a deity. And as for religion conceived as a purely personal concern, he maintains that he as a Positivist is in fundamental agreement with all real religions that have ever existed in that he believes that religion fundamentally implies the union of souls in common faith, common worship, common doctrine, and common discipline. On the contrary, Sophistes is really in agreement with only a few of the later mystics or spiritualists. Were Sophistes correct, there would be no relation between religion and morality. Indeed, if every man were to insist on his private, unique relation with his God, he in time would become his own God.

Finally, Sophistes quotes Pattison's charge that the Positivists are as biased against intellectual progress as the Inquisition itself had been. All systems of philosophy and theology, because they are systems, are of necessity false. Phaedrus asks whether Pattison has ever heard of Comte's Calendar of Great Men. Also, has any living

Englishman a more encyclopedic knowledge of all the sciences which Comte thought essential to a real education? When Sophistes urges that Comte tried to pin science down to its state when Comte died, Phaedrus vehemently answers that Comte's purpose was to organize and arrange our knowledge, not to compile an encyclopedia of facts in order to stereotype all knowledge. Comte even mapped out areas that should be open to human discovery for centuries to come. He attempted to establish a relationship within our knowledge for the sole purpose that it be connected with human life. He thought the object of man's intellect is to glorify the harmony and beauty of human life, not "to soar idling about space like a truant seraph or a runaway Pegasus" (*CL*, 187). The latter approach leads but to helplessness, cynicism, indolence, and despair.

Catholicism Minus Christianity

As mentioned above, it was Frederic Harrison who wrote the first article that led to the strong condemnation of *Essays and Review*, convinced that Christianity was approaching the point of extinction, too ruinous to be repaired. He had wanted the Reviewers to openly reveal themselves as the Positivists they really were and honestly profess the Religion of Humanity, hoping that it would absorb Christianity, not vice versa. [13] The thought of the Religion of Humanity was in the air everywhere. The idea of evolution was implicit throughout the writing of Benjamin Jowett, although he never specifically mentioned it. Like Comte, he argued there are two witnesses to the Being of God: the order of Nature and the progress of the mind of man (Comte, of course, would probably say "religion" instead of "God"). He was a student of Hegel and Comte, as well as of the Tübingen school. [14]

One of the landmark works in the field of anthropology, Sir James Frazer's *The Golden Bough*, was published in 1889. In the second edition, Frazer made clear the thought that religion stands in opposition to science, illustrating that the course of nature is not determined by the passions or caprice of personal beings but by the operation of immutable laws. He leaned, like Comte, toward a new faith in the moral, intellectual, and material progress of humanity, and he was convinced that any obstacle placed in the path of scientific discovery is a wrong to humanity. Charles Gore, in his important *Lux Mundi: a Series of Studies in the Religion of the Incarnation*, published just a year before Frazer's work, attempts to study the development of theology following *Essays and Reviews*; he well understood that belief in science and its method was the most original thought in Victorian England and that the ideal of service was beginning to turn from God to man. Emphasizing the centrality of the Incarnation in Christian belief, he was especially concerned with God's imminence in history rather than in man's deliverance from sin. It is interesting to note that when Huxley became president of a club for scientific and philosophic men in London who desired to know and speak the truth and spread sheer common honesty throughout the world, such churchmen as Charles Kingsley joined it. [15] It was in this atmosphere that Frederic Harrison felt that the right time for the development of the Religion of Humanity had arrived. It was his hope that he might steer a midway course between the moral agnostics and the traditional churchmen, who respectively represented his intellectual side, on the one hand, and his emotional, on the other.

Comte obviously realized that Positivism needed something more than a philosophy of science, or even of sociology, to effect a new way of life for mankind. Student of history that he was, he ironically found the answer in an institution that epitomizes the absolute cast of mind more than any other: the Roman Catholic Church of the Middle Ages. It was Huxley who trenchantly observed that Positivism is Catholicism minus Christianity, to which the Positivists rejoined: it is rather Catholicism plus science, or a human Catholicism. Comte became convinced that system is absolutely essential to the success of any scheme for reordering the social life of mankind. And, in his opinion, no other institution in history had ever evolved such an effective system as the Church, despite its reliance on gross superstition and exploded dogmas. Harrison once heard a well-known editor tell a leading Catholic prelate that were the Pope to become converted to Positivism, he could rule the whole world (*PER*, 141). [16]

Fundamental to the Catholic system are the Sacraments, which Positivism has adopted but has enlarged and ennobled, Harrison believes (*PER*, 131). The Positivist Sacraments confirm the believer's acceptance of a new social and religious consecration at each of nine stages of his career through, and even after, his life in this world. Harrison believes that some of the Catholic Sacraments are not truly sacramental in essence; and he notes that the Protestants have narrowed them down to two, whereas the Positivists have expanded them to nine. They testify to the religious significance of each stage of a person's career, and they require systematic observance. The initiation of the fetichist savage into manhood and the consecration of the chief or medicine man are early examples of the social utility of these ceremonies. The ninth Positivist Sacrament, Incorporation, occurs seven years after death, when the life of the deceased is consecrated to union with living Humanity (*PER*, 131–32).

Harrison firmly believes that no real religion can exist without sacraments or without a priesthood to administer them. The moral and social value in this institution is indispensable to a genuinely organized society. Confession is an important adjunct to the sacraments and is one of the vital functions of a priesthood. At its best, Harrison believes, Catholic confession is efficacious, but he has contempt for the secret, unofficial confession of the high Anglicans. The Positivist confession should not be either surreptitious or occasional, and it should be made to an authorized, married elder of much training and experience (*PER*, 134).

Celibacy might once have had some advantage, but Harrison fears that it does lead to a professional clericalism with its own vested interests. In order to make a priesthood free from incorporation into the power structure of the world, he believes that it should be divested of the cares of social and wealthy display. Ideally, it should be a true spiritual body of simple men who become incorporated within the laboring masses of the population (*PER*, 134–35). The fanaticism associated with monachism, fasting, and penance, and the harshness and severity, even arrogance, that mar the reputation of the Church really come from its visionary, arbitrary, and antisocial creed. But the Church did rein in human passion with an admirable self-constraint that is unique in human experience (*PER*, 135–38).

Ritual of the Church, though often tedious and formal, Harrison concedes, is nevertheless splendid in its appeal to the senses. Although England has long been suspicious of it, more recently as dogma is fading, a visible and dramatic ritual is developing in English churches. Even a Protestant church of the time has more ritual than high Anglican churches did sixty or seventy years earlier. (*PER*, 138–40).

But it is in its organization, Harrison agrees with Comte, that the Church reveals its deepest sagacity. It has successfully adapted itself to many climates, lands, races, and periods of history. Its principal liability, again, is its irrational and basically unsocial creed. The Church wisely permits, in his opinion, no election in anything but the choice of the Pope. And its authority is hierarchical, without any vestige of local control such as is found in, say, the Baptist church. The Positivist finds in the organization of the Church a permanent organization of spiritual power. In our modern social chaos, this is the element most signally lacking (*PER*, 140–42).

Carlyle had understood the same thing and in *Past and Present* looked back to the Middle Ages for his model. Comte is no more inclined to democratic liberalism than he. Although Comte thought he should take lessons from the medieval Church and borrow some of its institutions with important modifications, he refused to copy anything or to adapt anything without having first purged it of extravagance and vice. Above all, he felt as alien to its creed and dogma as did Carlyle. But quite unlike the great Scotsman, he desired to substitute a scientific, real, demonstrable creed, else all social and moral effort in the world would be wasted.

The Anglican Church is no more than agnosticism veiled in evangelical sentiment and hypocritical respectability, Harrison believes (*PER*, 152). Its articles of belief are Calvinist, its ritual is Catholic, and its organization is Erastian.[17] But it is actually no more than a toy model of the Roman Catholic Church. Everything is "dummy." Notwithstanding this strong judgment, he goes on to say that the Church of England is the most cultured, sociable, learned, and enlightened Christian denomination in the world. And its Bible and liturgy are far superior to the Roman. Unfortunately, it is virtually a bureau of the State, protecting the rich and the powerful and lacking in independent moral action. However, it remains the most tolerant of all churches, with no testing for membership; it even buries famous agnostics and selected Temple, one of the contributors to *Essays and Reviews*, as Archbishop of Canterbury (*PER*, 151–52).

Dissent, also, rests on a foundation of unintelligible mysteries and miracles. Its intensely arbitrary scheme of salvation destroys human, moral, and social values. Despite all this, though, Harrison asserts, Nonconformity has a way of finding out where the money is (*PER*, 171). Otherwise, its fantastic creed is foreign to the realities of human nature. Above all, should the teacher be chosen by the taught? It is the democracy of Nonconformity that results in the control by the most narrow and ignorant.

The Nonconformist opposes prescribed rituals and formularies, preferring the spontaneous and extemporaneous. However, Harrison cites a number of advantages of ritual and liturgy (*PER*, 173–81). The ecclesiastical, sacerdotal, and artistic concept of worship depends on the stirring of the soul by congregational communion with its moral and spiritual inspiration through both beautiful and familiar language, through the thaumaturgic power of tradition. As the fiery, Gospel-inspired spontaneity of prayer and worship begins to diminish in intensity, it is gradually replaced by an increasingly ritualistic form of worship. And once the Bible is no longer held to be the sole revelation of God, the Nonconformist cannot fall back on tradition, antiquity, Church, organization, ritual ceremonial, art, or even poetry. For Harrison, the Roman Catholic Church is the only permanent and essential form of Christianity. When the Bible goes, Protestantism must also go.

Neo-Christianity is, for Harrison, the adroit compromise of the English church in the modern age, although it has itself been the church of compromise from the beginning (*PER*, 183). Actually, he explains, the Religion of Humanity is a kind of Neo-Christianity, but carried to its logical conclusion. Simply put, Neo-Christianity attempts to retain the ethical and emotional spirit of the Gospel, while at the same time dropping the miraculous and divine revelation. It exalts the humanity of Christ and the nobility and goodness of the Bible's teaching. All this is the idea of the Religion of Humanity, too, Harrison readily acknowledges. However, the Religion of Humanity also recognizes all the great leaders and teachers of mankind, not simply one. Unlike atheists, it reveres the essence of Christianity and considers it as an essential part of its own religion as it has developed organically through the ages. Not only does it levy on Christianity, but also on paganism and fetichism, as well. Harrison marvels that the Neo-Christians would attempt to amalgamate these ideas with those of the present Church Establishment. As he puts it, it would take many Cranmers to adapt Neo-Christianity to the Calvinistic articles of the Establishment creed (PER, 186–87).

Harrison, like the Neo-Christians, finds the Incarnation, the miracles, the Atonement, the Resurrection, and the Ascension quite unbelievable in the nineteenth century. And the Bible is a medley of miscellaneous things, haphazardly collected and compiled over the centuries and differing widely from one another. Paul himself had substituted a higher law for that of Moses. And Roman Catholicism is a more solid thing than Christianity itself, for the Church has wisely abandoned the beautiful hyperboles of Jesus in the Sermon on the Mount, which is the essence of Christianity. Harrison finds Comte's "Blessed are the rich in heart, for theirs is the Kingdom of Earth" far higher than Christ's "Blessed are the poor in spirit, for theirs is the Kingdom of Heaven" (PER, 199). And that the meek shall inherit the earth he believes to be sheer nonsense. All that is better in Christianity comes at a much later period in its history. Actually, he is convinced that Christianity rests entirely on the divinity of Christ. And if there be no miracle, there can be no divinity. Therefore, Christianity without the supernatural would be nonsense (PER, 202–203).

But Theism (PER, 209–32) does not offer the masses of men a basis for religion, for it is so fearful of being anthropomorphic that it ascends to a sphere of metaphysics that is not altogether dissimilar to Herbert Spencer's Unknowable.[18] Harrison is neither a Theist nor an Atheist for he believes that he has no means to decide on the mystery of Creation one way or another. If anything, the hypothesis of Omnipotence is less unintelligible than that of Self-Creation or Chance. Further, the latter leads to egoism, conceit, and hardness. Even so, for the Religion of Humanity the object of reverence is the comprehensible, not the Incomprehensible; this planet, not the Universe; the relative, not the Absolute; the natural, not the Supernatural; the human, not the Divine. It is more important, Harrison avers, to know how the twentieth century will end than how the Universe began. What, after all, is the value of a belief in a "sort of something" that lies beyond all knowledge? Why not make, Harrison asks, a religion of Space and Time or of Arnold's Stream of Tendency? Actually, there is no "science of God," either (*PER*, 214—15). Theology is a vague presumption, whereas Humanity is an unmistakable reality. Paradoxically, the Absolute Almighty Being ultimately becomes a "preternaturally magnified Self" (*PER*, 228).

With small consolation to the orthodox Christian, Harrison grants that Christianity will survive only because it is as basically anthropomorphic as any true religion must be if its goal is to capture the human heart (*PER*, 230). The true goal of all religions worthy of the name will find historical fulfillment in the Religion of Humanity, to which they all lead up. Now they will receive the one thing needful: a true and honest scientific basis. Granted, all men crave worship, a creed, a scheme of salvation, and a church. But in the Religion of Humanity one does not have to achieve the impossible: that is, to reconcile both Divine Justice and Divine Mercy to a creation that ordains death, waste, and confusion. No longer does one's creed depend on the suspension of laws that obviously reign throughout the sphere of nature. Providence is no more or less than each man's individual destiny in this world from birth to death (*PER*, 231—32).

Nothing is more important to Christianity than the doctrine of the immortality of the soul and its reward of salvation in Heaven. No less than Thomas Henry Huxley himself, Harrison believes there is nothing in man that is not also a part of his physical organism, including the faculties of mind, feeling, and will. These faculties depend on the physical organs of the body, and it seems to him pure nonsense to talk about their continuing their functions when the physical organs no longer exist (*PCS*, 190—93). But he believes that the spiritual and moral energies of the individual may live even more intensely after his life than during it. The researches of Newton were destined to transform the philosophy of mankind after his death (*PCS*, 220). Ironically, many of the greatest moral, intellectual, and spiritual results of life begin only when the animal life has been satisfied and the small weaknesses and pains of the flesh have disappeared. The results of the care of father and mother often become apparent in the

child only long after its progenitors are already in the grave. As
Harrison says, John Brown's body lies a-mouldering in the grave, but
his soul is still marching right along (*PCS*, 222). Even the humblest
life sends a wave through the course of human society down through
the centuries, the millennia.

As for heaven, Harrison thinks that those savages who deny the
reality of death are at least more rational than civilized Christians who
envision immaterial souls flying about in space. For the Positivist,
not a single act or thought ends in itself. This concept of life seems
much nobler and worthier than that of awaiting a future of ceaseless
psalmody in an immaterial heaven. This vague yearning, based on no
definite evidence or conception, irrationally fancies it casts out the
devil of selfishness by direct appeal to the personal self and its reward.
Harrison considers this unwholesome emphasis on the perpetuation of
the personal self nothing less than the rankest materialism. The
Positivist idea of living for others not only in life but also in death
emphasizes the permanence of those activities that give happiness to
others rather than the mere preservation of self. The orthodox Christian is essentially saying, "I want to feel life; I want my personality;
therefore, I want my senses, and, consequently, my body" (*PCS*,
228). But is not perpetual worth more desirable, he asks, than an
eternity of vacuous consciousness?

As Harrison at the Metaphysical Society once told Richard Holt
Hutton, Lord Blachford, and others who defended the orthodox view,
nothing could be more forbidding than a Christian heaven that
consigns us to an infinity of apathy, without objects, relations,
change, or growth—"an absolute nothingness, a nirvana of impo-
tence" (*PCS*, 229). What can life and affection possibly mean with the
absence of every condition by which they might become possible?
Harrison agrees with Huxley that a functional relationship exists
between every fact of willing, thinking, and feeling, on the one hand,
and some molecular change in the body, on the other. Therefore, it is
hard to think of the existence of sensation, thought, and energy
without this corresponding molecular change that accompanies them
(*PCS*, 245).

Harrison argues that the affections, too, depend on conditions
coming from an external world to act in, yet these conditions are quite

impossible in the orthodox Christian idea of heaven. The concept results in a "mystical and inane ecstasy" for "this paradise of negations" (*PCS*, 237). He wryly comments that one might as well talk of a higher civilization without any human beings or of redness apart from its connection with anything that is red (*PCS*, 236). And he reminds Hutton that to be simply conscious forever, yet to lie thoughtless, with every human activity paralyzed within, must be the ultimate torment (*PCS*, 238). One recalls the Greek myth of Tithonus, who was granted immortality without release from old age or senility.

It is only in our relative world that the highest human moral activity becomes possible. Without labor and death (our twin inheritance from Adam), Harrison continues, the grandest qualities of human nature would be forever inconceivable (*PCS*, 239). The reason that Hutton is pessimistic about life and the future of the race is his enervating dream of a celestial glory. And Harrison reminds Lord Blachford that absence of molecular attributes might be awkward in interstellar space, adding that a life without those practical activities that form the sum and substance of life has to be nothing much more than a trance (*PCS*, 240–41). Lord Blachford seems to think that the tune goes on after the fiddle has been destroyed. Harrison, like Comte, believes in what he refers to as the subjective, not the objective, immortality of the soul. Thus the very core of Christian doctrine is lacking in the Religion of Humanity, although much of its spirit does remain.

The Religion of Humanity

In his second volume of the *Positive Polity*, Comte makes an exhaustive study of religion, in which he examines thoroughly just what a religion must do in this world and just what the foundations of all religions are. He believes that a true religion is the condition of harmony that is associated with the real conditions of both human nature, individually and collectively, and the world about us. It orders human life so that it realizes to the full both its inner and outer functions. All religions, at bottom, Comte avers, strive to attain this very goal, but only Positivism advocates real solutions rather than fanciful dreams. Whereas the growth of knowledge is anathema to all other religions, it is the very bone and tissue of Positivism, which is unthinkable without it. Peace, harmony, and the healthy function of the human organism are the goals of all religions, but only Positivism can actually achieve them. Religion should depend on neither fiction nor detachment from life and the earth. The goal of Positivism is continuous progress based on the foundation of order. Not only is religion a personal preoccupation but also an essential social attribute.

One defect of theology, Harrison contends, is its very narrowness, its deprivation of many important human faculties (*PER*, 243). Humanity offers the grandest field for expansion of the intellect, the most practical sphere for every expression of human application, and the most gratifying satisfaction of all human feelings. As Harrison says, man, after having groped for so long after the Truth in so many strange and diverse ways, always in vain, now has the chance for the first time in history to make his inner and outer life coincide (*PER*, 238). The ambition for millenia has been to gain some comprehension of an Absolute Principle, through rational means or otherwise, but Harrison asserts that the highest idea of life implies a sound Dualism, an action and reaction involving Humanity and the World (*PER*, 239−40). Comte also rejects any notion of monism. Religion now, for the first time, surrenders its immemorial claim to enter into a relation with the Absolute Principle of the Universe. The dream of Christianity has always been to shun the things of this world as vanity and to concentrate on things beyond the life of this world. It has never made any attempt to appeal to the whole nature of man (*PER*, 238).

Man must, of course, have belief, Harrison contends, not in the Incomprehensible but in his own ability to carve out his destiny in the real world, which is all he really knows very much about. It now behooves him to learn more and more about the nature of the world in which he really does live and to which he can apply all his natural energies. He should understand the connections between the sciences, the general course of human history, and the foundations of human society and morality. Religious belief should not be confined to a conjecture about the origin and nature of the Universe but should be based on a never-ending education in what actually is. It almost comes down to the fact that a completely uneducated person cannot be, in the full sense of the term, religious, for he has no adequate way to develop his own nature and his own understanding of his duty to collective Humanity, which it is his duty to serve. Education in science and philosophy may not be religion, but it is the essential foundation for it. It is the surest protection he has against his being lured by fantastic hypotheses and gross superstitions. Harrison believes that man must be made to comprehend the very grand and complex Providence which is the foundation of his whole life at every conceivable level (*PER*, 243–44).

And, of course, there must be worship in man's life that springs from his heart and feelings, not from his repeating a few formulae once or twice a week at a church (*PER*, 246–47). Harrison assigns a much more important role to worship. It should imply the habit of domestic tenderness—the loving converse of the entire family. It should encourage one to reflect on his work and duty in society. It should involve the spiritual use of noble poetry and music. It should establish communion with all noble spirits in public acts, past and present. And it should revere every generous act that springs from a full heart. It involves a thousand habits and institutions, of which congregational worship is but one. And it extends far beyond any single set of propositions and through the entire gamut of education from birth to death. Harrison would agree with Bertrand Russell, who said that, although Christ tells us to become as little children, little children would be baffled by the differential calculus, the principles of the currency, and modern methods of combating disease.[19] What is the advantage, morally or intellectually, of being beguiled by sheer illusions?

During the latter half of the nineteenth century, the worship of Humanity was in the air. The poet Swinburne recognized no religion but that of Humanity, with his pity for its sufferings, admiration for its achievements, and faith in its future.[20] As with so many in Britain, though, his principal difference with the Positivists was his love for liberty in a way that Comte would never have approved. But he was neither Christian nor Theist. The exception that Mill took, otherwise a partisan of Comte's, was essentially the same thing: Comte's addiction to system in preference to liberty. But there was one important American who did come close to Comte's Religion of Humanity in his own proposal for a Religion of Solidarity. He was Edward Bellamy, famous for writing one of the most significant utopian socialist books of modern times: *Looking Backward, 2000—1887* (1888). Less well known was his sequel, *Equality* (1897).[21]

Harrison contends that hell is really an inseparable part of the Christian religion and that there is no orthodox doctrine of extenuating circumstances (*CL*, 74—75). There are those who insist that fear about one's personal salvation is the only sure basis of an effective religion, an argument that dovetails with the claim of the social usefulness of such a belief. Fear of damnation keeps the individual up to the mark. But, says Harrison, heaven in the nineteenth century no longer attracts, nor does hell terrify any more than did Pope and Pagan in *Pilgrim's Progress*. These twin agents are no longer instruments of religion (*PER*, 23). As a matter of fact, heaven no longer is made to appeal to our gross physical senses and personal enjoyment but to the triumph of a good conscience and spiritual fellowship; in short, it has been idealized away and divested of the orthodox authority which it formerly had. The subjective future envisioned by the Positivists, on the contrary, incorporates the life of the individual with the future of Humanity as a whole. Personal salvation, therefore, is not the highest dream man can have. The Positivist regards social salvation as a higher and more worthy aspiration. As for the attainment of a sort of "hyperaesthesia of consciousness" after death, the Positivist does not adjudge dogmatically. But he does marvel at a state beyond this life without nerves or a corporeal system of any kind, for emotion without organs is something surely beyond any experience that we presently can have had (*PER*, 27).

But, most of all, the Positivists morally object to the idea of the continuance of the self. In contrast, the orthodox Christians attempt to elevate the noblest of human emotions, the benevolent instincts, by encouraging our self-love, or the hope of self-preservation in the Beyond, which then becomes the prime motive of our religious and moral life. Harrison excoriates this vaunted spirituality as unreal, unmanly, cynical, hysterical, antisocial, and even brutalizing. The idea of personal salvation abets an immoral principle in the very heart of Christianity, urging the individual to become self-righteous rather than religious. The Humanist ideal of religion is that Providence, unlike the Christian concept of it, is the sum total of civilization, the social organism of collective Humanity. Its goal is to maintain supremacy of social over selfish aims. In essence, it is an enlarged and ideal form of patriotism. The only kind of hell is a bad conscience in the incurably vicious and worthless (*PER*, 30−31).

The Bible is for Harrison great literature, but hardly the result of divine inspiration. Except for a few letters of St. Paul and some invectives of the later Hebrew prophets, it is doubtful that a single other piece of the Bible is what it purports to be (*PER*, 36−38). But these old creeds have remnants of the spiritual force that the Positivists need to absorb and use. They are at least closer to the convictions of orthodox believers than to those of the Deists, Theists, or Unitarians (*PER*, 44−45). For one thing, the unorthodox are no more successful in adjusting a Perfect Creator to an imperfect Creation than the orthodox, because they, too, adhere to the Absolute rather than to the Relative. And the illogic of an Absolute Will is that It can desire nothing better and fear nothing worse; neither can It gain anything It has not already got, nor can It obtain something that is not already. The Absolute necessarily is already perfect and unchangeable, and therefore there can be no progress and no improvement. How can even the will be predicated in the I AM? The great advantage of the orthodox over the unorthodox is that the past has always been on the side of some kind of organization or system of society. Harrison asks whether the future will be with unlimited fancy, instead (*PER*, 66−71).

He claims another advantage for Positivism: it is the only religion that does not despise its predecessors. It regards all religious and social institutions as transitional and imperfect. Even Fetichism is the origin of the institution of the family, which Harrison regards as the center of society. It also developed the quality of sympathy in its sense of relation between man and nature. And it led to the earliest fundamental inventions that made civilization possible. Our Calendar, anniversaries, reverence for places and for the dead—all are the survival of a thousand centuries and are incorporated in Positivism. Our very poetry is pure fetichism (*PER*, 76−82).

The Religion of Humanity is all-inclusive and synthetic. Unlike the exclusive adoration of the Creator by theistic systems, the worship of Positivism is as universal as that of Fetichism. Also, Positivism rejects any absolute, metaphysical Oneness, or monistic view of reality, even the monism of Humanity itself. Everything is dual: ego and nonego, objective and subjective, Man and the World, Man and Humanity, Induction and Deduction, Statics and Dynamics, Order and Progress, the Past and the Future, Man and Woman, material and spiritual. Positivism consecrates the Earth with religious reverence as the cradle, the home, and the tomb of the human race. It even adopts the rich imaginativeness of Pantheism with its poetry, myth, and fantasy. In short, it is all-inclusive (*PER*, 85−87).

Up to this point, I have used those ideas of Comte and Harrison interchangeably which they hold jointly. Now it becomes necessary to indicate an important divergence. In addition to being a Victorian, Harrison is also a man of independent judgment. One may well wonder why he did not join John Stuart Mill, who finally renounced the later writings of Comte, although earlier he had been a warm supporter. It must be noted that Harrison, who had had only one personal contact with Comte, always reserved the right to demur whenever he felt it necessary to do so. He pointedly never referred to himself as a "Comtist," but rather as a "Positivist." And he specifically disclaimed accepting all Comte's details, admitting that much remains to be resolved in the future. It was in the fundamental principles that he agreed, not necessarily in all Comte's specific prescriptions (*PER*, 253−55).

Harrison insists that Comte never meant, when he spoke of Church and priesthood, the use of arbitrary authority. The priests will be the teachers, artists, and philosophers, without inspired books, mystical Church, wealth, state establishment, political authority, or legal monopoly. They offer no heaven to promise, and no hell to threaten. They will have nothing but their knowledge, their usefulness, their high character, and their sweetness of nature to exert their influence (*CL*, 222−23). Harrison denies that Positivists attribute to Comte any kind of infallibility or ability to determine finality. He predicts that, like all other things, the program of the movement will constantly have to be modified, reformed, and enlarged with the growth of thought and the progress of knowledge. "Too much has been made of the deductions and corollaries of the human faith by those who have assailed it, and perhaps to some extent by those who have maintained it. The details, the utopias, the suggestions and illustrations of

Comte have been criticized with ridiculous minuteness, and with exaggerated importance. No one of these critics has ventured to dispute the great central Principle of a Human synthesis for thought and life. . . ."[11] (*CL*, 220–21).

Comte believed that the Religion of Humanity would become the religion of the whole human race. After achieving intellectual agreement throughout the world, it would then aim at the systematic cultivation of sympathetic feelings of love and gratitude. It would have both private and public expression. Woman, as domestic goddess, would be the object of private worship, and Humanity, in its public form, would be periodically celebrated in commemorative festivals and pilgrimages. The Positivist Calendar, which dates from 1789, the beginning of the French Revolution, indicates the dates throughout the year of the days dedicated to particular great men who have contributed to human progress.[22] Not only did the Positivists at Newton Hall often commemorate the centennials of great contributors to Humanity, but also they made pilgrimages to national shrines like the birthplace of Shakespeare or Westminster Abbey.

Alfred North Whitehead thought the two greatest intellectual movements in the nineteenth century were Jeremy Bentham's Utilitarianism with its "greatest happiness of the greatest number" and Auguste Comte's Religion of Humanity. Most of what has been effective in morals, religion, and political theory from their day to this has derived from one or the other of these two men. Although their theoretical formulations have been largely rejected, their "practical working principles" have virtually dominated the world of the twentieth century. They have swept away the claims of privilege formerly based on mystical intuitions with origins in religion or metaphysical philosophy, and have revived the spirit of the ancient Roman Stoic intellectualism. Whitehead believes both men extended the scientific revolt against metaphysical theory by Newton to the areas of moral and political theory. Discarding metaphysics in these fields, they accepted nothing but clear matter of fact, requiring no ultimate understanding of their relation to the rest of the things.[23] In the Renaissance we had a fusion of Humanism and Christianity in Spenser and Milton, who have usually been referred to as Christian Humanists. But Comte in the nineteenth century founded a distinctly Humanistic religion without any dependence on Christian doctrine. As Comte often maintained, Humanism and Positivism are synonymous.

Chapter Four
Vision of a New Social Order

No subject was more important than history at the Positivist center in London, Newton Hall, where Harrison was president for several decades. Here he gave extensive series of lectures on history, in which he emphasized the Positivist idea of filiation, illustrating the growth of society in the same way that branches issue from the trunk of a tree. In *Order and Progress*,[1] he explains Comte's theory of the static and dynamic conditions of human society: the one depends on the order found in nature; the other, on the evolutionary, developmental process that is always in operation, which history is an expression of and which leads to the positive stage of social evolution. In *The Meaning of History*,[2] Harrison discusses not only the use of history but also the great books on the subject that Positivists are encouraged to know.

In *On Society*,[3] composed largely of lectures he had given at Newton Hall, Harrison describes the kind of society that Positivists envision, as he also does in *Realities and Ideals*[4] and in *George Washington and Other American Addresses*.[5] The Positivist polity is based on a kind of moral socialism, far removed from the class warfare or the necessity of violent overthrow as prescribed by Marxism. It steers a midway course between communism, which would abolish private property, and capitalism, which would champion competition and private greed. Positivism would substitute social cooperation for mutual rivalry. It reposes great faith in the efficacy of right education that leads to altruism as the basis of human social behavior.

Like Comte, Harrison places reliance on the role of women, the Positivist priesthood, and working classes in effecting the Positivist utopia, representing the harmony, respectively, of feeling, mind, and action. Countering the criticism of Mill, Huxley, and Spencer—liberals with whom he shared many causes—Harrison disavows any attempt to form a new cult or sect or to implement ceremonial practices which Comte outlines in the fourth volume of the *Politique*. He does not feel the time is ripe for a Positivist polity. For the present, he aspires to achieve nothing more than imbuing receptive spirits with the ideals of the Positivist life. Believing in evolution rather than in revolution, he is convinced that the future is on his side, for ultimately Humanity will pass into the positive stage.

Newton Hall: Positivist Center in London

Only a little more than a century ago, the work of Auguste Comte found many receptive spirits. Harriet Martineau condensed and freely translated the six volumes of the *Positive Philosophy* (1853), finding the vast range of knowledge therein a "prodigious treat." She was so excited that she tried to average around twenty to thirty pages a day, and very often tears fell onto the pages as she worked at white heat. She shared with Comte the same love for order and system, and she wrote with the intention of correcting what she considered to be malicious and certainly uninformed opinions of his novel theories. The reception of his works in France had been so adverse that he suffered a breakdown and had to spend a period of time in a mental home. When a friend of hers in France asked who and what he was, she was told that he was an impoverished lecturer who had a ragtag following of several hundred vagabonds.[6]

Martineau's translation was one of the first works by Comte that Harrison read, although he spoke and read French very readily. Like her, he became enchanted with the Positive philosophy, and he made its propagation the main preoccupation of his extremely active and varied life. When Richard Congreve, his former tutor at Wadham College, split with Pierre Laffitte, the heir to Comte himself, Harrison and others, favoring Laffitte, decided to form a separate group. In 1881, they leased for twenty-one years an old hall of the Scottish Corporation in Fetter Lane. Although Harrison had wished to acquire a permanent place of meeting, he obligingly took the lease of this historic old building in his own name. Because Sir Isaac Newton, one of the Positivist saints, as President of the Royal Society had purchased the ground there, the hall was duly named by the society after him (*AM*, 2:258−60).

Harrison was invited to contribute a paper to the *Pall Mall Gazette* as part two of an article on centers of spiritual activity; part one had been contributed by Dean Church on St. Paul's Cathedral to the same article, which appeared on November 29, 1883. In his paper, Harrison described his new meeting place, which, in the preceding century, had belonged to the Royal Society and in which were stored materials that would become the first nucleus of the collections of the British Museum. He described his Positivist community as being very unlike other religious organizations the public was familiar with. There were no rituals and no priest. And although it might appear to be a night school or a political club, it was deeply animated by a genuine religious idea (*AM*, 261−64).

At the meetings in Newton Hall, audiences listened to lectures on science, philosophy, social organization, education, politics, history, and art. The connecting thread that ran through all the discourses was the relation of the subject, in every case, to the progress of mankind. They were all sermons on one text: the improvement of man's life by way of a scientific understanding of his powers and limits. The prime method was education. The core of the subject matter was the study of science. One of the society's slogans was "The end of observation is a knowledge of laws; and the end of knowledge is to enable us to act" (*AM*, 261).

Practical issues of the day, including foreign affairs, were freely and thoroughly debated at Newton Hall. Social communion was promoted through friendly meals in common, musical gatherings, and concerts by the society's choral union. It was not unusual to find in progress there the celebration of the birth of a great man, a trip to a national shrine, the presentation of a child to the Positivist community, or a commemoration of the dead. Throughout all the activities, however, the Positivist mottoes were driven home: "Live not for self, but for the world"; "Order and progress"; and "Live in the light" (*AM*, 263). Everything at the hall was open and free, and anyone could come and go whenever he wished. No one was paid for giving a lecture. And there was no distinction of social class, for all met on an equal footing. Tolerance was the order of the day. Harrison could never concede that the spiritual life is something too wide or too narrow for the many-sidedness of human life. He feared that in concentrating on ontological problems, the Churches, in their anxiousness to be spiritual, were no longer human. The Positivist tries to make every human act a religious one; thus he grows not less religious but more so (*AM*, 264–66).

Twenty-one years later, when the lease on Newton Hall had run out, Harrison was asked by the *Nineteenth Century* to write what the society had accomplished over those years at the Hall, the venerable place where Coleridge had delivered his twelve lectures on Shakespeare, the last ones he ever gave in public, and where Dryden, Dr. Johnson, Tom Paine, Hobbes of Malmsbury, and Otway had lived in the close vicinity. The Positivist Society had decorated the walls with its mottoes and had installed busts of many great figures celebrated in the *Positivist Calendar* from Moses to Bichat. And in the center there was the Positive Library of two hundred and seventy works, ancient and modern. At the front there were the grand piano and organ that once had been the property of Charles Darwin, and, yes, there was a large copy of the Sistine Madonna (*AM*, 268).

Harrison writes that they had had no apocalyptic dream of a Utopian New Heaven and Earth in their own lifetime (*AM*, 269). Never had they used the name of church for their society. Humanism and Positivism are synonymous terms, and religion extends to a belief in all solid truths, spiritual and physical, which inspire one to personal and social duty, as revealed by science. In 1881, Harrison had said in his inaugural address at Newton Hall that under their direction it would be simultaneously a school, a club, and a chapel, with special emphasis on scientific training as the prerequisite to real knowledge. It was a people's school, not dissimilar to a mechanics' institute as a seat of education in useful subjects, in certain respects (*AM*, 271–72). But it was always absolutely free. Also, it did not pretend to prepare people for the useful trades or professions, and it did not dispense desultory or miscellaneous information. Finally, the course of study was designed for a religious purpose, that is to say, for the purpose of training everyone there to serve Humanity. Least of all was it intended to aid one to gratify his vanity or to help him get ahead in the world of economic competition.

The courses included the study of the sciences, taught by specialists in the field, usually professors at the universities or doctors of medicine. Professor Beesly, of Mumbo-Jumbo days, during some twenty years gave a continuous and systematic course in both ancient and modern history. And Harrison, as well as many others, conducted systematic courses in world history. Above all, the lectures were never suited to the undergraduate who wanted to get some "tips" for his examinations. Even lectures on Euclid or conic sections, which would have no meaning for the religious teaching of Christians, Moslems, or Jews, substantiated the Positivist religious emphasis on the absolute necessity for scientific demonstration as the foundation of any permanent and valid religion. The supreme purpose of the society was to commemorate the great men of history—be they Moses, Mohammed, or the Buddha—who have shaped the course of human civilization.

Art was another important subject at Newton Hall. The society would visit and study collections of pictures, statues, and famous buildings. The works of great composers—Bach, Handel, Beethoven, and Mozart, for example—were either sung by the society's choir or performed by visiting professional artists. No means that might arouse the emotions to a stronger devotional spirit was neglected, that would appeal to the sense of man's dependence on the human Providence that surrounds every thought and activity of his life from the cradle to the grave. Members of the society had written hymns, without any theological or mystical implication, for such special occasions as birth, death, marriage, morning, evening, and New Year's Day.

The point of the human sacraments is to associate the great typical yet crucial events in the life of the individual with the life of Humanity as a whole, via the use of some public sanction, not unlike the oath of the Roman soldier of old. It is no more than a public pledge to fulfill some duty, with no mystical significance at all. The sacrament of Presentation, for example, involves the public dedication of the child by its parents or sponsors to the life of Humanity. Initiation inaugurates the child's commencement of systematic education. Admission is the beginning of a young man's life as an adult. Destination concerns his adoption of a career in the community. When one of the society received an appointment to the Far East, there was a public ceremony for him at the Hall. Of course, there are the sacraments of marriage and burial. In these, as in the other sacraments, there is no ritual or formal ceremony other than a commemorative address, such as the funeral discourses Harrison gave for Cotter Morrison and Grant Allen, prominent members of the society. Each of the nine sacraments has some social meaning. Harrison insists that no crude parody of Roman Catholicism was intended, although Comte would be the first to pay honor to the high ideal of the medieval Church.

Positivist Theory of History

Harrison and Comte consider history to be the handmaiden of social philosophy (MH, 138). In it, one can catch some idea of the central lines of human evolution. It should be, in the larger sense, the bible, or the manual, for a philosophy of human progress, a practical guide of life and conduct. It should be considered as an unceasing development of the organism in which all of mankind are the cells. We should come to know more and more those moral and social links that connect us with our ancestors. The best way to acquire this sense of unity in the course of our civilization and of the organic evolution of its gradual growth is to study the great historians, ancient and modern (MH, 117).

Harrison wonders whether the more remote history, perhaps with the least resemblance to our own, may not be the more useful (MH, 85). Of course, our own history is valuable, he concedes, but there is danger that we will know little else, content with narrow customs and prejudices bred in us through habit, and thereby we may neglect vast forces and possibilities latent in human society. The very history of other races and of different systems may prove to be the very best corrective of our insularity. We may become aware, as in no other way, of the endless permutations and combinations possible in world civilization. The actual object of the study of history should be to comprehend the life of the human race in its fulness and its continuous evolution (*MH*, 79). Overspecialization by historians all too often warps and distorts this overview.

History is the biography of civilized man, quite intelligible, as Harrison often insists, without depending on our loading our minds with endless facts, dates, and names. The major divisions seem to be clear enough. There were the early Oriental theocracies, the great stationary systems held in place by powerful religious system and immemorial social custom. These systems thrived in most of our planet for many centuries, though perhaps the era of the early fetichist nature-worshipers, without recorded history, was the longest of all. It was not until the theocracies that history as recorded fact was created by the great state sacerdotal organizations.

Harrison next credits the Greek republics with the development of intellectual activity, personal freedom, and self-assertion—in a word, the Hellenic spirit. A subsection might be the rise and fall of Alexander's brief empire (*MH*, 81). Next, there was the rise and development of the Roman world, separable into two periods over a thousand years. The republic lasted until Julius Caesar, and the empire until Justinian. Following Rome, even rising from its ashes, the Catholic and feudal world emerged. The next period, the formation of the great European states, included the Reformation and the Renaissance of learning, or Humanism. And, finally, there has been the political and industrial revolution of the modern world, which includes the consolidation of Prussia and of the United States; the intellectual, scientific, and industrial revolutions of the eighteenth century; the development of the worldwide empires and international communication; and democracy and socialism in their various forms.

Of course, Harrison realizes the obvious truth that there is much overlapping, although when seen as an entire process, the divisions become fairly distinct. There is a suggestion of a quasi-teleological process discernible in both Marx's inevitable evolution toward a classless society and Comte's inevitable development toward a positive society. Both favor a linear concept of history as opposed to a cyclic theory of the kind envisaged by Vico, Spengler, and the ancient historians. The linear, or straight-line, theories of Marx and Comte, respectively, are mundane transformations of the first of its kind made possible by Christianity in the *Civitatis Dei* of St. Augustine.

Oswald Spengler, in his *Der Untergang des Abendlandes* (1922),[7] developed perhaps the most formidable cyclic theory in modern times, using the analogy of the four seasons to trace the rise, development, and fall of successive cultures, each one proceeding rather much in the same way from spring through winter to inevitable death. Though the inner soul of any culture is intrinsically and peculiarly its own, its organic unfolding, or morphology, is comparable to that of any other. As in any individual organism, there is a natural limit to its duration, after which it must die. With an encyclopedic knowledge of virtually every field of knowledge that rivals Comte's own, Spengler studies and compares the features of the great cultures that we know something about in world history—the Egyptian, Chinese, Hindu, Classical (Greek and Roman), Arabian, Mexican, and Western cultures. Through his study of comparative morphology, Spengler is confident that he can demonstrate that in terms of religion, art, politics, social life, economics, philosophy, and science, close counterparts can be found in the same chronological position in each culture cycle.

Spengler believes that the telltale symptoms of the decline of the West are clearly to be seen in the Positivism of Comte. For the reformer, nothing has value but that which can be justified by reason. The *philosophe* comes to power, the most destructive force in history, he thinks, and the banker eclipses the baron. The rise of machines, destroying both peasant and aristocrat, and the growth of huge cities lead to the replacement of Culture by Civilization, of soul by intellect. The great philosophical system-making up to Kant is replaced by ethics and psychology. By about 1800, the line of change becomes apparent as art gives way to science.

All truths, continues Spengler, become relative, and certain philistines make a religion of progress as they talk about the accumulation and transmission of culture. But culture cannot be given to the mind, for it must be rooted deeply in the soul. That which is transferable is civilization, the tools and technical methods: this is not progress, but only change. The superficial intellect replaces profound instincts, and the air is full of slogans such as World Peace, Humanity, and the

Brotherhood of Man. The parallel in the Classical cycle is the Pyrrhonism of the Alexandrian age and Buddhism in the Hindu. Religion is not dead, but only has ceased to be organic, has ceased to be the soul of the culture.

But Comte and Harrison did not believe in the cyclic theory of history. The positive stage is eclectic in that it absorbs the contributions of its predecessors and is altogether dependent on them. One who has read Plutarch, Harrison says, knows quite a bit about Greek and Roman history (*MH*, 21). If he reads about the Middle Ages, he will learn something about feudalism and chivalry. But, looked at separately, all this is confusion, for that which is otherwise desultory must be combined into a living whole. It can no more be taken to pieces than a human frame can be left without its circulatory and nervous systems. Although no form of civilization endures, its consequences are evident in our daily life, whether they be the amazing invention of the alphabet (from which all the other alphabets derive), the institution of the family, the development of the calendar, the worship of the gods, the discovery of agriculture, the rise of literature and art and music. The inimitable intellectual and artistic accomplishments of the Greeks and the legal, social, and political legacy of the Romans are the very foundation of Western thought and practice. This is the Positivist theory of filiation.[8]

After the fall of Rome, it was Charlemagne who, like some former Roman emperor, built a new Germanic empire and civilization and developed feudalism into a methodical form, a reciprocal organization of duty and privilege (*MH*, 63−64). This system was not only material but also moral and religious, for the Church grew into one of the great institutions of all time. Harrison says that the Church was Greek in its creed, Asiatic in its worship, and Roman in its constitution. When Rome fell from her material greatness, her social genius survived in the Church, which continued to be the center of the civilized world.

The Church stood between the conqueror and the slave, telling them that they are all children of one Father in Heaven, inculcating in them all a new sense of a higher life, of a brotherhood among men, of the gentler qualities such as the world had never before seen (*MH*, 66). She taught reverence for women, personal self-denial, dignity of labor, and benevolence to all. Her humanizing power in the Middle Ages was especially felt in her desire to educate and in her development of the arts. It was this humanizing role of the medieval Church, apart from the worldly and political power of the Empire, that captivated both Comte and Harrison. The Church had no theocratic power over the state, yet all the while it enjoyed its own tremendous moral and spiritual power. The two powers were complementary, neither one significantly encroaching on the other. It was the kind of separation of powers that Comte envisaged for his own prospective Positive rulers and priests: here it was in actual practice.

But the Church was doomed from the beginning by its false theology, which led to a visionary ideal of human life and a selfish asceticism. Its indifference to science and progress later became horror and detestation. Harrison compares the Church to one of its own cathedrals, building for many centuries but never completed and falling into ruin while still unfinished (*MH*, 69–70). Like the Roman Empire before her, she degenerated into a prolonged convulsion of corruption, cruelty, ignorance, and tyranny. And upon the ruins of feudalism, which declined along with the deterioration of the Church, rose the great monarchies of Europe.

With the rise of the sciences, society passed into its final stage of industrial existence. The new knowledge was spread by the printing press, itself the product of the movement. The moral and intellectual guidance of mankind passed from the hands of the priests to those of the scientists, poets, philosophers, and journalists. Then came the great convulsion, the French Revolution, pulverizing the last remnants of the old feudal, aristocratic, and hereditary systems of the past (*MH*, 74). Harrison believes that the ground has been prepared for a new world, the materials for which are on every hand. The Positivist must harvest the riches of the older forms of civilization, extract their essence, and harmonize them with the new. With the knowledge, variety, activity, and humanity of modern life he dreams of combining the Greeks' zeal for truth, grace of life, and radiant art and poetry; the Romans' deep social spirit, genius for government and law, and noble sense of public life; and the Church's discipline of devotion to its faith, belief in the spiritual union of mankind, and tenderness and zeal for an ideal transcending self.

Finally, Harrison urges the study of the great historians. He speaks much of the especial genius of Herodotus, who had that observant and critical eye unknown to all the wisdom of the empires of Egypt, Babylon, or Persia, that ultimately would develop Greek philosophy and science. Thucydides was both a strictly scientific historian and a profound philosopher. No more truthful historical portrait exists than the one he painted of the age of Pericles in Athens. The history of the Peloponnesian War resembles a portrait of Titian, with the outward and inner life of man put before us in its living reality (*MH*, 91—92). Harrison also recommends Xenophon and Plutarch, as well as the great Roman historians. From the modern historians he discusses, I shall mention Gibbon, whose *Decline and Fall* he calls the most nearly perfect historical composition that exists in any language. In it, Gibbon weaves "for one third of all recorded time the epic of the human race" (*MH*, 101).

Sociocracy: The Positivist Polity

Whereas the essence of the old polytheistic religions had been the veneration and stimulation of the public qualities of mankind, Harrison believes, the focus of Christianity has been placed on the spirit within the individual. Christianity has made little attempt to regenerate the practical life (*OS*, 111—12). Since Positivism believes that life belongs to Humanity, it has attempted to restore the religious foundation of the public and practical activities outside the home, for it regards all active life beyond the home as public. Unlike the ancients, however, who restricted the public life to a small minority of free citizens, Positivism recognizes all adults in the community as citizens, whose public life is an extension and enlargement of their private life. Its whole organization exists for industry, not for war, repudiating the slavery and privileged caste system of the ancients, as well. When the French Revolution of 1789 proclaimed that men are free, equal, and independent, mankind had passed one of the turning-points of the history of Humanity (*OS*, 115). And Positivism, a child of the Revolution, insists that society exists for the people as its first underlying aim.

There are certain fundamental conditions requisite for the achievement of such a goal. There must be public education common to all citizens. A social and religious character must attach to every form of work and industry. The government must rest on the opinions of the public at large. And industry should exist for the production of all the things requisite for the highest possible cultured existence of mankind (*OS*, 118−19). I cannot help thinking of Edward Bellamy's socialistic technocracy in *Looking Backward*, in which the vast amount of available leisure time was spent on cultural activities that would cultivate the inward spiritual life of mankind; because all work was useful and all citizens cooperated in performing it, no matter how menial or disagreeable, no one had to work more than a few hours a week (Comte's goal was a minimum workday of seven hours).

Menial work in the ancient world had been done by slaves, and in the Middle Ages by serfs. But with the rise of democratic capitalism, the free labor market was born. There seems to be regression, however, in the coming to power of communism to a kind of neo-serfdom, in which freedom of choice is as severely limited as it is in military life. But even democratic capitalism has never overcome the social stigma attached to the lower levels of occupation. As Harrison has observed, idleness and useless sport in England have long been the pursuits of gentlemen. The ideal of Positivism is that all work is ennobled and ennobling, for men labor not for themselves but for society. Obviously, society could not continue without the hard work of the bricklayer, the farmer, and the seaman. And surely their wages do not compensate them for what they do, any more than the soldier can be adequately compensated for surrendering his life for his country (*OS*, 121). How can one ever assess economically such service? All honest labor has social consequences beyond calculation. And the antecedents of wealth and birth have been so complex and widely dispersed in the past, so arbitrary and so accidentally conferred, that they cannot be reckoned at all in terms of social value (*OS*, 123). The sole worth will be measured in terms of the value of service to the community. It is clear that Harrison sees the family as the microcosm of society, as the form of the complete life.

Finding that no known political form suffices, not even the democracy of the time, Comte devises the term *sociocracy* to convey the idea that the organization of the state should serve the collective interest of society, not the interest of any special class or caste. Sociocracy differs from the contemporary democracy in that it recognizes that all men are not equal in their power and capacity to serve society more genuinely, and it does not pretend otherwise. Also, it is concerned with future generations of Humanity more keenly than it is with the passing claims of the masses at any one given time, which, Harrison believes, is the root fallacy of Marxism (*OS*, 127).

Comte's trump card, of course, is the Religion of Humanity. Communism disavows religion altogether, concentrating entirely on the material side of reality. Christianity deals with only one part of man's nature and deals contemptuously with what it calls "natural" man. But the stumbling block for Positivism, as well as for Communism and Christianity, is clearly understood by Comte to be self-love. He refers to it as "the great infirmity of our nature, an infirmity which unremitting discipline on the part of each individual and of society may materially palliate, but will never radically cure."[9] The seventh and last science of his hierarchy is Morality, which Comte was working on up to his death. He freely concedes that the personal instincts outnumber the social ones by seven to three and are also the stronger. But he remains optimistic that the Positivist morality contains all the advantages of spontaneity and demonstration, of being so intensely human in all its parts. It is clear that his reliance is on education, on the training of the heart, with which intellect must cooperate. As I shall show later, the two elements essential for spiritual power arise from the sympathetic influence of woman in the family and the systematic influence of the priesthood on public life. The Church had attempted to capitalize on these advantages, but the synthesis on which its hope was based was imperfect and unstable, lacking the fusion of intellect, feeling, and action.[10]

Capitalists will be the temporal chiefs of modern society as the nutritive organs of Humanity, which collect and prepare the materials essential for life and distribute them, always modified by a central organ. Their personal powers are essential to sustain the vigor of their energy. But in order to check their consequent hardness and resort to authority, derivatives of personal power, Comte looks back to the medieval world for an answer, when temporal and spiritual power were separate and existed in a state of balance and equipoise.[11] The one thing both Harrison and Comte equally abhor is resort to external force. Harrison insists that thought, in particular, must be free from any legal restraint and subject only to conscience and public opinion. The moral and spiritual power will be exercised by the priesthood and never by the ruling capitalists, whose expertise, however, is indispensable to the successful conduct of the material affairs of society. But all classes will be imbued from the cradle to the grave by the precedence that social duty takes over natural rights (*OS*, 284−85).

All theologies are, at bottom, selfish and thereby antisocial, based, in the final analysis, on individual man's own soul and his superterrestrial hopes. They draw man's hopes away from Humanity. The Religion of Humanity throughout life holds out the idea of the duty of the individual to Humanity. The horrors of nineteenth-century industrialism, Harrison believes, are caused not by unusual wickedness but by mere anarchy and unprincipled principles. It is not the rulers and exploiters who are vicious but the system of which they are inevitably a part, if system it may be called (*OS*, 343−44).

Positivism would revive the ideals of the feudal ages, emphasizing the sense of reciprocal duty that should prevail throughout the social organism. The honorable sense of *noblesse oblige* should enable the powerful to protect the weak and the less able to respect the more able. Every laborer should own his own property. Public education should be free, as well as access to art, architecture, music, painting, drama, as in Athens (*OS*, 349). Positivism is a moral socialism, the socialism of free opinion. How can all this be attained? It cannot be done, Harrison emphasizes, by a system of selfishness, by a vision of personal salvation, by dreams of the beauty of the Cosmos; it can be achieved by no theology, by no metaphysics, by no pantheism. But it can be attained by a real religion, one of unselfishness, a human religion (*OS*, 350).

In Comte's *The Catechism of Positivism*, there is a dialogue between a woman and a priest of Positivism, in which the priest explains that the idea of rights must disappear from the political domain as completely as the idea of cause should from that of the philosophical. The reason for this prohibition is that the will is placed above discussion, with the implication of the necessity for a supernatural source.

Nothing should take precedence of human discussion. The ideal of rights is basically anarchical. Positivism admits of nothing but duties of all to all, whereas the ideal of rights suggests individualism. The idea of rights implies some previous earning of them, whereas the longest life could never enable one to repay what we have received, the countless obligations we have accumulated from our predecessors and owe to our successors. The Positivist priest holds that all human rights are so absurd that they are quite frankly immoral. Now that the idea of divine rights has been exploded, the foundation for unearned human rights has also disappeared.[12]

Harrison concedes that the prime objection to the system of regeneration proposed by Positivism is that it is visionary, utopian. He explains, however, that the weakness of other schemes, socialist and religious, is that they are only partial attempts to deal with the wholeness of human life and society. The Gospels, for example, leave thought, industry, politics, and art aside, and even communism is a "hole-and-corner" affair. The strength of Positivism is that it deals with human nature as a whole, offering a synthesis based on a general harmony of everything. The nostrums of today in England are no more than patchwork solutions for individual problems, not in the least pretending to usher in a millenium (*OS*, 158–59).

Of course, Positivism has much to do with specific reforms, but admittedly it is a utopia, a vision of what human life could and should become, a religious belief in an ideal. And Harrison advises that all the great things that have ever existed are usually the results of ideals, often seeming rather strange at the time of their first expression. The Gospel itself is one long appeal to do things that would appear ridiculous and insane in the ancient Roman world where it originated, yet it overwhelmed the world, in time, and recast man's entire civilization (*OS*, 160). That tremendously influential work, Rousseau's *The Social Contract*, taught a crude, wild dream of social utopia, based on the most dubious of premises. The other ideal utopias—those of the Buddha, Confucius, and Mohammed, respectively—all seemed equally strange at one time (*OS*, 161). Even the most fictitious of ideals have transformed the practical life of mankind. And there are Russian nihilism, Henry George's single-tax theory, and communism, which are also visions of a social future. In short, the charge that Positivism is utopian in no way diminishes the possibility of its adoption in the real world (OS, 162−63).

Harrison concludes that Positivism is the only present scheme of life that has a future before it. It substitutes social cooperation for mutual rivalry; unselfish standards in place of selfish; a foundation of science, history, and the law of evolution in all things in place of sheer fantasy; an appeal to deep social passion, generosity, and reverence for envy and hate; duty for self-interest; and religion in the place of utility. It provides the image of eternal Humanity from which man derives all that he has and all that he will leave behind him. It is only just, therefore, Harrison reminds his critics, that man give all that he can to this ideal, which represents everything he is and everything that he has (OS, 183).

Woman, Priesthood, and Education in the Positivist Polity

Comte believes that the regenerating elements in society will be the working classes, the philosophers (or priests), and women, who represent, respectively, action, thought, and feeling. Feeling is the motivating power of our being that brings the other parts into unity. It is a more spontaneous and lasting spring of inspiration than either action or intellect, and it provides the constructive quality, preventing the waywardness of the intellect and the undermining tendencies of our active powers. But like the philosophers and the working classes, women modify rather than govern. [13]

Throughout the animal kingdom, the male surpasses the female in physical and in intellectual force, and practical life is controlled by action rather than by affection. Success in great efforts depends more on energy and talent than on goodness or affection. However, in what Comte considers the highest attributes of Humanity, woman is superior. It is in the family that woman is dominant, the primordial unit of society that is so much more important than the individual. The home, says Harrison, is "the primeval and eternal school where we learn to practise the balance of our instincts, to restrain appetite, to cultivate affection, to pass out of our lower selves—to Live for

Humanity (*OS*, 42—43). Home is the place where the characters of men are formed and where the great personal problem of how to reconcile self with non-self has to be solved. And here woman is the trainer of all the feelings that come from our instincts and our hearts, woman in the various roles of mother, wife, sister, daughter, and domestic. As Harrison continues, she is our nurse in infancy and in illness, the helper in our work, the comforter in our wrath, the teacher and advisor, the companion of maturity, and the inspirer of our deepest sentiments and highest thoughts.

There could be no more Victorian concept of woman that this Positivist one, which Harrison, of course, embraces wholeheartedly. And he invokes as examples the great female creations of literature— Antigone of Sophocles, Jeanie Deans of Sir Walter Scott; Cordelia, Ophelia, and Desdemona of Shakespeare; and, of course, Beatrice of Dante. Then there are the women of the Bible, including Ruth, the Virgin Mary, and Mary Magdalene. Naturally, marriage is the center and the root of the family, the profoundest expression of living life for others, resulting in the moral refinement and elevation of man through the sympathy of woman. And society is the combination of families, the place where the very root of social morality can first be found (*OS*, 46).

The family is really a society within itself, depending on the same distribution of function, organization, and government. Unlike the supporters of the Equal Rights for Women movement of today, Harrison believes it is the duty of the man to financially support the woman, who should naturally remain in her rightful province within the home. The home is the center of education, compared to which the instruction we receive from books is but an acquirement. No part of our education is more important than that which we absorb before the age of fourteen.

Individuals do not live a separate social life as they do a separate physiological one. They are not independent social organisms, for there is no such thing as an independent, self-supporting living individual. Brains and stomachs cannot live in separation, nor can individuals. As Harrison explains, the mind, the nervous system, and the digestive system are mental abstractions, unable to live apart. As the primordial unit of society, the family is the source of religion and of morality. Most anarchical theories derive from our looking on men in terms of individuals rather than of families. The family contains the basic elements of society: succession, combination, and distribution (*OS*, 36). By succession, Harrison means the transmission of thoughts and ideals as well as of useful knowledge and things down through the generations. By combination, he means the coordination of mutual effort toward a common end. And by distribution, he means a distribution of the different faculties of differently qualified individuals for the attainment of the common end in view.

Animals seem to have some of these attributes in a minor degree, but the one social ability that man has that marks him off from the rest of the animal world is the transmission of experience from generation to generation. The family has a far larger meaning to the Positivist than the immediate group of man, wife, and children, for it includes ancestors, descendants, domestics, and even the animal adjuncts to it (*OS*, 41−42). The family is the organism that creates Humanity, and it is only in the home that Humanity is fully developed in all its nobility, beauty, and tenderness. Although it is true that the home can be perverted into a den of selfishness, it is only in a sound and healthy home that the three kinds of affection—attachment, reverence, and sympathy—can mature in all their intensity and purity. And, of course, the immediate relationship that expresses all three in their deepest form is that of marriage (*OS*, 48−49).

Comte adopts the method of dialogue in his *Catechism of Positive Religion* as the most effective form of communicating religious instruction, deeming it superior to the method of direct exposition. After considering several possibilities for his interlocutors, he devolves on a woman (really Madame Clotilde de Vaux) and a priest (himself) (see above, pp. 41−42). Because Clotilde had been taken from him after so short an acquaintance, he will now accomplish subjectively that systematic preparation he otherwise would have endowed her with. She brings to the conversation nothing more than those unformed opinions found in most women on such subjects, and in most of the working classes, as well. Women are the mediators between man and society, the ones who influence man to the highest point of cultivation. His moral guardianship is in the hands of mother, wife, and daughter, who respectively imbue him with three qualities essential to unity with contemporary fellow-citizens—obedience, union, and protection. Also, these three relationships, respectively, connect man with the three stages of continuity in life—past, present; and future. [14]

Following Comte's line of thought, Harrison fears that the absolute assimilation, or equality, of men and women would guarantee the destruction of both home and family, which, in turn, means the elimination of the womanliness of woman and the humanity of man (*CL*, 315 − 16). Marriage is a religious act quite as much as it is a civil one. In addition to those valuable personal relationships between the two members themselves, there is the formation of a new and fundamental unit of society itself, and so marriage is called a sacrament. Quite as rigid as the Church itself is in the matter, Comte feels that since marriage outlasts death itself, one can effect a marriage union only once in a lifetime. The husband leads in the force of his superior strength in public work and activity, whereas the wife leads by her moral and spiritual persuasion. This relationship is a symbol of the twin material and moral power, the world of action and that of feeling, and that of state and church. We must all learn to live for others as we learn to live for our own flesh and blood. To live only for the family would be a form of selfishness akin to that of the individual's living only for himself (*CL*, 316 − 18).

Like the family, society, too, is an organism that has to be treated as a whole. We may reason in the abstract about the different functions of the state, but in fact they all form one whole and cannot be detached. Underlying the entire structure must be a supportive public opinion which itself rests on an organized education that will be common to all, an education that is both moral and intellectual. Without this correlated and unified public opinion, all social and political plans are nothing but so many nostrums. The Positivist is less concerned with the specific form of organization of the state than with the spirit of public opinion that is its vital essence. Harrison hopes to obtain this alternative to having to increase the power of the state by providing for all the people an education that is complete, by reducing working hours to provide more leisure time for life in the home and for self-development, by increasing the opportunity for workmen's clubs and meetings to have political discussion, by submitting all political appointments to public approval, and by guaranteeing complete freedom of speech. Just as the main influence on education is moral and spiritual cultivation, so must the main influence on political activity be public opinion (*GW*, 170).

Harrison envisages a society without class distinction, a condition that depends almost entirely on equal education for all. It will make all men gentlemen, for Harrison believes that status is the criterion for entering that social class. This education will be given gratuitously by an independent body maintained by gifts and endowments, not by the taxpayers' money. By priesthood, Comte means such an independent body of educators who teach everyone freely; and by church, he means a teaching institution independent of privilege, monopoly, and state authority. The function of the priests will be very different from that of contemporary professors. They will be concerned with religion as much as with science and philosophy, and they will perform all the public ceremonies of the human sacraments. It will be the duty of the priests to inculcate a systematic comprehension of the physical and moral sciences, so unified as to prevent the dissemination of distortions and misinterpretations (*OS*, 126–29).

Harrison obviously is contrasting the ideal education by the priests to that currently being given by the schools and universities in his era. In the nineteenth century, no gentleman ever sends his son to an "elementary" school any more than a working man sends his to a "public" one. Pride of caste forces a gentleman to cling to a false so-called Humanistic education that teaches the student nothing but what is utterly worthless: quoting Latin without false quantities and writing doggerel in Greek and Latin verse (*R&I*, 326, 327). The main purpose of it all is to win prizes and honors, but the end result is a pressure system which destroys all genuine interest in, and understanding of, the great works of antiquity. Further, serious studies become secondary to competitive games. Above all, guidance and inspiration are needed, not bludgeoning and squeezing. Education can enable a man to form his mind, but it can never create it for him (*R&I*, 329).

Drill is good in its place, as are discipline, punctuality, and good order, but, says Harrison, it can better turn out good troopers, dockyard workers, and able seamen. As for contemporary higher education, since it rests almost entirely on a purely intellectual base, it neglects the moral and affective side of human personality and emphasizes purely material and pecuniary motives, together with testing by way of visible "marks" (*R&I*, 325–26). The goal has become ultimate success, money, applause, and superiority. The teacher, instead of attempting to improve the student's mind, is frantically preparing him for the race to success on competitive examinations given by overworked examiners who have never seen either student or teacher. Such an inhuman system may change an honest fellow into "a selfish, dull brute, or leave a weak brain softened and atrophied for life" (*R&I*, 321).

Unlike the professors and the priests who preceded them, the priests, or philosophers, of Humanity would combine a moral and an intellectual influence, subordinating every subject of thought to the moral principle. They would lead mankind to accept a complete and homogeneous synthesis. The primary reason for their spiritual authority is their refusal of political power, thereby keeping the theoretical and the practical apart just as the spiritual and secular authorities of the Middle Ages were kept separate, avoiding the danger of the kind of theocracy which earlier empires had unfortunately fallen into. By rising above wealth and worldy ambition, the priests, or philosophers, of Humanity would enjoy a moral power most like that of the medieval Church. But the moral power of the priests of Positivism would be based, not on theological fiction, but on demonstrable truth. They would regenerate and synthesize all the functions of science, poetry, and morality in the life of Humanity to the point that our political action will be devoted to their service. As we come to know the Great Being, or Humanity, so unlike that absolute and incomprehensible Being of theology, its worship would become the distinctive feature of our whole life—political, social, and otherwise. [15]

One of the most important ideas that runs through his *Mutual Aid* (1902) had been inspired by a lecture Prince Peter Kropotkin had heard by a Russian zoologist at the University of St. Petersburg, which emphasized that, in addition to a law of Mutual Struggle as taught by the Darwinians, there is also in Nature a law of Mutual Aid. This law might well be as important in the struggle and progressive evolution of the species as that of mutual contest. When one grabs a bucket of water and rushes to help put out the fire consuming his neighbor's house, this generosity springs from an instinct of human solidarity and sociability. Struggle may be replaced by cooperation, which may result through the development of those moral and intellectual faculties that would actually create in the species its most effective means of survival. Animals, Kropotkin argues, which acquire the habit of mutual aid are fitter to survive than those that are constantly warring against one another. As a result, mutual confidence and individual initiative make possible intellectual progress, which is more vital than mutual struggle to the evolution of human society. Kropotkin's theory of the law of Mutual Aid would lend valuable support to Harrison's reliance on the importance of the altruistic principle that is fundamental to the Positivist theory of human nature (see above, p. 104). The entire system of Comte and Harrison depends on whether the attainment of altruism in the social life of Humanity is no more than a vain utopian dream.

Communism, Capitalism, and Positivism

Harrison criticizes the Church for its historic inability to solve the problem of labor and industry. Justinian's code treated the institution of slavery as though it were as eternal as that of marriage. And now that the institutions and discipline of the medieval Church have considerably disintegrated, there remains scant possibility that they will bring an answer to the modern problem. And for that "queer bit of affectation called Christian socialism," which interprets Christianity as essentially the Sermon on the Mount, he writes that such a spirit is more pertinent to the personal life of the individual than to the public life. With its "Lay not up for yourselves treasures on earth, take no thought for your life, take no thought for the morrow," its effect is paralyzingly antisocial (OS, 186–87).

There has been no more controversial problem in the Western world since the beginnings of the industrial era than that of work. The Italian writer Adriano Tilgher made a study of man's attitudes toward the subject down through the ages, from the idea of the Greeks, who conceived of it as a hardship, to the early Christians, who regarded it as punishment for Original Sin, down to recent times. In the modern age, the ideal of *homo sapiens* has become *homo faber*, for whom work has become the greatest and ultimate attainment of man.[16]

Positivism, Harrison writes, like communism, exalts work, proclaiming, however, that the first step toward a wholesome, human, and social religion is a religion that reveres labor (*OS*, 132). He faults Christianity, which has put the emphasis on loving, suffering, and meditating. But he also censures communism for failing to realize that not all industry is productive of merely useful material commodities. A great deal of energy must be devoted to many social activities which are not materially useful yet without which civilization would be inconceivable. And if the State alone possesses all the instruments of production and all the capital, every person will be required to do the kind of work the State requires of him. Harrison says that Positivism opposes this kind of "cast-iron Utopia" because it would suppress not only human freedom but also the foundation of family life. It could assign a million workers as it sees fit to any location it chooses. In a socialist society, he continues, a Darwin, a Spencer, a Tennyson, or a Ruskin would be treated as mere idle malingerers and would probably be forced to become second-rate carpenters or bookkeepers. It is imperative that our creative geniuses be permitted to live free lives, working out their own ideas without external interference (*OS*, 134).

It is true, Harrison continues, that both Positivism and communism are indignant at the present state of society—the low wages, the cruelty and indifference, the waste, the selfish struggle for wealth, and the vicious strife promoted by competition. Both glorify the worker as the prime consideration of society and treat capital as the true property of the community. But whereas the Communist proposes solving problems in an absolute way through use of law and force, he emphasizes, the Positivist attempts to achieve in a relative way a change of feeling and habit through opinion and moral influence. Ideally, the Communist seeks to absorb the family into the State, to remedy the abuses of capital by abolishing it, and to eliminate the bad side of property by eradicating even the good side of it. The Positivist, on the other hand, would strengthen the role of the family by making it the actual center of the life of society. He would convert capital to a commodity for the public good and property to a tool for social good. Unlike communism, then, Positivism is a moral and religious socialism (*OS*, 136).

Perhaps the greatest divergence between communism and Positivism, Harrison continues, is their respective positions on ownership of property. Ideally, communism would eliminate the possession of property by private individuals, but Positivism regards all wealth as the creation of social cooperation and holds that it should be used in the service of society. For Positivism, although property is not a moral right but only a legal convention, it approves of its personal possession only if there be the understanding that it is a moral and social convenience which comports with the activity essential to social progress. It is the abuse, not the use, of appropriation (i.e., the acquisition of property) that is harmful, because it is the basic condition for social and moral life. Our very human existence depends on a certain amount of both personal and social appropriation. Without it, we should all be slaves, without moral freedom, and wholly dependent on the will of the state. It is the basis of any dignity of life, successful activity, or even goodness and generosity. Far from being theft, property is the joint creation by many workers within the entire social context (*OS*, 138).

The very existence of the family and the home is based on appropriation. Of course, no modern Communist proposes to eliminate the family and to institute a community of wives, husbands, and children. But the family's perpetuation from the past into the future obviously depends on appropriation, which carries "the sentiment of property to its most passionate and enduring form" (*OS*, 140). To eliminate property is tantamount to abolishing not only the family but also human nature, as well. The poetry of life is closely associated with the possession of beloved things. To abolish the household and its possessions is to deprive daily life of its humanity, freedom, and stability (*OS*, 140).

Harrison believes that true communism in the land involves the production of food for the nation by migratory laborers who most closely resemble the *latifundia* on the great estates during the decadent days of the Roman Empire. As he clearly saw almost a century ago, fixity of tenure is the first condition of moral life and of productive efficiency (*OS*, 147). In 1920, he is able to write (as he is reviewing Harold Cox's *Economic Liberty*) that socialism is the negation of liberty: "Be my brother or I will kill thee!" exclaims Lenin (*NV*, 115). Harrison also attacks the fundamental Marxist theory of Surplus Value. Although only a moderate amount of his profit is retained by the capitalist, the laborer is told that he is plundered by the capitalist—"a silly falsehood by Marx" (*NV*, 93). And he further says, "We can all see how a crazy social gospel of new industry converts a magnificent and populous city into the dying wilderness of Leningrad" (*NV*, 92).

But the ideal of capitalism, or competition, is no more promising than that of communism, Harrison contends. Here the emphasis is quite candidly on the motivation of selfishness, whereby every individual is out for his own advantage. The gulf between capital and labor grows ever wider, with the working classes who produce the goods living lives unfit for civilized beings (*OS*, 165). It has become morally right that the strong and aggressive forge to the top, whereas the weak and the helpless sink to the bottom. Wonderful inventions are made that would seem sure to relieve the drudgery of millions, but the result has been something horribly different. Usually, as he points out, a technological improvement has only made the work of the millions more monotonous and soulless than before (*OS*, 167). It increases the quantity of production but not the income of the poor. The cities have grown blacker and more polluted, and life has become more regimented. Competition has only succeeded in creating immense wealth for the few and scant distribution of it to the many.

Positivism would do away with the absentee landlord, and everyone, be he manager or laborer, would have his own property secured to him. Workers would receive a fixed wage per week, plus one that is varied, depending on the state of the market. The hours of labor would be reduced to seven or eight a day. The masses of the people would receive a free education until the age of twenty-one so that workers socially might be treated as gentlemen and scientifically as philosophers. Everyone would receive free recreation and access to art, libraries, museums, and galleries, as well as to pure air and water. All work would be treated as honorable and deserving of respect (*OS*, 150–52).

Everyone would be taught constantly that the use of capital is a social duty and that the capitalist has the same responsibility as does the general of an army. There would be a social stigma attached to the idleness of the rich, as well as to their selfishness and oppression, their wanton luxury, and their desire to do nothing but obtain large fortunes. The opinions of the people, guided and taught by the priestcraft, would be the final court of appeal. Everyone would be thoroughly instilled with the idea that all capital and all labor belong to Humanity (OS, 153). To the Socialists and Communists who wonder how this aspiration could be made real, Harrison replies that this religion of social duty would be inculcated from the cradle to the grave. The flaw in the schemes of the Socialists and the Communists is that they play with only the fringe of the problem (OS, 153). The Positivists, on the other hand, face the entire problem of human nature by proposing a religion, a philosophy, and a polity, all based on social science. They believe that the transformation of the human heart can be achieved by the Religion of Humanity, without which no utopia would be possible (OS, 156–57).

Criticism of Comte's Social
Theories and Harrison's Reply

John Stuart Mill, perhaps one of England's most gifted philosophers, was for a long time a correspondent with, and an advocate of, Auguste Comte. Even after they had broken off their relationship, Mill still helped secure financial support for Comte, who, until the end of his life, suffered from considerable poverty. But, unlike Harrison, Mill could not overlook what he took to be Comte's later change of direction. He thought the central flaw in Comte was his obsession with unity, or system. This addiction errs in its excess. Everything is regulated down to the most minute detail, many of which prescriptions are ridiculous. Unfortunately, Comte betrays a singular lack of wit or humor. Mill notes that the only humorist in his *Positivist Library* is Molière, and he is honored for his wisdom, not his wit. [17]

Nothing is more reprehensible to the usually tolerant Mill than Comte's sacrifice of democratic, or representative, forms on the altar of system. The whole human race will have one Supreme Pontiff in the Religion of Humanity. It is obvious that now progress would be sacrificed to order, whereas formerly the two were kept in a state of equipoise by Comte. It would appear that the constant development of life was encouraged until the triumph of Positivism, after which the principle of regulation of activity becomes fixed. No longer does Comte desire the further development of human mental power but rather submission and obedience. Mill asks who can judge whether certain researches are useless? Comte grows distrustful of demands for proof as though they were almost an affront to the sacerdotal order. And he seems suspicious of all books other than those one hundred chosen for the basic *Positivist Library*. He even goes so far as to suggest that everything, including species of plants and animals, that might be injurious to man be rooted out. One man—the high priest—decides which problems are to be pursued and which to be ignored. Mill wonders whether the present intellectual anarchy and chaos are less to be desired than such an absolute monarchy.

In his frenzy for regulation, Comte, Mill charges, indulged in his superstitious reverence for numbers, planning to change the decimal system to the septimal. He even imposed on himself extremely artificial rules for writing, such as permitting no sentence to exceed five lines of print and no paragraph to have more than seven sentences. He decided that it would take thirty-three more years for the establishment of Positivism, before the close of the century, to be divided into periods of seven, five, and twenty-one years each. Of course, each number has a particular significance. Mill also attacks Comte's later sympathy for fetishism and the Oriental theocracies. Whereas Comte ascribed the ultimate failure of the theocracies to their fusion of the temporal and the spiritual authority, Mill blamed it on the very onus that Comte himself was trying to impose on his own system: the stifling of free investigation through the imposition of a tyrannical unity very much his own.

One further point should be made. Mill ironically and very percipiently notices that Comte, who usually looked to the discipline of the medieval Catholic Church for his model, failed to do so at a crucial juncture. The Church has always had two standards of morality: one, which suffices for the salvation of the ordinary, and another, which demands the sanctity of the saint. Unconsciously, for he has no respect for Protestantism, Comte followed the path of the extreme Calvinist here by requiring that all believers shall be saints "and damns them (after his own fashion) if they are not."

Comte so thoroughly condemns any suggestion of egoism as opposed to his ideal of altruism that again there is no half-way house, no intermediate ground. Mill suggests that life is not so rich in enjoyments that it should neglect the cultivation of all those that have the misfortune to verge on Comte's classification of the egoistic side of man's nature. Rather than eradicate them on the ground of egoism, Mill proposes that we should rather cultivate the wish to share them with others as much as possible. Mill oppugns only one gratification absolutely and that is the love of domination, or superiority for its own sake.

In two lectures (reprinted in *OS*, 203—58) at Newton Hall in 1893, Harrison deals in some detail with Mill's attack on Comte's later writings. He observes that this is the most important criticism ever made of Comte, for it is the source of most of the other criticisms that have since been directed against him. Because no other critic combines both his knowledge and his philosophical skill, to answer Mill is to answer them all (*OS*, 203).

The crux of the difference between Mill and Comte can be simply stated, Harrison thinks. It is the individualist school versus the socialist. Should society be regenerated by an organized effort or by an individual one (*OS*, 205)? Comte, however, specifically prevents the philosophical class from wielding state authority. It should have no state monopoly, wealth, or privilege. It should have no heaven to promise nor hell to threaten, and there should be no power to interfere with it from either state or court. Its only authority should be its own moral weight and intellectual usefulness (*OS*, 252—53). Even Mill admits there is a need for a philosophical class to educate the community. His real objection is to permit all education to be handed over to a central authority. If that were done, says Harrison, no one should protest more than he (*OS*, 250—51).

Harrison is surprised that Mill would say that the *Positivist Library* consists of only 100 books instead of 270, amounting to about 500 volumes.[18] Probably no more than three men in all England could master this library. And, of course, Comte never said a word about proscribing all books other than those in the Library (*OS*, 223—24). As for Comte's distaste for wit and humor, Harrison recalls that the Library includes nearly all the greatest humorists of ancient and modern times, instancing Aristophanes, Aesop, Lucian, Juvenal, Boccaccio, Chaucer, Rabelais, Swift, and Sterne, for a few. Comte often refers to Cervantes, Fielding, and Goldsmith. And he includes the entire works of Molière in his Library. As for the wit of other religious leaders, Harrison notes that the Buddha, Jesus, and St. Bernard were never known for being especially playful (*OS*, 220—21).

As for choking off free thought and investigation, Comte wrote three years before his death, "It was for me to institute the Positive; it was not for me to constitute it." Neither Harrison nor M. Laffitte ever regarded Comte's *Polity* as final (*OS*, 225). Far from insisting that all Positivists become saints, Harrison alleges that of the ten human instincts, personal and social, seven of them are personal and they are the more energetic ones. The social instincts are supposed to control, not eradicate, the personal ones (*OS*, 234). Harrison agrees with Mill that Comte had put too little emphasis on introspection as a means of discovering the laws of the mind, but even so, this deficiency, like all the others, does not invalidate the main principles of Positivism (*OS*, 229—30).

Harrison admits that Comte was too often overconfident, as when he entertained the extravagant illusion that by 1854 the era of war had ended. He honestly concedes there were a number of other such absurdities, including some dangerous suggestions of moral discipline. But, again, the *Polity* was never held to be inspired as the Mosaic Law and the Puritan Bible were supposed to be. Understandably, Mill did take some illustrations to be laws, for there can be no doubt that Comte did too often slip into prescriptive language (*OS*, 224).

Harrison pays the highest tribute to Mill as friend and teacher, and he contends that, in the main, Mill subscribes to Comte's basic theories. For example, Mill has always enthusiastically supported Comte's general conception of a possible science of sociology. Mill had written in his *Logic* in 1843 that Comte alone had understood that it is possible to base a true science of social phenomena on a sound historical basis. Of course, Comte never pretended that he had actually created sociology as a science, as Mill has mistakenly charged, but simply developed the general conception of it. Harrison cites Mill's own uncompromising acceptance of the Law of the Three States and his general approval of the Classification of the Sciences. Mill even agrees with Comte's synthesis, or philosophy, of the sciences (*OS*, 208−209). And it was Mill himself who supplied methods of proof that Comte thought his own synthesis was in need of, methods that Comte himself had not worked out. And Mill accepted Comte's division of sociology into the theory of statics and the theory of dynamics (*OS*, 209).

Harrison further says that Mill adopts Comte's dominant law of human evolution on the theory that progress is determined by intellectual advance, defending the idea against criticisms by Herbert Spencer. Mill also accepts Comte's relating moral progress to intellectual progress as opposed to Buckle, who doubted the reality of moral progress.[19] And Mill cannot be too complimentary toward Comte's theory of history, which he thinks, next to the philosophy of the sciences, is Comte's greatest achievement. The compliment is all the more impressive when one realizes how vast and complex is the entire course of human civilization, to which Comte devoted over sixteen hundred pages, with innumerable judgments and analyses (*OS*, 210−11).

Mill even approves of the general scheme of the *Positivist Calendar*, with its list of 558 benefactors of mankind. Mill says that Comte included every important name in science, art, religion, and political science. Despite his criticisms of Comte, Mill believes that the Religion of Humanity fulfills the basic conditions of a religion. A religion should claim authority over the whole of human life. It should attempt to control human conduct, and it should be crystallized around a concrete object. He thinks that Humanity is an adequate center for a religion. He highly approves of the cultivation of altruism as the basis of moral discipline and the end of religion. He accepts the principle that a cult is essential to a religion and that it should have spiritual power in a social sense. There should be a social aim in all intellectual pursuits, and he is not averse to the supervision of education by a philosophic class (*OS*, 212−13).[20]

The main strictures Mill employs against the theories of Comte relate to what he deems to be their excessive infringement on freedom. However, it seems that in his *On Liberty* (1859) Mill's reliance on the efficacy of freedom of discussion in modern parliamentary government is quite as idealistic as the presumptions that he takes Comte to task for. In this justly famous work, which may well be the high-water mark of Western liberalism, Mill gives place to no other serious philosopher in holding out such hope for free discussion. It is all the more remarkable when we recall that he served in the House of Commons on various committees and commissions where he surely must have constantly noted that politicians can seldom proclaim what they really think as they serve the interests of their party, their constituencies, and powerful special interest groups. However, it must be said that Mill himself always maintained his own personal integrity by practicing what he preached.

Harrison is distressed that Thomas Henry Huxley, though a friend of thirty years standing and a fellow-participant in many a debate at the Metaphysical Society, has continued to lampoon him as "pontiff, prophet, general humbug, and counterpart of Joe Smith, the Mormon" (*PCS*, 295).[21] Harrison cites from his various addresses at different times to convince Huxley he has consistently urged that Positivism should exclude all blind trust in authority and in all "cut-and-dried" formulas. He had specifically warned against treating Comte's fifteen volumes as a new divine revelation with a biblical kind of authority. The one lesson that Positivism should teach is that one should accept nothing as verity without demonstration. The Religion of Humanity does not involve the substitution of a human God for a celestial one nor the worship of a Supreme Being at all. Further, he reminds Huxley that he himself has advocated, to use his precise words, "a reverence and love for the ethical idea" (*PCS*, 299).

At Newton Hall, Harrison continues, there were no ritual, no test for orthodoxy, no director, no rigid scheme of belief or worship, and no sign of "revised popery." "Would he [i.e., Huxley] be angry if I wrote a book about him as an orthodox 'Haeckelist,' and suggested that he kept in his back-yard a stuffed gorilla, which he was wont to reverence as his primordial ancestor?" (*PCS*, 300).[22] He reminds Huxley that men of science of high international reputation like

Lafitte in France (who succeeded Comte as leader of the movement) and Dr. John Bridges in England were deeply devoted to the movement. As to Huxley's own espousal of Agnosticism, Harrison has to say that it is necessarily a thin and temporary phenomenon as a religious philosophy. Huxley, indeed, does not pretend that Agnosticism is a creed but rather admits that it is no more than a method.

Harrison recalls that he used to attend Huxley's lectures on physiology many years ago, and he is pleased to say he has consistently admired his great contributions to human thought, as well as his unique ability to make alive everything he discusses. But Harrison is especially gratified that Huxley thinks the natural and permanent type of true religion is "service of humanity," for that is exactly what Harrison himself believes in and lives for. Huxley, then, really does seek a solution for the religious problem in the human and social direction rather than in any Absolute philosophy, on the one hand, or in Agnosticism itself, on the other. They both, it seems, equally repudiate Herbert Spencer's attempt to develop a philosophy of evolution. Intellectually, both men are on the same side, he contends. Huxley is really a Positivist without knowing it (PCS, 306–307).

Harrison had always objected to making Positivism at that early period into just another cult or church, having split with his former Oxford tutor, Richard Congreve, on that very matter and having only reluctantly participated with the Newton Hall group later. In view of the small number of active Positivists at the time, Harrison preferred that the movement concentrate on education of the public in its philosophy. He insisted that Positivists recognize a spiritual life that does not depend on mystical enigmas or imaginary figments. This spiritual life is essentially the consensus of faculties that reside in the human organism. And despite his disavowal of blind trust in or worship of Comte or any other man, he reminds Huxley that he has never written or spoken a single word of disrespect for either Comte or the genuine reverence of Humanity (PCS, 316).

Chapter Five

Literary and Historical Interests in the Ancient World

In addition to his numerous polemical writings on current foreign and domestic problems, as well as on Positivism, Harrison also published an historical novel, a tragedy for the stage, literary criticism, biographies, historical studies, and travel sketches. In *Theophano: The Crusade of the Tenth Century*,[1] he decided to present historical materials in the form of the novel. The rich color and the tragic action of events in tenth-century Byzantium come through vividly enough. And his novel remains so close to historical records that it can scarcely be called fiction, except for verbatim conversation. Using the same materials, he later wrote *Nicephorus: A Tragedy of New Rome*[2] in blank verse.

It is certainly helpful, and almost essential, to become familiar with Harrison's several articles on Constantinople before reading his novel and drama. He published in the *Fortnightly Review* "Constantinople as an Historic City," and "The Problem of Constantinople" (both essays were republished in *MH*, 309–67).[3] He also republished his Rede Lecture, "Byzantine History in the Early Middle Ages," given in 1900 at Cambridge, in *Among My Books*.[4] After reading these accounts, one can understand not only the background of his literary efforts but also the reasons why he attached such importance to the general subject. He thought that the Byzantine civilization formed the link between the ancient and modern worlds, yet ironically it is little known, even by the intelligentsia.

In his *De Senectute, Among My Books, Choice of Books and Other Literary Pieces*,[5] and *George Washington and Other American Addresses*,

Harrison develops the Comtean idea that the great heroes of Humanity may be not only men of public affairs but also scientists, religious leaders, philosophers, and literary figures. Comte thought that the three great creations of Humanity are philosophy, poetry, and polity, with poetry developing from the first and culminating in the third. And he believed that feeling not only is the highest principle of existence but that it also must always be constrained within the existing order of reality, which it may wisely modify but never subvert. The unity of human nature finds its fullest expression in art, which is in the most direct contact with the basic elements of human nature: feelings, thoughts, and actions. Art does indeed hold a mirror up to nature. Poetry, by which the other arts may be ranked by their affinity with it, is the noblest, the most comprehensive, the most spontaneous, and the most popular of the arts. It idealizes the most and imitates the least.

Adopting Comte's theories on art in their entirety, Harrison thinks that the choice of our books for reading is really the choice of our education, of the formation of our moral and intellectual ideals, and "of the whole duty of man" (CB, 20). But books in themselves are not any more education than laws are virtue, for a shallow person may also be well read in books. Great books afford us capacities rather than materials and should appeal to the reader's imagination, his memory, and his reflection. They should bring to us the wide range of human thought and the innumerable variations of human nature.

To find the best books requires no specialized research and no immensity of learning or scholarship. Humanity has long since determined almost unerringly the first-rate books of the past, judgments on which generations of able critics have concurred. There may be some dispute about the third-place and the fourth-place but not the first and second. The great masterpieces of the world are "the master instruments of a solid education" (CB, 25). Harrison deplores the plethora of books that issue forth today that all too often vitiate the taste for immortal works of human genius. "Greece gave us the model and eternal type of written language, not only in epic, tragic, and comic poetry, but in imaginative prose, and in pure lyric" (CB, 32).

Theophano and *Nicephorus:* Harrison's Ventures into Creative Literature

It is the sequence of history that the Positivist especially dwells on. And no other city, Harrison observes, other than Rome itself, can claim so unusual a sequence of historic interest as Constantinople, or Byzantium, as the Greeks have always called it (*MH*, 309). For nearly a thousand years it had been a Greek city of considerable importance before it became the center of the Roman Empire. It remained the capital of the Empire for more than fifteen hundred years, longer than any other imperial city in known history. And it remained the city of the sultans from the mid-sixteenth century until the early twentieth century. Rome was the center of Empire for only four centuries, and the royal cities of the Euphrates, the Ganges, and the Nile were abandoned after some centuries of splendor. There have been many great cities, but without such a sustained continuity of empire. And the great cities of Europe—London, Paris, Vienna, Madrid—are but creations of yesterday. Throughout the vagaries of life and history, only one city in world history has endured for fifteen centuries as the continuous seat of empire (*MH*, 310−11).

Until the latter half of the nineteenth century, historians were fairly oblivious of the significance of Byzantine history, be it Greek, Roman, or Ottoman. After some meritorious work in England, first by Finlay and later by Freeman, it was J. B. Bury who presented the English-speaking world with a systematic account of an era of which even Gibbon had given no more than excellent sketches based on limited materials (*MH*, 312). Much light has since been thrown on those romantic and tremendous events of a thousand years. The period from Theodosius to the Crusades was the one that has been most neglected by Western historians, when for seven hundred years Byzantium alone handed down the ancient world to the modern and when it was the most civilized city in Europe. Before the Crusades, it had already defended Christian civilization for four centuries.

If the Moslems had earlier succeeded in erasing the empire of the Bosphorus, the whole history of mankind would have taken a different turn. Harrison wonders where we would have elsewhere discovered

Roman law, Hellenic art, ancient poetry and learning, the complex art of organized government, or the traditions and manufactures of a cultured civilization. It is true, he writes, that Byzantium had her share of human weakness, meanness, corruption, and pedantry, but no other civilization was richer in heroism, skill, and intellectual energy (*MH*, 315). From Constantine to the Crusades, a period of seven centuries, when Rome and every other ancient city of Europe was stormed and sacked, Constantinople remained intact, always the most populous, wealthy, and cultivated city in Europe. Travelers during those days testified to its uniqueness in wealth, splendor, and power. All the while, it was placed in the midst of inveterate enemies from all sides: Western Christendom on the west, the Slavonic enemies and their incessant attacks from the north, and the Moslem foes on the east and the south; yet it never ceased being the great mart and clearing-house between East and West and North and South.

On no other spot on earth was there so ideal a location for a city destined to become the mistress of the world. Not only does it stand at the crossroads of civilization, but also it is impregnable to attack by any invading fleet from either the Black or the Aegean Sea. Harrison considers Constantine's recasting of the Empire both politically and religiously—his changing it from the ancient to the modern world, from polytheistic paganism to Christianity—to be one of the several crucial events of history (*MH*, 327). Some of Harrison's best writing is his descriptions of such cities as Constantinople, Paris, London, as well as of the artistic and architectural treasures of Europe, reminding us at times of Ruskin himself. His fascination with Byzantium, which he knows thoroughly firsthand as a visitor and historically as a student of both ancient chroniclers and contemporary scholars, is the basis of his several ventures into creative writing.

There is no extant architectural structure that so enraptures Harrison as the Church of St. Sophia, the Holy Wisdom, one of the most daring and triumphant buildings in the history of man. It unites sublimity of construction with grace of design, surpassing in glorious effect even the richest of Western gothic cathedrals. Justinian and subsequent emperors ransacked the pagan temples of the Roman Empire for its inimitable treasures. Harrison marvels that it is almost without parallel that the Moslems adopted the Holy Wisdom without serious injury or alteration within. Very unlike them, the Greeks ignored the form of Egyptian and Syrian temples; the Christians preferred the form of the law-courts to the temples of the polytheists; and Protestants have no use for the cruciform churches of the Catholics. This oldest cathedral in Christendom is an architectural example of Comtean filiation in that it has become the type of a thousand mosques. Small wonder that Justinian is supposed to have exclaimed, "I have surpassed thee, O Solomon!" (*MH*, 334).

Harrison notes that nowhere in Europe could there be equipped such fleets and armies as those of Nicephorus and John Tzimisces in the tenth century, nor indeed is there anything else to be compared in art or wealth or civilization as a whole, for actually Byzantium would stand alone at that time, virtually without any real competitor (*MH*, 354). It is in this period of the true beginning of the great Crusades against the False Prophet that Harrison places the setting of his novel and of his later drama. His first intention had been to write a monograph on the state of southeastern Europe and its relation to the advancing tide of Islam, the first historic confrontation between these vast powers that would be carried on by the West for several centuries somewhat later. It was J. B. Bury's *The Later Roman Empire* that first brought Harrison to the study of the Byzantine historians themselves.

Harrison, referring to himself as vice-president of the Royal Historical Society, dedicates his novel *Theophano: The Crusade of the Tenth Century* to J. B. Bury, Regius Professor of Modern History in the University of Cambridge. Instead of writing the historical treatise he had planned, he decided to produce a "romantic monograph," as he calls it, employing as his principal characters real figures of history and basing his story on contemporary records. Despite utilizing much history—replete with rich description of places, military events, ceremonies, and customs—Harrison conveys a remarkable sense of the crisis of important historical figures of that misty era, the entwining of character with stark and often terrifying fate. The historical thread of the earliest Crusades against the Moslems of the Near East runs throughout the story, including profound issues of Church and State, the relationship between East and West, the internal court intrigue involving powerful pressure groups and leading personalities of the age, and the sinister role of Theophano. This lady reminds us of the unscrupulous Byzantine empress of the ninth century, Irene, who blinded her son Constantine VI and usurped the rule of the Empire, although there was no precedent for female rule there. Theophano's violent passions were also above the law and contemptuous of custom, no matter how sacred.

Not only does the tale follow closely the contemporary authorities, but also many of the speeches and descriptions are literal translations from the Greek, which Harrison read with facility. Whereas the texts of contemporaries are constantly consulted, the scenery of the palaces is based mainly on Harrison's personal observations. Harrison attempts to recapture the glowing color of the life of the age, not just the succession of political events. An especial element the reader remains conscious of is the State Church, which little resembles the Papacy and its relation to the Empire of the West. Although the dependence of the Byzantine Church on the State caused much loss of freedom, morality, and spirituality, Harrison believes that it gave to the emperor powerful and lasting strength, investing him with a halo of majesty. The Byzantine Church, together with the inheritance of tradition and prestige of the old Roman Empire and of the wonderful language and the versatility of the Greek genius, was able to sustain the Byzantine civilization for nearly a thousand years (*MH*, 350−53).

Theophano had once tended the young heir to the throne when he had received a wound in a boar hunt. Refusing to be his mistress, she becomes his lawful wife. Harrison gives a sumptuous description of the coronation of Romanus II as emperor and of Theophano as empress, in which he is saluted as Caesar, even as Trajan, Constantine, and Theodosius were also hailed. After this ceremony, they appear for a great celebration in the Hippodrome, which held a central place in the city's history. After this auspicious ceremonial, the leading general of this supremely military period of Byzantine history, Nicephorus Phocas, is seen in confession to the monk Athanasius, revealing that he wishes to withdraw to a monastic cell because of his overpowering passion for this new Theodora, this second Irene. However, Athanasius refuses to give him absolution unless he promises to march to protect the Empire from the impending threat of the Moslem infidels. As Harrison succinctly puts it, he thereupon goes to his ultimate ruin and death.

Joseph Bringas, the lord high chamberlain, a eunuch and the mortal enemy of Theophano and Nicephorus, nevertheless advises Romanus that only the great general can recapture Sicily from the Saracens, who for 150 years have remained a constant threat to the Empire. Meantime, Theophano, who is as artful, as unscrupulous, and as self-serving as the Eunuch himself, insists that the weak Romanus send his sisters and mother to a convent so that neither they nor their possible children would ever pose a threat to herself or to her own future children. Harrison has Theodosius the Deacon compose his *The Conquest of Crete* in iambics, which describes the journey and the conquest, including an interesting account of the use of the Byzantines' secret weapon, "Greek fire." Theophano had told Nicephorus that he would be a new Belisarius, the master of New Rome and of its mistress, as well. "And so, with wild hopes, resounding cheers, and solemn anthems of prayer and blessing, the great Crusade of the Tenth Century sailed forth to do battle with the Saracen" (*Theo*, 80). Harrison spares no detail of horror to describe the reality of war and the picture of carnage after the defeat of the Saracens, including the dramatic storming of the fortress of Chandax on the island.

Nicephorus sends his Warden Digenes, a young man honestly devoted to him, to visit the Caliph of Spain to settle on a *modus vivendi* with that dignitary. Here Harrison gives us a picture of Cordova and the Spain of the caliph that sounds like the world of Haroun al Raschid, quite rivaling Constantinople itself in splendor. Digenes meets a beautiful daughter of an emir from Crete, Fatima, who falls hopelessly in love with him. Unfortunately, he is in love with a young sister of Romanus, the princess Agatha. Meanwhile, the poetic Deacon wonders whether in learning, magnificence, and general culture, Byzantium could rival all this. With his love for city planning and government, Harrison gives a full, detailed picture of Cordova, especially praising the Arabs as the leading engineers of the age.

When Nicephorus plans to enter a hermitage after his huge military success, Theophano, looking "down on him majestic and inspired like the Cumaean Sibyl in Raphael's fresco at Rome" (*Theo*, 137), asks who but him could protect not only the city but also herself and her babes. Rushing away with tears, she leaves him "quite dazed, drunk with perplexity, and mad with passion" (*Theo*, 137). Joseph

Bringas, the Eunuch, in his jealousy of Nicephorus, persuades the Emperor to order the general to the Asian frontier, after taking good care to load him with honors first. We meet in the general's tent for the first time John Tzimisces, the rival and later the successor of Nicephorus, an Armenian noble of the highest rank, a distinguished veteran who is famous for being even more romantic and reckless than Nicephorus himself. In council, Nicephorus speaks more like a priest at the altar than the leader of a mighty army, whereas John is bold and impetuous.

Nicephorus has compiled his famous *Handbook of Tactics*, which Harrison has him read from, explaining in some detail his three main military principles: (1) rapidity of movement; (2) exact knowledge of all the facts; and (3) foresight of every detail. His next move is to invest the city of Aleppo, in Syria, an important Moslem center. Just after the city proper falls and he is attacking the citadel, Theophano, having just had her fourth child, sends him an urgent appeal to return, for the emperor is dying, to which Nicephorus responds: "I come." Meantime, she has secretaries record the emperor's will. As Joseph Bringas is forcibly thrust back from the death chamber, Romanus designates Theophano as regent and Bringas as her minister; she plies him with forbidden wine to make him confirm Nicephorus as Lord Domestic of the East. After the emperor dies, his end hastened by the wine, Bringas shouts that the will is a false, forged document. The patriarch engineers through the Senate a compromise, by which Theophano does become regent but does have to accept Bringas as a power in the State.[6]

When Bringas sees Theophano and Nicephorus embracing, he realizes his danger but is resolved to win. There is a magnificent celebration of military victory in the Hippodrome, during which, in the procession, fragments of John the Baptist's camel's-hair tunic are carried. Having been captured at Jerusalem by Omar, the caliph who had transformed Islam from a religious sect to an imperial power in the seventh century, these fragments would remain at Constantinople for two and a half centuries until carried off to France by European conquerers in 1204. While basking in imperial glory, Nicephorus again yields to his urge to become a monk, feeling that Theophano wants him more as a tool than as a husband. Theophano opportunely arrives in the disguise of a hermit to persuade him to escape to the Holy Wisdom for sanctuary under the protection of the patriarch, for Joseph Bringas has orders for him to be dragged away.

Nicephorus, just on the point of crushing the Saracens, receives an urgent appeal from Theophano and a personal urging from John Tzimisces in his tent to rush back to the capital, for Bringas has issued letters for his arrest. After brooding many hours, he determines, as Harrison puts it, to cross the Rubicon. The city goes up in the flames of open revolution, the mob burns the eunuch's palace, and he is forced to seek sanctuary in the cathedral. Of course, Nicephorus is crowned emperor. The eunuch is deported to a distant place in Asia, where he lives in obscurity the rest of his life without further punishment. Nicephorus constantly wears a hairshirt under his imperial robes, forswearing the use of meat and wine as he feels himself to be a monk on the throne.

Now he makes the mistake that will ultimately destroy both himself and Theophano: he marries her, despite the warning of the Prelate Anthony, the same churchman who had prevented his becoming a monk. The patriarch forbids the new emperor the rites of the Church for a year and a day as penance for having married the wife of the former emperor. The emperor faces the priest at the altar, and the emperor retreats.[7] Meanwhile, Nicephorus lavishes on Theophano every possible gift, but the patriarch, by a technicality, catches Nicephorus in the sin of incest. He had acted as godfather at the baptism of Theophano's infant son; the Church under the Iconoclasts had prohibited the godfather from marrying the mother of his child-in-God. but Nicephorus flung himself into Theophano's arms, "that paradise for which he was willing to brave eternal damnation" (*Theo*, 186). It is later determined that Nicephorus's father was the child's real sponsor, however, and the wound is partially healed; but the scar remains permanent between Church and State for the remainder of this reign.

As the story moves along, Theophano more and more interferes with Nicephorus's plans for his military campaigns, causing some terrible disasters by persuading him against his better judgment to let others conduct his military affairs for him, as in the disastrous Sicilian campaign. Harrison uses the device of having Eric the Norwegian conducted through the fortifications of Constantinople, enabling us to learn about them in rather technical, but nonetheless interesting, detail along with Eric. Amid all this unique military and naval power, Nicephorus is being progressively undermined. Theophano tries to poison Digenes because he is planning to marry Princess Agatha, whose blood line would have a claim to the throne; then she tries to thrust a poisoned stiletto into him as she catches him in an embrace, but he falls into the arms of Nicephorus, who has just come into the room.

Successive beacons are burning in the distance, beckoning Nicephorus to come to lead the army, as Eric the Norwegian is told how the Greeks had used this method of signaling in the *Agememnon*. From now on, Theophano will be watched, as Nicephorus leaves his beloved aged father a regent in his absence, despite her frantic pleading. Thenceforth she will cease to be his wife, although to the world she will appear as his Empress. Even so, he cannot fully quench the love that he has always felt for her. Now Nicephorus launches his final campaign aganist the Infidels at Antioch, granting no quarter, for he is a sharp and severe disciplinarian, proud of the fact that the word "tender" is not in the vocabulary of the Roman Army. A captured document reveals to Nicephorus there is a treasonous liaison between John Tzimisces and Theophano, and again he is forced to leave a crucial battle because of her. He summons John, who protests his loyalty, but Nicephorus is never seen to smile again.

Nicephorus sends a delegation to Old Rome, where they meet the successful German emperor Otto and his representative, the Lombard historian, Liutprand. Harrison gives a marvelous picture of life in Old Rome in A.D. 967, in which he also contrasts the Hagia Sophia (the Holy Wisdom) to the old St. Peter's, much to the advantage of the former. The Byzantine delegation are especially impressed by the fact that Old Rome has so imitated their culture that their very words and phrases are heard everywhere. Otto has dreams of uniting the two empires and churches, planning to send Liutprand to Constantinople in order to arrange for the marriage between the princess Theophano and his own son, who will become Otto II. The embassy arrives under Liutprand in 968, but Nicephorus is furious with Otto for having attacked his Italian provinces in the south and for having claimed to be the Roman emperor. Further, he demands that Liutprand prostrate himself before him as the true Roman emperor, and he treats Liutprand with undisguised hauteur and contempt, reminding him that he is not a Roman but a Lombard.

Otto, infuriated, attacks the Byzantine colonies again in southern Italy, but Digenes is ready for him. The reader is reminded of similar scenes in the *Iliad* and the *Aeneid* as Harrison relates the meeting between Digenes and Count Pandulph in single combat, in which Digenes is killed, and the grief-stricken Princess Agatha retires to a convent. Now Nicephorus has lost his most trusted friend. From now on, he seems to be rushing downhill to his destruction, with nothing going right. In addition to his intensely religious nature, there is something of the fierce pride of Coriolanus in him. As he plans a third Asian crusade, he disdainfully ignores the crowds who gather to protest his high rates of taxation to support his military adventures. Agitators openly complain about his severe measures. And not the least cause of his troubles is his determination to rid the State of hordes of useless monks, whom he calls cowards and idlers. Of course, he would not interfere with genuine cells where men seek a godly life of prayer, but the Church protests nearly everything he recommends, even his living apart from Theophano. It also protests his plan, resembling that of the Moslems, to reward as martyrs those who fall in battle fighting the Infidel. However, he does make one concession: he agrees, reluctantly, to permit Theophano to live in the palace, where she immediately proceeds to agitate actively against him.

Even when he puts on an elaborate show in the Hippodrome to celebrate victory against the Moslems, terrible riots break out, for which he is blamed. Now he feels a curse has fallen on him. He nevertheless launches a violent campaign to capture all of Syria, including the tomb of the Savior. Having captured the head of John the Baptist and having broken the power of Islam in that part of the world, but once again hearing of Theophano's plots, he has to rush back home, only to see hatred against him everywhere. Even General Bourtzes, whom he left to complete the destruction of the Moslems, turns against him as had John Tzimisces and Theophano.

In the final scene, the two generals secretly meet Theophano in her room, where she stands like the image of Here as created by Scopas.

As she leads the conspirators into the room where Nicephorus lies sleeping on the floor, Harrison compares her to Clytemnestra as well as to a lovely Gorgon. They stab his body many times, crying "Tyrant!" and mutilating his body beyond recognition. And his battered head is dangled from a chain to swing in the wind, whereas his mangled body is thrown to the ground below the window. Knowing that the Patriarch would never approve of his marrying Theophano, John coldbloodedly rejects his partner in crime, else the Patriarch would have anointed General Bourtzes as emperor instead. He consigns her to a convent in a distant land and conducts a vigorous and successful military policy against the Russians to the north and the Moslems to the south during his very able few years as Emperor.

Harrison's indefatigable research bears comparison with that of Flaubert for *Salammbo*, an historical romance of Carthage in the third century B.C. *Theophano* is also an erudite reconstruction of an almost forgotten age of grandeur. Although it may lack the brilliant coloring of Flaubert's unique work, it does seem less like merely animated history. Harrison reaches the effects of tragic grandeur that Bulwer-Lytton achieved, both having been similarly affected by Greek tragedy. Like Bulwer-Lytton and unlike Sir Walter Scott, Harrison makes leading historical characters the principal actors in *Theophano* and combines powerful tragic passion with impressive reconstruction of past history. Harrison also obviously strives for some of the dramatic, pictorial scenes that James Anthony Froude created in his memorable *History of England* (1856), an imaginative historian who could often rival Gibbon and Macaulay in his panoramic effect. As we have noted in his dialogues, Harrison is especially able to bring off confrontation by way of quite natural conversation without its falling into the sententious or grandiloquent. Doubtless, this facility is what will decide him to convert the same general material into a drama the next year.

Why did this historical novel, then, not achieve any notable popularity or even significant recognition? Perhaps in the early part of the first decade of the twentieth century the dominance of the psychological, the realistic, and the naturalistic novel eclipsed interest in the panoramic, historical novel that focused on grandiose characters with a mythical aura. After all, Bulwer-Lytton's *The Last*

Days of Pompeii was published in 1834 and *Rienzi* in 1835, Disraeli's *Tancred* in 1847, and Flaubert's *Salammbo* in 1862. The Byzantine civilization is so little known, even in our own day, that the reader senses no landmarks, as it were, in a vast trackless region of *terra incognita*. Even Hamilcar in *Salammbo* stirs ever so faint a memory in the educated reader, but what can be said for Nicephorus Phocas or John Tzimisces? It is gratifying that Harrison's only intellectual thesis in the novel is to recover a vital connecting link in the chain of cause and effect that works through the unfolding of world history; otherwise, he is not foisting on his reader a dogmatic commitment to any religious, political, or philosophical idea, not even the Positive. He does a creditable job, in general, of creating character, but especially in the case of Nicephorus, whose complex personality emerges satisfactorily, especially from the struggle within him between the military genius and the religious recluse.

It is Harrison's realization that Nicephorus stands out as his most successful characterization in *Theophano* and that his ability to develop live, natural dialogue would especially suit the drama that leads to his casting the same general materials into *Nicephorus: A Tragedy of New Rome*. In an edition limited to 450 copies, Harrison stresses the fact that here he is not precisely following historical events or characters; in short, the play is not supposed to be a dramatized version of *Theophano*. Designed for the stage, it avoids poetic elaboration and ornamental diction, attempting primarily to create characters of idealized tragic, heroic dimensions through the medium of blank verse. But, as in *Theophano*, Harrison wants to draw attention to the basic elements of human tragedy and heroism involved in the long neglected Byzantine struggle to check the dynamic advance of Islam.

The general story, then, is now familiar to us. It is divided into five acts, each containing some four or five scenes, the more incidental ones resorting to prose. There are soliloquies devoted to expression of inner thoughts at points of crisis, as when Theophano, in the second scene in Act II, admiring the manliness of Nicephorus, deplores her fate to be married to Romanus, a weakling, a puny gamester, feeling she is deserving of better things. When Nicephorus confesses her power over him to Athanasius, the churchman says he must bear the full weight of his sin by fighting for Christ till death as penance.

Joseph Bringas is even more prominent in the tragedy. Just as he orders that Nicephorus Phocus be carried off to have his eyes torn out, Theophano intervenes with her commission from Romanus, which makes her regent; having just given birth to her fourth child, she faints into the arms of Nicephorus before the Eunuch. The third scene of Act II opens with a soliloquy by Nicephorus before a huge icon in his oratory:

> Would all were ended—and my storm-tossed soul
> Had found its haven! How the thunderclouds
> Roll round me, prophesying anarchy,
> Blind passion, and dishonourable death—
> Crimes piled on crimes—rebellion—a dog's fate—
> A Phocas stained with treason—my bright sword,
> Which kept its edge true in a hundred fights,
> Broken and hacked in some vile palace scuffle!
> No! sheathe it, son of Bardas! Thou has wrought
> The task that Christ appointed thee
>
> Rome breathes again, and Christendom is saved—
> Thy mission's ended—. . . .

In the tragedy, John Tzimisces and General Bourtzes are favorably portrayed, rushing to help Nicephorus in his struggle with the Eunuch and disclaiming their own competence when he offers to let them assume the rule of the State. Also, Theophano comes in with the patriarch and offers to share the throne with Nicephorus. However, the patriarch, as in *Theophano*, refuses to approve the marriage, but in the play the real reason is concern over incest, not the trumped-up belated technicality of the novel.

In Act IV, there is an especially good soliloquy, in which Nicephorus laments the degeneration of the Byzantine populace: "At each new tax they sputter insurrection, / And find the cowl less irksome than a spear." Digenes has a more prominent role as advisor of Nicephorus, warning him against despoiling the Church as Nicephorus defiantly insists that his loyal Armenian guards will keep the peace. Theophano is as devious and diabolical as she was in the novel. Nicephorus becomes convinced that she had originally sought him only to betray him, luring him to ruin, despair, and madness. And Nicephorus has an impressive soliloquy on the madness that goads men to seek a throne, the endless striving that brings naught but endless waste. There are effective passages in which Theophano protests her innocence to a doubting Nicephorus, all the while plotting his downfall.

In Act V, Theophano, General Bourtzes, John Tzimisces, and the patriarch exchange their lists of grievances. But only Theophano plans the assassination, for the others think only in terms of banishment, as they demand that no harm come to Nicephorus. However, John does swear, at her insistence, to disavow his own betrothed and to marry her. As Nicephorus lies unconscious on the floor before the shrine of the Virgin, Theophano brings in four guardsmen, who slaughter him brutally. The others had wished only to have him face his judges, not to wound him. But Theophano draws aside the curtain, taking pride in her accomplishment. When she reminds John she is now free to marry him, he exclaims she is a fiend risen from hell to slay Rome's noblest warrior. He banishes her forever, as the patriarch arrives to cut her off from all communion with the Church. She wildly attempts to stab John, accusing him of violating his oath, for which deed he shall be punished in hell below. Nicephorus now is honored as a man of God who saved the Church from the False Prophet, and his body receives solemn burial by Church and State. It is this scene that is the most radical departure from the novel.

Although Harrison is clearly not a master of blank verse, the portrayal of character and the structure of plot are well handled. The reader badly needs the background that the novel provides in order to appreciate the action of the tragedy, yet he cannot avoid being somewhat disturbed to encounter the changes in conception of character, especially in the final scene. It must be remembered that Harrison found the material so colorful and dramatic that he believed it could be more adequately presented in literary form. For both drama and novel, however, the time was not right, as no one knew better than Harrison himself.

His passion for revering the great spirits of the past, literary as well as any other, is clear from his espousal of Comte's *Positivist Calendar* and *Positivist Library*. Ironically, his Positivist Society, to which he devoted the main energy of his life, achieved no more immediate success than did his one novel and his one play. Byzantium, so important once but now nearly forgotten, nevertheless for Harrison vindicates the Positivist conviction that no energy is ever lost in the sum total of the life of Humanity—past, present, and future. It is doubtless this thought that always served to sustain him in his indomitable optimism.

Harrison's son Austin attests that his father never set out to do a thing from any motive of personal advantage, having very little commercial sense and almost no earthly vanity. As we have seen, he intensely disliked specialization. When he wrote *Nicephorus*, he disdained to consider stage technique and was even surprised and a bit wounded when Sir Herbert Beerbohm Tree explained to him the difficulties of staging an "historical essay." Had he not also attempted to express himself in literary forms, as he had done in nearly every other way, his very nature would have remained to that extent inhibited. Austin says that his life was, indeed, his pen: "Of few men can it more truthfully be said that 'he was what he wrote,' and probably no man of his time ever wrote more or better with less material ambition or advantage" (*FH*, 131).

Criticism of Ancient Literature from Homer to King Alfred

Austin Harrison believes that the classics and the arts were to his father what the old deities were to the pagans. The Greeks and the Romans became Austin's first heroes, and all around his father's library there were rows of their busts with which he became familiar from earliest childhood. He came to associate Marcus Aurelius with his father in thought, deed, and character, still retaining in later years the copy of the great Roman Stoic emperor's *Meditations* which Professor Beesly had given him. He always thought that Aurelius was the first practical Humanist, whose system of life was morally associated with the sociology of Comte (*FH*, 162−63).

In his preface to Comte's *The Positivist Library in the Nineteenth Century*,[8] in the edition of 1886, Harrison explains that in this volume there are about 270 works by 140 authors which Comte chose as books of permanent value for constant use by all educated men. This systemization is in line with Comte's teaching that all intellectual training should comport with a central synthesis and should reach the entirety of human nature. Such a carefully chosen body of the world's greatest books forms an important part of Comte's scheme of reorganizing education, which is the foundation of the entire Positive system, or Polity. This list, necessarily provisional and very much subject to future revision, consists of four sections devoted to (1) poetry and fiction, (2) science, (3) history, and (4) religion and philosophy.[9]

Wherever Comte is too narrow, Harrison is not behindhand in expressing his own qualifying opinion. The important legacy of Protestant thought is, for example, represented in the *Library* only through the obviously prejudiced writings of a Catholic theologian, as Harrison properly observes. However, as usual, Harrison agrees with Comte in theory, if not in specific application, contending that true literary judgment should be based on a weighing of each work and each writer in relation to the sum total of human cultivation and to the advance of the human spirit through the ages, doubtless with some suggestion of the fundamental static and dynamic principles of all life. He believes that the consensus of all the nations throughout their history proves, in the final analysis, to be right. As he puts it pungently, "It is unlikely, to say the least of it, that a young person who has hardly ceased making Latin verses will be able to reverse the decisions of the civilised world; and it is even more unlikely that Milton and Molière, Fielding and Scott, will ever be displaced by a master who has unaccountably lain hid for one or two centuries" (*CB*, 75). The ultimate court of appeal is, then, Humanity itself.

The highest works of poetry and fiction, Harrison believes, are those which may be read many times and the true value of which can be gained only by frequent and habitual reading. The immortal and universal poets must be reread until their music and inner spirit become a part of our own nature and until within them we can see the strength and beauty of Humanity transfigured in its joys and sorrows, dignity and struggles. Harrison contemptuously notes that if the highest works are difficult to any sincere reader, they are clearly impossible to the "gluttons of the circulating library." One may be a veritable devourer of books in great quantities but all the more incapable of reading one hundred lines of the wisest and most beautiful poetry (*CB*, 79).

Just as the railway bookstalls will never overwhelm Fielding and Scott, so will the armies of research in Europe and America never make Gibbon obsolete, he writes. "As an old man, I stand by the old Books, the old Classics, the old Style" (*AMB*, 123). Although the "Separators" deny that the *Iliad* and the *Odyssey* had a single author and the "Smashers" break the poems up into small fragments written by many poets, Harrison feels in his bones "that the poem as a whole is the immortal work of a mighty and sublime genius" (*AMB*, 125). He attempts to deal with the problem as belonging to the world of literature, not to that of pure scholarship. As we saw in his two creative works on Byzantium, he did his best "to master the arguments of scholars, historians, archaeologists, and mythologists" (*AMB*, 126). For thirty years, he says, he has been fascinated with his literary activities, during which he has three times visited Greece, together with its islands on either side. He has read his *Iliad* in the original and pondered on its problems while watching the plains of Troy and the wooded hills of Chios, and he has read the *Odyssey* on a yacht voyage to Ithaca. He has studied the ancient remains of prehistoric Greek art on location as well as in the museums of Athens, Naples, Paris, St. Petersburg, Berlin, Copenhagen, as well as in those of England and of America (*AMB*, 127).

Just as he is dubious about the latest "new" discoveries in this "new Trojan War" (i.e., of scholarship), which have not changed the meaning or value of Homer one whit, so is he dubious that wholly new and original forms of literature will be discovered in the twentieth century. He feels that the basic forms of literature through which genius can find expression have, for all practical purposes, been exhausted during the three thousand years since Homer. Despite myriad changes that will take place, the essential forms of human expression are not infinitely numerous or variable. There are types, standards, and canons of beauty both in literature and art. How odd it seems that this very radical Victorian, so often at odds with public opinion throughout his life, pronounces that it is no more than a cry of feebleness and conceit that extols the invention of some new art and new literature and that denigrates "all that the good sense of mankind has hitherto loved as beautiful and pleasing" (*AMB*, 123). But we must also remember that he is a Positivist, who reveres past heroes of Humanity, and, as such, he similarly parried the blows of the Agnostics against the traditional religion and the Church. Paradoxically, he is both revolutionary and conservative. Was it not the radical John Bright who defended the Queen?

The *Positivist Calendar* dedicates its second month, called Homer, to ancient poetry, with each of its twenty-eight days assigned to a Greek or Roman poet or artist. Following as it does the month of Moses, dedicated to the founders of antique theocracies, it demonstrates the Positivist's sense of the relative nature of human life in that the emphasis passes from absolute systems of theology to men of individual genius who give beauty to human life. In short, the Positivist reveres all forms of human sympathy and sense of oneness, all the higher instincts of human nature. It must be the task of any complete religion, Harrison explains, to understand and honor the role that all parts of our nature play, including that of sensitivity to poetry and art. Man's artistic creativity is as essential to the fullness of Humanity as are the primitive theologies, and Homer is the equal of Moses in his influence on mankind. Further, poetry is everywhere antecedent to prose, and it is more closely associated with early religion. Though Shakespeare and Dante may be equal to Homer in genius, neither has exerted so vast a sway over the imagination of mankind. Sounding rather like Shelley, Harrison asserts that whereas the codes of Moses and Confucius have passed away as living forces, Homer, after three thousand years, remains unaffected by novelty or age. "The Poets alone are immortal. All other men, however great, pass away into a dead past . . ." (*AMB*, 147).

Harrison considers Homer to have been a poet of "transcendent genius," who, in great poetry, transfigured for his people their religion, their morality, their patriotism, their grace, and their marvellous vitality. When he was alive, the other arts were in their "rudest infancy" among "the most poetic race in all human history." It was Homer who, with "a sensuous abandonment to freedom and to joy," glorified a manly and spacious life, appealed to memories of the past, and envisioned a future of national glory that Harrison believes

was not realized until the appearance of Alexander six centuries later
(*AMB*, 148). He became the poet and teacher at a critical point in the
evolution of Humanity. No poet, Harrison is convinced, has ever
approached Homer in his influence over the education and tone of the
lives of men. He appeared at the crucial point in the history of
mankind when there existed a civilization for the first time capable of
artistic expression, simple enough to be conveyed through the medium of a superb epic, and sufficiently primitive to be free from
revolutionary discord. And it was just on the point of turning from a
stationary to a progressive society. Homer probably lived between the
period of old-world theocratic fixity and the new world of freedom
and change, yet too young to fall into the anarchy of mere change or
into the vices of a complex civilization. He is close enough to the
theocratic society to retain some of its best moral qualities but far
enough away from it to be free from its rigid and exclusive spirit
(*AMB*, 153).

In Homer there is uniquely no touch of affectation or fustian.
Harrison, far from recommending nothing but the study of books,
emphasizes the emotional and imaginative side of literature as the
most necessary for daily use, for relishing the very aroma of life. Old
Homer, he adds, is the very fountainhead of pure poetic enjoyment.
He is the eternal type of poet, and in him alone of all poets is
transfigured a national life, wholly lovely, happy, and complete,
where care, decay, and worry are unborn: a secular Eden of the natural
man, unfallen and unashamed. Unlike all later writers, Homer painted
a world as he actually saw it (*CB*, 26–27). Harrison especially
deplores the sort of person who chatters about latest archaeological
finds and feels a "literary prurience" after new prints and "early
copies," all of which "unmans us for the enjoyment of the old songs
chanted forth in the sunrise of human imagination." Whether in "the
resounding lines of the old Greek, as fresh and ever-stirring as the
waves that tumble on the seashore," as Harrison describes Homer's
dactylic hexameters, or some English poetic or prose translation, he
always remains fresh and rich (*CB*, 27).

Harrison has much to say about translations, as did Matthew
Arnold in his *On Translating Homer*, a work which Harrison admits to
having studied carefully (*DeS*, 106–107). In the main, he agrees

with Arnold's comments, except that he disagrees that a translation should be done in English hexameters. He prefers Lord Derby's translation of the *Iliad* into blank verse, which was done after Arnold's essay had been written. He thinks this translation lacks the stiffness, awkwardness, and commonplace quality that Arnold objects to in other translations; it is rapid-moving, as well as plain and direct, and, most important of all, "eminently noble." Even though Harrison thinks that ancient languages can be translated into blank verse, their precision, subtlety, and reliance on fewer words make English equivalence impossible: there is "the structure of our tongue, with crowded consonants, crashing vocables, and paucity of vowel endings, [which] makes imitation of the ancient metres hopeless" (*DeS*, 107). The *Iliad* is composed almost entirely of dactyls and spondees, which English has few true examples of. "An English dactylic hexameter is too long, too jumpy, too much a ballad for a grand epic" (*DeS*, 108). The Greek dramatists, on the other hand, wrote mainly in iambic, which is the natural meter of English verse. Harrison believes the translation of any great poetry into English should be in unrimed blank verse. Unfortunately, however, the strength and the delicacy of foreign lyrics are both lost in translation.

On one of the greatest problems of literary criticism and exegesis of all time, Harrison has, as usual, quite decided opinions. It was Wolf's *Prolegomena* in 1795 that opened the war over Homer and led to the Higher Criticism of the Bible that, together with evolutionary theories, underlay the gigantic clash between religion and science in the Victorian age. It will suffice to mention a few of Harrison's conclusions on the matter. He doubts that the Greek language was ever written in Greece proper until the seventh century B.C. The poem might have been composed during the era of transition and settlement between the Mycenean age (anterior to 1000 B.C.) and the beginning of the commencement of historic Hellas around 700 B.C., that is, midway between the unrecorded mythical, heroic age and the historic, democratic world. Doubtless, Homer imposed a unity on generations of fluctuating lays currently in circulation, and the *Iliad* was very likely reduced to writing in the Athens of the sixth century, without the originality of the poet or the essential unity of the poem having been seriously affected. Just as Milton used Genesis and the Bible, as a whole, so Homer welded current myths and ancient lays into a single, unified poem, "the grandest Epic in the whole range of human genius" (*AMB*, 131).

It was John Addington Symonds in his *Greek Poets* who finally convinced Harrison of the unity of the *Iliad*. Admittedly, the *Odyssey* is clearly unified around the one character, Ulysses. However, he readily concedes that the *Odyssey* was very likely a later poem, written by a different, yet still a single, author. The tone and the *ethos* of the two poems are indisputably different. The *Odyssey*, unlike the warlike *Iliad*, fairly breathes the peaceable, social, domestic, and affective life, with family, servants, and pets playing a part that is totally alien to the *Iliad*. The tone is as different as that of *Paradise Lost* from that of *The Faerie Queene*. Finally, the scene of the *Iliad* is laid exclusively in Asia Minor, whereas the action of the *Odyssey* passes entirely in the western islands and the Ionian Sea, that is, the western and southern Mediterranean. Harrison speculates that not only might the second Homer have come several generations later than the first but also that he might well have been inspired by the first. All great poems are usually filled with anachronisms and improbabilities, but all great poets live in the world of their imagination (*AMB*, 137–39).

Religion, Harrison concludes, must again become human and poetic as it is in Homer if it should ever hope to again become the guide of human life (*AMB*, 162). Because both pedantry and skepticism have served to separate religion from poetry, poetry has become a literary amusement and religion a mystical quietism. It is only through poetry (as Harrison sounds rather more like Matthew Arnold) that religion can be made real and human. No religion can reach man's life unless it speaks through great poetry. The mission of the epics was grander and even holier than that of the Psalms, Harrison ventures to assert, for the simple reason that they sprang from a fuller and more humane sympathy with human life as a whole.

But the great dramatists of Athens come closer to this fundamental human religious spirit than did Homer himself. It was Aeschylus who founded his tragedy in religion, for it was in substance a religious ceremony, full of religious symbols and forms. Harrison estimates that the loss of the seventy plays of Aeschylus is probably the most terrible loss that literature has ever suffered (*AMB*, 165). Aeschylus and his successors in Athens exceed all others in the sheer massive, elemental form of the tragedy, in which every word adds to the pathos and in which the spectator is held spell-bound throughout with a sense of pity, sympathy, and dread. Although Harrison considers Shakespeare to be the greatest poet of all time in his range of genius, encyclopedic thought, and witchery of language, he thinks Aeschylus is the unchallenged master of the pure, severe, unalloyed tragedy, the grandest, most genuine form of the tragic art. Only once, he thinks, did Shakespeare approach this kind of tragedy, and that was in *Macbeth*, but his audience would not tolerate it (*DeS*, 79–80).

For the Greeks, tragedy had a sacramental sanction, inspired by an intense patriotic fervor that was free of any mercantile motive. It was a free gift to all Athenian citizens from both State and private sources. Harrison says that he has stood on the stage of the theater of Athens and Syracuse, reciting passages from the tragedies that companions in the top benches could hear clearly. He recalls that in this age of poetic polytheism, there was no manager watching the box office, no actor playing to the gallery, no thirst for buffoonery, blood, or torture (in the tragedy proper). The entire day was devoted to worship of the god, national pride, and the highest conceivable art. Of course, he admits the many limitations of the Greek stage as compared to ours. The conventions of the Attic drama, with its masks, buskins, "inevitable messenger," and moralizing chorus, obviously lacked breadth, freedom, variety, subtlety, and even humanity of the modern stage since Marlowe and Shakespeare. But even Shakespeare's versatility and depthless insight into every recess of the human soul diverts the spectator from the unrelieved tragedy of concentrated pity and awe we sense in the great catastrophes of Aeschylus and Sophocles (*DeS*, 81–85).

Harrison holds *Lear* to be the profoundest embodiment of Shakespeare's genius, yet it is an epic, a "human apocalypse," rather than "an acting tragedy," an art-form in which actual scenes are literally laid before our very eyes in all the substance of their agony and truth (*DeS*, 87). Ancient drama grew out of the chorus, which remained close to the activities of worship and festival. As a public act of solemn ritual, or sacred consecration, it gloried in its great declamations of moral intensity, without the trappings of florid ornament or embellishment. It would be impossible for us today to recapture the effects of the sacred fire on the altar, the pious chants to the deity, and the procession of elders and virgins. Dithyrambic poetry seems inappropriate to moments of great deeds; it may be great as poetry, perhaps, but intrusive on direct action. In Marlowe, this kind of poetry becomes "superb rant," and in all the Elizabethans it quickly deteriorates into "an almost farcical storm of big words and sesquipedalian declamation" (DeS, 91). The tendency is toward euphuism. Whereas all the characters in Hamlet speak high poetry, Sophocles would put these speeches into the chorus.

As a Positivist, Harrison prizes Aeschylus as the creator of tragedy as an art, making the theater a new way of exhibiting moral struggle in the destiny of Humanity. In the fusion of civic and religious dedication it reaches a new note of sublimity that no other poet has ever attained. But such a high spirit in the theater was shortlived. Before Aeschylus had reached old age, the judgment of his own city (and of Aristotle later) preferred the exquisite literary refinement and nearly perfect form the younger Sophocles developed. But Harrison is quick to add that Sophocles is as matchless and faultless as a statue of Praxiteles. Lacking the Titanic imagery as well as the passionate inspiration of Aeschylus, Sophocles imbues his great tragedies with an exquisite and intensely moral kind of religious feeling. Only later did drama degenerate into nothing much more than literary amusement (AMB, 165–73).

Euripides, with his splendid versatility, subtlety, and pathos, supplied the laws, forms, and even ethic for the French and Italian tragic drama, as well as for Dryden and Otway. But despite his overwhelming genius and influence as a poet of the highest order, he destroyed, as a social revolutionary, the sanctities of the ancient age. His dramas are cynical, argumentative, skeptical, and sentimental, reminding us of the scorn and contempt of a Voltaire and a Swift, for he is the most modern of the ancients. Harrison does not for a moment deny Euripides' lyricism, psychological subtlety, pathos, and boldness of thought, but he sides with the judgment of Aristophanes in The Frogs against him. Harrison agrees with Aristotle that the function of tragedy should be to purify the soul through pity and terror. He further believes that it should cleanse the human spirit of its sordid, selfish, and mean qualities and touch its dormant sympathetic feelings for fellow man (*AMB*, 174—75).

Harrison thinks that Aristophanes, especially in *The Frogs*, created the most amazing combination of delicate lyricism, limitless fancy, and ageless satire that any dramatist has ever done. Even Swift, Rabelais, and Molière never achieved anything like this, and not even Shelley painted more ethereal pictures of the heavens than we find in the choruses of *The Frogs* and *The Clouds*. Growing more rhapsodic still, he thinks Keats himself never surpassed this luscious music in the song of the Nightingale nor did Goethe exceed him in flights of fancy. Harrison thinks that only Shakespeare can be compared to Aristophanes in ancient or modern times. No one else has his "dithyrambic audacity," his "aerial music," or his wild laughter, not to mention his uncanny ability to touch every nerve of man. As we might well expect, this greatest of all comedians has one inexcusable fault: his outrages on decency (*AMB*, 177—79).

Although Greek classics suit his humor more often and more readily, Harrison does relish the Latin classics, too. No English translation does much justice to Latin poets, and least of all to Virgil, whose subtle music of phrase haunts us like a Beethoven melody. Although there is a monumental quality in Virgil's Latin, he has such a persistent sadness that one thinks of him as a "sensitive invalid" (*AMB*, 18—19). There is no Roman Homer. However, the genius of Roman poetry is in its form; therefore, translations are, of necessity, futile. There is the same loss in translation that we get in a photograph. Only Edward Fitzgerald, Harrison believes, reads as though he is an original (*CB*, 38—39). How could one capture in a translation, he exclaims, the unique felicity of language that we find in the original Latin of Horace? We enjoy in Horace the concentrated essence of good sense and sheer simplicity that not even Pope at his best can capture, superb as he is in epigrammatic English poetry (*AMB*, 18—20).

As for prose, he thinks that Plato's prose style is the most nearly perfect in all literature, reaching its epitome in the *Phaedo*, but he cares very little for Plato's metaphysics. He much prefers those prose writers who, in the ancient world, were already coming close to a truly human religion. Writers like Plutarch, Seneca, Tacitus, Epictetus, and Marcus Aurelius—in their humane morality—were more akin to Hume, Adam Smith, Condorcet, and Comte than were the Christian writers of either Rome or Byzantium. Harrison regrets that these forward-looking ancient spirits were not able to overcome the slavery and debauchery of the world around them and so obviate the centuries of monkish tyranny and ignorance that later were imposed on the world. Only a few centuries after they had written, their world was fairly swept away, together with its laws, arts, learning, culture, and religion (*AMB*, 32).

Harrison is especially cognizant of the startling similarities between the world of the later Roman times and our modern Western world. He quotes Leslie Stephen's essay in the *Apology* to the effect that we have just what they had in the time of the Antonines: "Theosophical moonshine," "rationalistic interpretation of orthodoxy," "the galvanizing dead creeds," sundry "philosophic moralities," and "many strange superstitions" (*AMB*, 34).

The work of Lucian is strangely modern yet also very characteristic of the late Roman world. Harrison finds him as racy and entertaining in his banter as Thackeray in his *Book of Snobs*. Petronius, "the Oscar Wilde of Neronian aestheticism," paints a vivid picture of the "smart" world of Rome—of New York—of London—of Paris. "Vulgarians are immortal." In Apuleius we find the strange mélange, in the Rome of the second century A.D., of "bestial and frivolous licence, spiritual mysticism, ideal aspirations for a new Heaven and a new earth, fierce asceticism, and preaching of the Sermon on the Mount. Apuleius touches on all" (*AMB*, 36).

With the sense of historic continuity that we saw in his interest in the Byzantine Empire, Harrison notes "the marvel of literary history" that Greek imaginative literature was continuous from Homer to Longus (beginning of the third century A.D.), a period of over thirteen centuries, with little break in continuity of language or tone. In the *Positivist Library*, Comte put that "last dying swan of ancient Greece," Longus, with his *Daphnis and Chloe*, along with Theocritus, Greek pastoral poet of the third century B.C. And in the *Calendar*, Comte placed both Longus and Theocritus in the month dedicated to Homer. Although *Daphnis and Chloe* is unabashedly erotic, the atmosphere is no more pornographic than a Greek statue in the nude, the Victorian Harrison concedes.

Since the writing of biographies was so important to Harrison, having done quite a bit of it himself, he writes that in the latter years of his life, as he is reading over again some of the favorite books of his youth, he has been rereading the two supreme masters of the thrilling art of writing the lives of famous men, Plutarch the ancient and Boswell the modern. Plutarch he considers to be the greatest of all biographers because he wrote more about the inner nature of man than about just the outer events of his life: that is, less about what he did and more about what he was. The most masterly portrait ever painted, he believes, was Plutarch's picture of Alexander the Great, himself the most superbly endowed human being in human history. He believes this estimate is just, even though he admits that Alexander was guilty of crimes, vices, and brutalities. Alexander also excelled in superhuman qualities of body, mind, and soul. More than that, no other man has ever inaugurated such huge secular movements throughout the globe. This portrait is far more true than all the laborious researches conducted by annalists, both ancient and modern. Boswell, the greatest modern biographer, did in miniature what Plutarch did on a far wider canvas and within a far mightier world (*AMB*, 70).

Harrison urges that by all means one should study the lives of the foremost men and women of ages past (*AMB*, 75). A goodly measure of the hero-worship one finds in Carlyle and Ruskin may also be seen in Comte and Harrison. For the Positivist Harrison, by studying parallel, though dissimilar, lives of great men, one may the better grasp the miraculous complexity of the history of civilizations and the seemingly unlimited capacity of human beings. And he recalls that for a number of years of his life he was busily engaged in editing a biographical dictionary of the lives of 558 men of eminence extending from Moses to Hegel. No work he had ever done was more enjoyable or more useful and instructive than his activities with this dictionary.

For him, no life is more fascinating than that of King Alfred, "the noblest, best, purest, wisest man in all recorded history—our own sacred hero, Alfred—the only name of a chief in all human annals on whose memory no blot, no defect, moral, intellectual, or even mythical has ever been alleged" (*AMB*, 69). Although no adequate biography has yet been written of him, his own writings are sufficient for knowing him. Much of Alfred's *Boethius* is his own reflections on life, duty, and religion, which Harrison deems among the noblest passages to be found "in the last immortal work of antiquity." He ranks it with the *Imitation of Christ* in spiritual elevation, although it is also the private manual of a military hero. In it we may search into "the inmost spirit of the best of kings and the bravest of saints" (*AMB*, 72). As a military genius, he built the first British navy, in the treaty of Wedmore (A.D. 878) he settled the foundation of England and converted the Danes to Christianity. This new Charlemagne, dreaming of an intellectual commerce between East and West, of a new imperialism not based on bloodshed, domination, and ruin but on sympathy, knowledge, and ideas, was as important to history as were Alexander, Julius Caesar, and Charlemagne, but superior to them in natural grace and beauty of soul. "Alfred, it is truly said, was the only perfect man of action in the annals of mankind" (*GW*, 42, 59–61).

Chapter Six

Appraisal of
Modern Literature

Harrison discusses modern literature—which, in his opinion, begins with Dante—in *Among My Books, Choice of Books,* and *De Senectute,* as well as in *Tennyson, Ruskin, and Mill and Other Literary Estimates*[1] and in *Studies in Early Victorian Literature.*[2] He cautions against the inclination to seize on some particular quality in a school or an individual for immoderate praise or blame, advising that the critic maintain a rational, a healthy, attitude by preserving a sense of due proportion (*CB*,74). True judgment, he maintains, consists of evaluating each work and each writer as a whole and "in relation to the sum of human cultivation and the gradual advance of the movement of ages" (*CB*, 75). In literary criticism, Harrison is as thoroughgoing a Positivist as he is in any other activity of life: this pursuit is an integral part of Comte's human synthesis.

Harrison believes that he is devoted to no one particular school. Like Ruskin, who would countenance no second-rate art, he simply favors the work of all great men and does not that of smaller men. Also, he is willing to stand by the judgments formed by centuries of reading and discussion. Above all, one should not seek out, "as collectors hunt for curios" (*CB*, 77), men of undoubted genius but distinguished only by some especial quality. And having read a work once does not qualify one to speak of it with any reliable authority. He has no more respect for the dryasdust specialist than he does for the snobbish but sophisticated aesthete with his poses and affectations. It is his fear that a revolutionary and democratic age like our own is only too likely to resort to perversity by proclaiming a new art or a new criticism by simply flying in the face of generations of mankind and by defying its good sense. It is his conviction that the main types and canons of art and literature have long since been formed, although naturally modification within the basic forms may be made (*AMB*, 123).

In his discussion of the literary figures of the Middle Ages and the Renaissance, Harrison finds too much has been made of some lesser figures. However, he has much good to say of many eighteenth-century writers in England and of the age as a whole; and he most of all has much to say about his own age, in which he knew most of the famous writers personally. Like Arnold, he fears that he may be too close to them to make definitive judgments, but much of what he does say has stood the test of time. His judgments are nearly always made clearly and sensibly, for he is nothing if not forthright. The reader never senses that Harrison is making a parade of learning, that he hides behind words or phrases, or that he is casuistical.

Although Harrison is at all times the Positivist, the reader is never annoyed even if he be aware of the fact. Were one unaware of it, he would not find Harrison's literary theories less worthwhile or less interesting. Although Harrison fairly often protests that he is not a thoroughgoing scholar or a great reader, it is obvious that he is conversant with every subject that he undertakes to discuss. If he appears to be rather hard on aspiring young writers of his own time, Arnold and Ruskin were not less so. Although he can be rather frank about Carlyle, Ruskin, Arnold, Tennyson, Browning, George Eliot, and many other contemporaries, he nevertheless speaks glowingly of what he considers to be their peculiar virtues, which he finds to be many.

From Dante and the Middle Ages to Shakespeare and the Renaissance in England

J. Oldham: "Well! and as for the moderns; you do not bar them, I hope?"

Onesimus Senior: "I bar none, my dear Dean. Dante and the great Italians who follow him, *Fabliaux*, *Morte d'Arthur*, old ballads, Milton, Calderon, Corneille, Cowper, Burns, Byron and Wordsworth, are the books I take up most often."

J. Oldham: "What! Not Keats, Shelley, Tennyson, and Swinburne?"

Onesimus Senior: "All these, of course! You might as well ask me if I do not sometimes open my Bible. The best nineteenth-century men are to be 'taken as read' in any decent library; and certainly in my library they are read." (*DeS*, 5).

This passage is found in "A Dialogue in a College Garden," in which Harrison is clearly the Rev. Onesimus Senior, D.D., former Rector of Felix-in-the-Weald, and John Oldham, M.A., College don and dean, a representative of the newer generation at Oxford. Onesimus has retired in peace, after seventy years in parish work, to a small plot of land and to a life in which books fill much of the time of a very old man. When J. Oldham asks him whether he keeps up with the new books, Onesimus exclaims that laudation by publishers of the latest genius leaves him cold. He still reads the old romances again and again—Scott, Fielding, Austen, Trollope, Thackeray, Disraeli, and Dickens. But he prefers to find the profound mysteries of human nature in Aristophanes, Cervantes, and Molière, for example. Of course, his chief reading is the Greek tragedy; did human speech ever sound such magical music?

Harrison thinks that just as Homer is the father of ancient poetry, so Dante is the father of modern European literature. As an undergraduate at Wadham College, he first studied Italian under Count Aurelio Saffi in 1849, one of the three triumvirs with Mazzini who came to power in Rome. Married to the daughter of an MP, Saffi was appointed to Oxford's Taylor Institution where he became the University's "revolutionary-in-residence" and an inspiration to academic radicals.[3] Later, Harrison studied Dante in Italian under Campanella of Milan, another colleague of Mazzini in the Revolution. Therefore, all Harrison's interest in Italian literature and history (medieval and modern) are concentrated in Dante, in whom he saw the Mazzinian vision of a great *Risorgimento*, the founding of a new, free, great Italy. His political interest in Dante undoubtedly was inspired by his teachers, the important Italian refugees. While living with his father, he would chant a canto of the *Commedia* of an evening in his bedroom, causing an elderly grandmother nearby to complain to his parents that Oxford had so demoralized him that he was chanting his prayers in Latin. It was the study of Dante that diverted him from a professional career in law when he should have been preoccupied with law reports.

Harrison discusses Dante in "Poets That I Love," *English Review* (1911–1912), reprinted in *AMB*, 42–64, and in "The Choice of Books," *Fortnightly Review* (April 1879), reprinted in *CB*, 1–93. If Dante is not the greatest poet for Harrison, he is surely the greatest philosopher who used poetry to convey his thought and "the most profound poet who ever idealized the whole cycle of previous history and learning" (*AMB*, 46). Harrison wrote a life of Dante for the *Calendar of Great Men*. Despite the admiration of Petrarch, Ariosto, and Tasso by Comte and his good Positivist friend from Mumbo-Jumbo days, Dr. John Bridges, Harrison never greatly enjoyed them, although he wrote the life of Tasso for the *Calendar*. But what Shakespeare is to the Teutonic peoples, Dante is to the Latin. Very often Dante recalls Plato, or Tacitus, or St. Augustine to the student of literature. The *Commedia* can be viewed as either a mystical vision, a religious allegory, or a political and historical satire; it calls to mind *The Pilgrim's Progress*, the Vision of *Piers Plowman*, the book of Job, the Apocalypse, *The Fairie Queene*, and *Faust*. Oddly, Harrison does not also mention Thomas Aquinas, whose influence is perhaps the dominant one. But he does say the poem conveys the whole picture of man and his culture in the Middle Ages through "the Catholic Camera Obscura" (*CB*, 49).

For Harrison, the *Divine Comedy* is a Gospel without divine revelation or canonical authority, but full of mystery and difficulty like its prototype. In nearly every part, as well as in the larger sections, of the poem we may find double and even triple meanings. Although he considers the whole library that has grown up on Dantesque literature to be comparatively needless, he does think the reader might do well to use translation and notes while reading it, especially Cary's translation, although it is scarcely poetry. His favorite translation is that by Lamennais into antique French prose with an effect that is weird and solemn. He praises Rossetti's translation of the *Vita Nuova* as excellent, as well. Criticizing the all-too-frequent assumption that the part of the poem we should read is the *Inferno*, and even just certain sections of that, he strongly asserts that the first third of the poem gives almost no concept of Dante's social ideas. For him, the *Purgatorio* is both the profoundest and the most beautiful part of the entire poem (*CB*, 50).

The first commentator on Dante, Boccaccio, came nearest to the prose of Plato, achieving the earliest perfect example of modern prose (*CB*, 50). And Harrison still regards Boccaccio's as the most beautiful of all modern prose, with its music and grace. Harrison remains solidly Victorian even as he bravely praises in Boccaccio's writing "the aroma of full-blossoming life" which we also scent in the Italian dramas of Shakespeare, although it is redolent of the whole fablieau literature from which it sprang and of the "libertine humanism which stamps the Renaissance" (*CB*, 51). However, he reassures us, many of the tales of the *Decameron* are comparatively free from offence, many selections from which are fit to be read by the young.

Shakespeare is the greatest poet of mankind, above even Homer, Dante, Milton and Goethe, because of his superiority in every type of poetry—tragic, comic, lyric, and gnomic. But despite owning the greatest poetic genius ever given to man, he was not able to rise above the conditions of his time. He played and wrote for hire, composed in order to appeal to low as well as to high, and filled his stage with corpses in grisly fashion. As versatile as he was (and no one was ever more so), he does divert us from the tragedy itself, filled as his great plays are with "this mystery in the convolutions of man's brain" (*DeS*, 85). The very demands of his audience compelled him to resort to melodrama very often rather than to tragedy. Harrison points out that Shakespeare occasionally had to work rapidly and therefore carelessly for an audience that was, in part, rather brutal and gross. It seems that he was never conscious of his exceptional genius and the possibility of his future fame.

As much as Harrison admires the poetic genius of Shakespeare, he denies the Romantic theory prevalent in the nineteenth century that his every word was inspired. Much of his work in the thirty-seven plays is below the best level, and the texts we presently have are oftentimes not altogether his. Seneca, Marlowe, and Kyd taught him to regard murder and torture as true tragedy, a lesson that Shakespeare has taught too many of us also to believe. The Greek dramatists keep lyric poetry for the choruses, and in Sophocles there would not be found a speech like so many in Shakespeare that strike Harrison as being extravagant and grotesque. Sophocles never "o'ersteps the modesty of nature," whereas Shakespeare, despite Hamlet's advice to the actors, often does.

Unlike the Greek tragedy, whose essence is unity of concentrated impression, that of romantic drama, like Shakespeare's, is variety and multiplicity of impression. Harrison illustrates his meaning with *Hamlet*, whose very brilliancy, variety, and wealth of psychological analysis only serve to lessen the intensity of the tragic impression; the sheer profusion of events and anxieties does not intensify the pity and sympathy we should feel. There is so much violence and brutality in *Hamlet* that Harrison calls it the "very Dance of Death" (*DeS*, 99). Unlike Greek tragedy, modern romantic tragedy makes character dominant and the action subsidiary. By focusing on the vagaries of character, it sacrifices the grave and tragic element to the spectacular. He concludes that Shakespeare, Schiller, Goethe, and Ibsen produce dramatized romances, not tragedies in the true sense of the term. In one respect, Harrison differs markedly from Hazlitt and Lamb: he strongly believes that we should see and hear Shakespeare on stage. It is hard, however, to believe that the acting in Harrison's day was markedly different from that of Hazlitt's; and who can forget Hazlitt's satiric portraits of the actors of his day and their lugubrious resort to rant and fustian?

Although the poet Shakespeare thrills him, Harrison could never develop much interest in the other Elizabethan and Stuart drama. He admires the music and passion of "that Caesar Borgia of our poets" (*AMB*, 101), Christopher Marlowe, but he deplores the extravagance and brutality of his plays. Despite Marlowe's occasional brilliance of language, he lacks Shakespeare's infinite variety and spontaneity. As for the fashion to dredge up anything that remains of the Stuart stage, Harrison feels it is nothing short of sheer decadence. These dramas are nothing much more than so many puppets, programmed so as to evoke violent sensations and to afford the opportunity to traffic in rank smut. And the dramatists like Otway and Dryden who were successful were primarily poets rather than playwrights. Harrison finds the main deficiencies in modern drama result from its dependence on long runs, elaborate pageants, costumes, mechanical devices, and a mania for shocking realism and for a brutal, depraved decadence.

One of the most flattering offers that Harrison felt he had ever received was made by Kegan Paul, with the blessing of Cardinal Newman, to translate the *Imitation of Christ* by St. Thomas à Kempis in a new edition, for the Cardinal wanted an accurate translation in perfectly pure English. This is one time that modesty overcame Harrison, for feeling the test too much for his literary capabilities, he declined the opportunity. He observes that he is passionately fond of not only this great Catholic literary religious masterpiece but also the equally great Protestant ones. Even Comte placed Bunyan alongside Thomas à Kempis, and Macaulay declares the *Pilgrim's Progress* to be the only religious work of its kind with a strong human interest. It is remarkable that Catholics, Calvinists, Anglicans, and Agnostics all alike fall under the spell of Bunyan's religious allegory, and there is a Catholic *Pilgrim's Progress*, minus the episode of Giant Pope. Dr. Johnson admitted it was one of the few books he could read through from beginning to end. The Positivists of Newton Hall made pilgrimages to Bunyan's grave and to his prison at Bedford, and they joined in raising the memorial to his memory at the Abbey.

The poet that Harrison most often turned to is Milton, whose life he wrote for the *Dictionary of Great Men*. The *Positivist Library* includes *Paradise Lost* and the lyrical poems, and, in the *Positivist Calendar*, the month of Dante ends with Milton. He quotes Comte as saying that Milton's inimitable epic is "the highest measure of Man's poetic powers." Only Homer, Dante, and Shakespeare have such sustained music and conceptions that one finds in Milton. From Newton Hall, Harrison once led a pilgrimage to the poet's tomb and another to the cottage where he retreated during the plague to write *Paradise Regained*.

English Literature of the Eighteenth Century

Harrison takes issue with Thomas Carlyle for his unending invective against the eighteenth century as "the age of prose, of lying, of sham, the fraudulent-bankrupt century, the reign of Beelzebub, the peculiar era of Cant" (*CB*, 351). How valid is it, Harrison asks, to launch a blanket indictment of a century anymore than to do so of an entire nation? He sees a filiation between the seventeenth and the eighteenth, as well as between the eighteenth and the nineteenth, centuries. He considers the eighteenth century to be the veritable turning-point of the modern world, the equal of any other century since the Middle Ages. It is in this era that the manifold life of the modern world really first came into being. But, to Carlyle, the one great occurrence during the century was the "most glorious bonfire recorded in profane history" (*CB*, 352), the French Revolution. However, Harrison notes that it is certainly ironical that, with the exception of Oliver Cromwell, nearly all Carlyle's heroes of modern times lived during that unspeakable epoch: Frederick, Mirabeau and Danton, George Washington, Samuel Johnson, Burns, and even Goethe himself. And Harrison adds Defoe, Goldsmith, Bishop Berkeley, Burke, Reynolds, Gainsborough, Handel, and Mozart. A century that begins with the *Rape of the Lock* and ends with the first part of *Faust*, with Gray, Cowper, Burns, the *Ancient Mariner*, and the *Lyrical Ballads* all in between, is hardly a century of mere prose. Of course, Harrison is averse to treating each hundred years as a natural period of history. Indeed, we are always, even daily, entering a new era and finishing an old one. Yet if we remain sensible, we can classify a century, as we do a yard or a mile, as a definite whole with a discernible spirit.

If the poetry of the century was not the highest, it at least created a new order of the medium. If its art was not the greatest, its music was supreme. And in science and philosophy it equaled any period that had preceded it. Despite the Reign of Terror and much social corruption, Harrison would call the century the "humane" age, when Humanity first realized its nearly illimitable possibilities in a serious, practical way. Perhaps no other age since that of Augustus has left such detailed and intimate pictures of its own daily life as this one: its frivolities, its cruelties, its caste arrogance. But a true picture of English life and character we do get from the pages of Addison and Steele, Defoe, Swift, Fielding, Smollett, Goldsmith, and Dr. Johnson. The human record in these and many more is invaluable, not only in itself but also for the humanistic development of the nineteenth century. Harrison thinks this eighteenth century was perhaps inferior to the seventeenth and sixteenth in poetry, art, and political genius, and it was far inferior to the nineteenth in moral, social, and material development. But in philosophy and science, the work of the century in all Western countries is hard to match. Its specific characteristic, or hallmark, is its genius for synthesis, for seeing things in wholes.

Gibbon has compressed the history of a thousand years in a work whose prose is as nearly perfect as it can possibly be. "He has combined the epic unity of [the Roman historian] Livy with the infinite variety of Herodotus, the vivacity and portraiture of Plutarch, and the punctilious truthfulness of Caesar" (*M & T*, 83). In the eighteenth century, he was less philosophical than many others (Hume and Montesquieu, for example), less conscious of social evolution than Condorcet or Burke, less artistic than Voltaire, less able in historical judgment than Robertson. Yet Harrison considers him to be the greatest of all literary historians. He can transform huge mountains of exact scholarship into a consummate whole, "glowing with life in all its parts" (*M & T*, 85). Carlyle could infuse vitality into exact materials of research, also, but Gibbon's scope is immensely larger, and his work is a more brilliant, organic work of art than even Carlyle's. Gibbon's work is like some interminable procession, say, a Roman triumph with treasures from all parts of the known world. But like the great Atlantic, Harrison says, it can be both grandiose and monotonous with its unending magnificence and continuous antithesis and balance. It lacks the clear simplicity of Voltaire and of Hume, the grace of Addison, and the pathos of Burke, but there was never such pith, such point, such vigor, or such precision, as well as such glowing color of the painter, in the writing of history (*M & T*, 86). In short, Harrison values the *Decline* as one of the great dramas of human civilization, seen through the virile imagination of a master of human speech.

Harrison is convinced that it is style, and style alone, that with its simplicity, ease, and grace, can lure the reader back again and again to read a book. From all English literature he chooses Goldsmith's *Vicar of Wakefield* as the Mozartian masterpiece of English prose, as the epitome of charm, grace, and feeling. It is free of the precious, the affectatious, the pompous, the sardonic, for too often in more ambitious works there is excessive use of "drum and trumpet in the orchestra" for pleasant reading over and over again (*AMB*, 111). The same felicity we find in Goldsmith is also evident in the letters of

William Cowper, the purest and most beautiful in English, expressing the sensitive feelings of a private heart to obscure parsons and women in the remote countryside. Gray's letters, too, are classics, though they bear too much weight of scholarship. Even though the writers of excellent memoirs in England, like Walpole and Mme. D'Arblay (Fanny Burney), are too numerous to mention, those of Saint-Simon and of Mme. de Sévigné in France are more wonderful still. The eighteenth century was indeed an era of the consummate letter and memoir.

It is Harrison's judgment that there are three definite types of English poetry in the century: (1) the satirical masterpieces of Pope, such as the *Rape of the Lock*; (2) the poetry of the home (wherein is found the power to serve the cause of Humanity) which sings the simple annals of the poor; and (3) the songs of Bobby Burns that herald the later revolutionary poetic outcries of Byron, Shelley, Wordsworth, and Schiller (*CB*, 380−81). Harrison considers Burns's songs the most ringing in our entire literature. Pope's poetry belongs to the age of Louis XIV. Coming later, Gray's famous elegy may be the most representative poem of the century, giving preference to magical pathos and unity of feeling and to simple humanity over the brilliancy, subtlety, and novelty of its predecessors. The poems of Burns augur a new age just over the horizon. Only Cowper partook of the qualities of all three periods, possessing the easy mastery of the rhyme and rhythm of Pope, the delicate grace of Gray, and the moral earnestness of Wordsworth and Shelley.

Not least of the contributions of this century to our culture is the novel. In an address to the Bath Literary Club, Harrison pays especial tribute to Henry Fielding as one of the great names of modern European literature (*DeS*, 137). He considers Fielding to be the real creator of the English romance of life and manners as well as one of the mighty masters of the English tongue. Not even Shakespeare surpassed Fielding in the intense realization of the truth of human nature in nearly every character in his novels, and even Coleridge declared that the plot of *Tom Jones* is equal to that of the *Oedipus Rex* of Sophocles. He regrets that Fielding allowed himself to use language that was current among the theatrical and idle people that he associated with, although there is no evidence that he was ever guilty of being a rake or a profligate himself. And he partially exonerates Fielding's "breezy coarseness" by preferring it to the "close sentimentalism" of Richardson (*DeS*, 147).

Nevertheless, he cannot completely forgive Fielding for some things that are so disgusting that they cannot properly be used as the subject of art, since the business of comedy and romance is to charm rather than to disgust. Harrison cannot excuse the introduction of unnatural vice either into the novel or onto the stage, such as a husband's selling his wife to a rich adulterer or a young man's selling himself to the purposes of a lustful harridan. But these faults in *Tom Jones* are atoned for in the admonitions Squire Allworthy gave Tom and in the purity and idealism of Sophia, as well as in the saintliness of Amelia and the agony of remorse in Booth in *Amelia*.

In philosophic power, Fielding was for him the equal of any other figure of his age and was perhaps superior to Johnson in his learning of a more varied and deeper kind. As a writer and as a magistrate, he endeavored to cure society of its more disturbing vices, and he gave us such enduring pictures of human nature as can be found only in Homer, Aristophanes, Cervantes, and Shakespeare (*DeS*, 151).

It took Harrison many years to learn to tolerate the cynicism and coarseness of Tobias Smollett, as well as the "priapic obscenity" that is also repellent in Sterne. But his brutal ribaldry is easier to endure than the "sniggering indecencies" of Sterne. Admittedly, the leading characters of Smollett are unmitigated villains. And his plots have none of the consistency that Fielding is so justly famous for. But, despite these objections to him, Harrison, in his later years, could speak well of him. First, as a great caricaturist in the line of Cervantes to Hogarth to Dickens, he has uncovered human curiosities from the lowest strata of life. Second, he is an honest historian of the dark side of his time, which, much more than Fielding, he knew firsthand, for he was of it. But, best of all for Harrison, Smollett has a sincere love of honesty and charity, and in his art of caricature and humor we discover depths of benevolence and tenderness (*DeS*, 154–55).

It may be appropriate to point out briefly that Harrison deems the whole gamut of music, with a few exceptions, as the creation of the eighteenth century: the complete development of the opera as an art form, the sonata, the concerto, the symphony, the oratorio, as well as the full use of chorus, instrumentation, march, and fugue. What with Bach, Handel, Haydn, Mozart, Gluck, and the early Beethoven, not even the age of the madonnas and the Sistine Chapel or the age that gave us Rheims and Westminster Abbey contributed more to the culture of Humanity. And during this century, music was not merely the amusement of leisure hours, but, Harrison says, was appreciated with the passion that animated the Red and the Green factions at the races in the great Hippodrome of Byzantium. It is such passion that marks the character of an age whenever art reaches its very zenith (*CB*, 383–85).

Nineteenth-Century Literature: Critical Considerations

Harrison explains that works of the first rank in both prose and poetry clothe great and vigorous thought in nearly perfect form, in which the range of the ideas is wide and the depth penetrates to the roots of nature and of life. The thought should be either superior or equal to the form and should be large, profound, and various. Further, the work should exert power and influence over diverse numbers, races, ages, and sympathies. In the greatest writers we find deep insight, immense imagination, and, not least, worldwide impingement, as we do in Shakespeare, Homer, Dante, for sure, and doubtless in Milton, Chaucer, Fielding, Goethe, and Scott, as well. In judging the works of his own century, Harrison realizes that it may be too soon to dogmatize with any confidence, for no definitive opinion is possible until over a century has passed. He especially guards himself against indulgence in eulogy for the people whom he has, in many cases, personally and even intimately known in the latter half of the nineteenth century. Also, he is conscious that virtually all writers, other than Milton, have left work much below their best, a fact that the critic should ever be aware of. Harrison is obviously conscious of what Matthew Arnold terms the personal and the historical fallacies, in these respects (*TR & M*, 190).

Harrison is aware of the differences not only among artists in a given period but also between the artists of one age and another. It is as difficult to think of *In Memoriam* in the age of Byron as of *Sartor*

Resartus in that of Johnson. The world of the Brontës and George Eliot differs widely from that of Edgeworth and Jane Austen. The types, aims, and essential ideas are recognizably different. The age of Pope, Johnson, and Gibbon was concerned with symmetry and the grand air of the classical manner, whereas the age of Byron, Shelley, Scott, and Coleridge indulged in color and romance, in mystery, legend, strange dreams, and revolutionary struggle. The style of the Victorian age differs from the classical style of the age of Gray and Johnson as distinctly as it does from the "resounding torrent" that pours forth from Byron and Scott. One important difference in Victorian literature is its serious concern for social and moral problems, as in Dickens, Carlyle, Ruskin, and George Eliot. Tennyson brings theological controversy into lyric poetry, and Browning brings psychological analysis to his dramatic monologue. Although Victorian literature strikes many notes, Harrison believes that the principal preoccupation is with social reform. But with all its earnestness and fine feeling, it is too largely indifferent to the highest reaches of the imagination and comparatively unconcerned with the vibrant action that belongs to drama (*SEVL*, 1–8).

If anything, Victorian literature is much too varied in form and style, with each writer striking out in his own individual direction. In preceding ages, one can detect the *Zeitgeist*, the peculiar spirit of the era, as a whole, in both diction and form. The Elizabethan age can be distinguished from the Restoration. Ciceronian diction and the heroic couplet predominated from Dryden to Byron. Harrison asks us to compare a page of *Sartor*, of Macaulay's *History*, of Arnold's *Literature and Dogma*, and of Ruskin's *Stones of Venice*, which differ from one another as widely as Tennyson does from Pope. The poets of the Victorian age evidence just as much disparity, betraying no common standard of form or meter. But there is one note that runs throughout Victorian literature as a whole, reflecting a profound characteristic in the *Zeitgeist* itself. It is the sense of change that permeates every activity of Victorian life: philosophy, political and social ideals, literary and artistic standards, theological concepts, and even relations between the sexes. Also, philosophic doubt colors every aspect of Victorian life. The principal philosopher of the age, Herbert Spencer, says that the divine originator and ruler of the Universe is the

Absolute Unknowable; and the principal poet, Tennyson—as much a theologian as Milton himself—assigns true faith to honest doubt. Indeed, most philosophers, scientists, poets, and even theologians, in their own way, say much the same thing. For Harrison, of equal importance is the fact that the nineteenth century repudiates all notions of synthesis. Do not speculate too specifically about what is behind the veil, but stick to aggregates of facts, which must be kept within their known boundaries. It is the age of special research. Even Spencer's grand Synthesis, the only one ever conceived by an English thinker, Harrison believes to be founded on a "substructure of hypotheses" (*AM*, 2:323).

Harrison thinks that the literature of the first half of the nineteenth century is superior to that of the second half, which, in turn, is superior to that of the first part of the twentieth. He asks us to contrast the names of 1910 with those of 1810. There has never been a time when second and third-class poems, quite graceful and beautiful, have been poured out so copiously as in the early twentieth century, yet there is not a poem of the first order like Shelley's "Ode to a Skylark" or Keats's "Ode on a Grecian Urn." Of the ten thousand women novelists, will there be one in the year 2020 who shall have written an *Emma* or a *Castle Rackrent*, despite the incredible increase in what passes for education? The immortal literature of Athens was created at a time when only a few thousand could judge literature and when there were only about a hundred books available to them. In the modern world, there is the urge to conjure up something new, to discard the old ideals, yet there is no correlative attempt to teach us how to make do without them (*AM*, 323–24).

In the final sections, I intend to devote as much space as possible to the writers of the Victorian age in England about whom Harrison says a great deal because he knows so much about them. Of course, he often acknowledges the preeminent writers of the Romantic era. He praises Wordsworth's gift of infusing a local patriotism into a whole countryside as he did in his Lake District. Byron perhaps thrills him most of all with his sheer intellectual power, although perfect lines are rare in his poetry. The incomparable lyricism, the melody, of Shelley is something found in few others than Milton, Shakespeare, and

Ruskin. Can the enthusiast of modern poetry genuinely feel the music of Shakespeare, Milton, and Shelley?

As for Keats, though he thinks less well of him than we do today, Harrison admits that he wrote odes that touch us like a canvas of Giorgone and a few short lyrics that compare with any other ever composed in English. Had Keats lived another twenty or thirty years, he might have reached a point of "painting in winged words" that might have placed him somewhere below Milton and Shakespeare. But we have no assurance that his powers of intellectual vision would develop along with his ability to produce luscious music. Even though he knew no Greek and had had scant formal education, he could, by the age of twenty-five, write sonnets that Milton would not scorn, lyrics that Shelley might have envied, and letters that even that master letter-writer Byron could hardly have improved on. In imagination, he was very nearly as Greek as Milton himself. In fact, Harrison uses Keats as an example to us that we should try much more to cultivate ourselves, to carefully use the books we have, and to be sure always to use none but the best books (*TR & M*, 195—98).

Of course, it is important to point out that Harrison never accuses the great Romantics of aestheticism, of a love of art for art's sake. He has no use for the dilettante who loves lace but sees nothing in a great statue, or who speaks learnedly of a painting but has no use for a sonata or a noble poem. The true zealot has a rational love of all beauty, and to narrow that love is to be guilty of being an aesthete. The infallible mark by which we can distinguish "an Osric," an aesthete, is his certain praise of a master whom few have heard of and his undisguised contempt for anything the rest of the world enjoys. Never for a moment would he place Keats or any other great Romantic in this category (*CB*, 291).

The profound and incredible change in English life from the time of the great Romantics until the end of the century, a transformation vaster than any that had taken place for many centuries before, has exerted a reaction on literature that has been far-reaching. Harrison, writing in 1895, divides the period from 1837 in two at 1865. The superior half in literature is the first. The old parliamentary system is over with the death of Palmerston in 1865, after which time Britain has been absorbed in deep constitutional problems (*SEVL*, 30−31). With the social ferment going ever deeper into the fabric of the national life, there is felt a universal yearning of the millions for more material improvement, a new social power is in the air, and all activities are affected by it. Harrison thinks this ferment diverts literary minds from the higher kind of imaginative work. A social earnestness colors all literature at this time. Since Shelley, no one has attempted to soar into "the seventh heaven of invention," and even in the drama no one has equaled Shelley or Byron (*SEVL*, 15). Social earnestness has inhibited a taste for dramatic passion. Although there is a very high average of merit, there is very little of the first rank.

Analyzing the change that has been developing through the second period from 1867 to 1895 (and doubtless beyond into the next century), Harrison lists several developments that serve to check the growth of an original literature. The very existence of a fairly high average of good work and of a rather considerable mass of it diminishes the possibility of brilliant successes in nearly every field. With thousands of graceful writers of verse, there is little evidence of any great poet. With torrents of skillful fiction, there is no great novelist. "Elaborate culture casts chill looks on original ideas" (*SEVL*, 28). A high average of culture and a mechanical system of education also militate against the spontaneous flow of an original literature. Violent political struggle is a negative influence. But the growing absorption in material interests and the general love of comforts are as deadening as anything else. And, more subtly, an increasing, acutely conscious self-criticism erodes the free spirit of creativity.

Comfort and material conveniences are not favorable to the essence of romance with its variety, contrast, and individuality (*SEVL*, 33). If society were leveled and every nineteen individuals out of twenty were made equal, the Britain of Fielding and of Scott, with its picturesque, boisterous, jolly world, would become passé. The world is growing less interesting, less mysterious, less various, less rich in color and in contrast. Modern democracy must end in a monotony and lowered vitality, which are naturally anathema to romance. Harrison insists that the novelist must use living models which he must interpret for his own age; he may not write merely for posterity nor occupy a dream-world of his own fantasy (*SEVL*, 36). He thinks that Meredith and Henry James seem to view life from a private box, very much unlike men who move down onto the stage of life and taste it firsthand. The true novelist must live in his own generation, for he can no more get out of it than get out of his own skin. However, Harrison makes some concession to the fine art of subtle psychology of the period. Although it may not be the highest art, it is nevertheless genuine and sound (*SEVL*, 38).

Unlike Carlyle and especially Ruskin, Harrison does not for a moment propose that we return to a medieval world or any other not consonant with the culture and civilization that we presently possess. He believes that the new democratic move toward greater equality and freedom is too valuable to Humanity and too certain ever to be dismissed for any reason whatever. The world, he concedes, does not exist for the creation of brilliant literature of the first rank. But he hopefully envisions an age in the future when color, romantic beauty, variety, and movement can once again be with us. The present desperate expedients will not do. Of course, we must be unavoidably disappointed when we are told by Harrison that the best we can do is to honestly delight in our own age and that somehow, someway, in the very far future, we shall be able to have our cake and eat it, too. In any utopian commonwealth, be it Edward Bellamy's or Comte's, one may well wonder whether art and literature would be more exempt from uniformity than from modern democracy or socialist egalitarianism. If Harrison chides late nineteenth-century writers for "topsy-turvy straining after new effects," we do indeed wonder what writers of that distant day under Positivist auspices will be doing, "we know not how" (*SEVL*, 38). Of course, in all fairness, it must be conceded that this is the kind of question that no man can really answer any more satisfactorily than Comte can convince us beyond the shadow of any reasonable doubt that man can make altruism prevail in human society or Marx that dictatorship of the proleteriat will gradually but surely wither away.

Yet, even so, Harrison provides us with an answer for the future of fiction. Romance, or the novel, he is convinced, is the special art of the modern world, for it is not found in either the ancient or the medieval (*CB*, 229). In this world without religious or social ideals, or at least where they are as varied and unstable as the ideas of modern man himself, it is, ironically enough, to this very kaleidoscopic intellectual and spiritual relativity that modern romance owes much of its liveliness and perpetual interest for modern man and woman. Fine shades of meaning and suggestions of mystery fascinate the mind that would escape Molière and Shakespeare as well as Aristotle, Bacon, Pascal, and Kant. Harrison confidently expects that, as with all other great arts, the day will come when romance will also be joined with genuine religious and social ideals. He speculates on whether Walter Scott, "our English Homer," would not have been able to realize his religious ideals transfigured as even Homer himself saw them. Would not Scott, George Sand, and Fielding have been even more glorious than they are had they had the advantage of religious and social ideals such as those Shakespeare, Calderon, and Dante enjoyed? Perhaps George Eliot, because of her spiritual and intellectual feeling for her art, anticipates the direction of the future of romance. Fiction, the unique creation of modern literature, may join that other uniquely modern art, music, which surpasses anything so far ever done in its general field, and also achieve triumphs that will far surpass these early tentative beginnings. Obviously, Harrison envisions this consummation with the inevitable evolution of the unified scientific, religious, and social basis of Positivism. Fiction must reflect such a coherent world, as have all other great forms of art, in their respective periods of world history (*CB*, 229–30).

Victorian Poets and Novelists

During the latter half of the nineteenth century, Harrison maintains, Tennyson has been the preeminent poet, with the same kind of dominance that Pope had in his day and Dr. Johnson in his (*TR & M*, 1). Criticism of him, nay, insufficient praise, has always seemed a kind of *lèse majesté*, for he had been "the poet" for the Victorian age as Homer was for all Greece or Hugo for nineteenth-century France. Although it is true that Tennyson with exquisite poetry has expressed the tastes, creeds, and hopes of much of the English-reading public of his day, his supreme accomplishment is the perfection of his form— lucid, simple, and musical—with unfailing precision. Avoiding the often ragged verse of Byron and the redundancies, at times, of both

Shelley and Keats and the too-frequent commonplaces of Wordsworth, Tennyson is hardly yet sufficiently valued for his masterly
perfection of our language, for a polish that only Milton can consistently match (*TR & M*, 2—4).

This perfection of language reaches its apex in *In Memoriam*,
perhaps more faultless than any other long poem in English. Though
not so glorious as "Lycidas," it shares with Milton's poem the mastery
of language (*TR & M*, 5). Its mode is more effectively the ideal form of
the reflective and elegiac poem than is the form of *Il Penseroso*. But
despite its charm and pathos, does it really reach the topmost peak of
the lyric that we can find in Shakespeare, Wordsworth, and Shelley?
Harrison believes that it is on the short lyrics that Tennyson's permanent fame will rest, for their wealth and beauty assure for him a top
rank over many centuries among English masters of the form. The
Tennysonian lyric reaches its perfection in such a poem as "Oenone,"
a "delicious Correggio," a picture like one in an idyll of Theocritus,
Tasso, or Shakespeare—done in a splendid, glowing chiaroscuro,
with sunlight playing sensuously through the glowing leaves, in a
simple rural setting of an idealized, romantic, legendary world
(*TR & M*, 30). It has a coloring that is the poet's own, at every
point evidencing his inimitable "dainty felicity of phrase, his faultless
chiselling, and his imperturbable refinement" (*TR & M*, 44). Tennyson has never been surpassed in mastery of the resources of nearly
perfect poetic expression.

Tennyson almost never descends to vulgarisms or mystification,
yet Harrison doubts that he ever reaches the deeper feelings as do
Byron, Shelley, and Wordsworth. Despite his frequent poetic sloven-
liness, Byron unites Titanic energy and intellect to create new imaginative worlds that have stirred the entire civilized world. Byron had
the essence of true poetry: a powerful, original imagination, which
arouses the deeper memory and richly colors the minds of men.
Nature in Wordsworth speaks to the human heart in a new language
with a new tone and a revitalizing power. Shelley has resurrected from
this age of strife and confusion a vision of a new heaven and a new
earth. Does Tennyson have this same powerful originality? He paints
honest doubt and faint trust as he exquisitely sings of death, creation,
and the perplexities of his age. Harrison cannot concede to Tennyson a

high place as the poet of human destiny or as a great creative master, but he readily accords Tennyson the foremost place in Victorian poetry. He stands with Milton as a master of poetic diction, he is second to none as a lyrist, and he has endowed the softer aspects of nature with a fanciful beauty which no man had done before (*TR & M*, 49—50).

As for the *Idylls of the King*, Harrison finds the poem closer to a modern romance than to an ancient epic. Launcelot has been transformed into a kind of Charles Grandison in plate armor, King Arthur into a court painting of the Prince Consort, and Queen Guinevere into a Parisian grand lady "with a secret" (*TR & M*, 18). They all talk in the way characters do in modern ethical and psychological novels. It is obvious that Harrison's underlying objections to the *Idylls of the King* are that it violates the genre of the epic and that its tone and significance are modern. As in so much else, the general objections of Harrison, and the first-mentioned one in particular, have been frequently maintained until very recent times.[4]

Harrison was frequently in personal touch with the laureate, but his papers delivered in favor of Comte at the Metaphysical Society perhaps estranged the poet somewhat. Harrison recalls that the problem of an afterlife beyond the grave haunted Tennyson like a nightmare, a matter he discussed with Harrison on their first meeting at the society. In 1871, Harrison, while living near Aldworth, was shown through the grounds and gardens of Tennyson's estate there. Over several decades, Harrison lived near the two homes between which Tennyson spent much of his time, and he became familiar with countless scenes recognizable in the poetry. Every landscape brought to mind some particular image or phrase, expressing Tennyson's inimitable exactitude and subtlety of observation. When he was alone with an acquaintance and unperturbed by his popular image of the sage, the poet's conversation was lively and interesting, full of entertaining stories. Only those who knew him at close hand could appreciate his intense dedication to making himself a poet and to living every moment of his life with that goal in mind. Only Wordsworth might have rivaled him in this preoccupation. Tennyson was rather indignant with Harrison for having once written that Byron had a far higher intellectual power than he (*AM*, 2:103—105).

Harrison recalls Robert Browning, with his "endless anecdotes and happy *mots*," at the Sunday-afternoon receptions at George Eliot's salon. No Victorian, he thinks, was saner or more original; he was versatile and spontaneous, as well as healthy and human. Although Harrison feels that Browning surpasses Tennyson in mental power, he falls far short of Tennyson in the poetical gift, which has to do with imbuing "fine thoughts in exquisite melodies." Browning seems to seek out cacophonies, repudiating melody as "an artificial cosmetic unworthy of a poet." Harrison laments the growing trend toward "barbarous, tiresome, and dissonant form" used by men of genius and high imagination, who express themselves in lines written as though they were verses. In the late Victorian era, he thinks, there are but three poets of first rank: Browning, "with subtle thought but no music"; Swinburne, "with luscious music and no deep or original thought"; and Tennyson, "who put his truly poetic ideas into exquisite, varied and harmonious cadences" (*AM*, 2:106–108).

Although Harrison considers Matthew Arnold to be primarily a critic, he grants that no Victorian poet has equaled him in general culture. No other poet in English literature, other than Milton, is so saturated with the classical spirit, and unlike other poets imbued with it, he never varies from the classical quality into the romantic and fantastic. Interestingly, Arnold's poetry, Harrison continues, is modern in thought yet indulges in the Wordsworthian fetishistic worship of natural objects. But he is classical in "the serene self-command, the harmony of tone, the measured fitness," together with the fine balance, lucidity, and Virgilian dignity. There is almost no excess anywhere. All the same, he is one of England's most contemporary poets (*TR & M*, 113–14).

Harrison realizes that Arnold's poetry has not yet received complete acceptance. But we must never forget, he reminds us, that the poetry is short on passion, and it is rather lacking in color and melody (*TR & M*, 115). On the other hand, it is reminiscent of Greek gnomic poetry, especially fragments we have of Theognis, with its disdain for vulgarity, its stoical firmness, its tendency toward elegy. He found his sustenance in Homer and in the great Stoics, Epictetus and Marcus Aurelius. Arnold occupies a higher region of philosophical thought than any of his contemporaries (*TR & M*, 118). Fortunately, unlike the Greek gnomic poets, he is never prosaic or tedious, although he lacks exuberance of fancy and of imagination, of the "rush and glow of life, in tumultuous passion, in dramatic pathos" (*TR & M*, 119). Ironically, although he left us innumerable quotable lines from his prose, he left us very little from the poetry. And Tennyson and Shelley would have been aghast at his cacophonies. But, most of all, Harrison finds Arnold lacking in that fountain of delight which the highest poetry must have, although he does indeed possess the high seriousness which he himself thought the best poetry should have (*TR & M*, 123).

Turning to the great Victorian novelists, Harrison finds that the popularity of Charles Dickens is as unassailable as that of Tennyson. And he confesses to being himself one of those devotees of the novelist, who has his own "accustomed nook at every fireside" (*SEVL*, 137). Although Harrison saw him almost daily for a number of years, strangely enough he never actually spoke to him; he did, however, hear Dickens read and speak in public, and the familiar haunts of the celebrated novelist were well known to him throughout his life. He was Dickens's neighbor both in London and at the seaside.

Harrison believes that the novels after *David Copperfield*, written when the author was thirty-eight, are inferior to those written during the years before that time. *Pickwick* he considers to be the purest Dickens, although it is without a plot, full of tomfoolery, and with more caricature than character. But its originality and vitality rival that of *Tristram Shandy* and *Gil Blas*. Dickens has not the style of Thackeray's crisp, modulated mastery of the English sentence. Harrison believes that he has mannerisms, but no style. And, of course, he lacks Thackeray's extensive reading. Everything in Dickens is in excess, hyperbolic, grotesque. The very key to caricature is distortion of nature, unlike the truth to nature in Goldsmith, Scott, or Thackeray. Exaggeration is perhaps the sole form of humor that he uses, and every character has some feature thrust out of proportion. Harrison does realize, though perhaps insufficiently, that Dickens is a poet in that he throws a halo of the imagination over the whole suffering world of the plain and the simple, finding beauty and joy in the most monotonous lives (*SEVL*, 142–43).

As a true-blue Victorian, Harrison especially values Dickens's purity, although he paints the dregs of society and many dreadful scenes of passion: "You will not find a page which a mother need withhold from her grown daughter." Despite his purity, Dickens's "exuberance of animal spirits" is inexhaustible, surpassing even Scott and surely any other Victorian in this respect (*SEVL*, 143). But Harrison fears that this endless gaiety at last begins to pall on the reader through frequent iteration in the same key, without the variety that one gets in Aristophanes, Shakespeare, and Rabelais. He will be remembered more for his unforgettable scenes and characters than for whole novels, for in his own particular kind of humor he has no equal in all literature. It is odd that Harrison does not make more of Dickens's radical attack on the institutions of society. And modern criticism has much more to say about the powerful symbolism, the very poetry of the comic, and the imaginative kind of realism that one does not find in a so-called realistic novel.

It is the style of Thackeray that Harrison especially enjoys. Carlyle is often grotesque, Macaulay pompous, Eliot pedantic, Ruskin hysterical, and Disraeli and Bulwer slovenly and bombastic. His style is as effective as Swift's but more graceful and flexible. It is natural, pure, delightfully modulated—the language of a cultivated English gentleman with his ease and self-possession (*SEVL*, 113). The language of *Vanity Fair*, Thackeray's masterpiece, is a "miracle of art" (*SEVL*, 119). And his forte is the comedy of manners. In all of *Vanity Fair* there is not a dull page, not a single example of padding; even Scott, Fielding, Austen, and Richardson have their failings here, whereas Thackeray's invention seems inexhaustible, clothed in a style that surpasses them all in polish and purity. Although he may not equal Fielding as the "prose Homer of human nature" (*SEVL*, 119), he writes an even finer and more flexible prose. In every kind of prose writing, he excels every other writer of his own age: in burlesque, comic song, critical essay, speech, comedy of manners, and extravaganza; in pathos or terror, in tragedy, in narrative, and in repartee. Of course, he never attempts the rich rhapsody of De Quincey or "dithyrambic melodies" of Ruskin, for his milieu is society (*SEVL*, 124).

The supreme accomplishment in *Vanity Fair* is Becky Sharp, who is more fully worked out than any other character in the English novel; above all, she is real, as are the other major characters. But unlike

Shakespeare, Scott, and Fielding, Thackeray has few women to revere, for nearly all of them are selfish, cruel, ambitious, spoiled, weak, or silly, and the men are not much better. Harrison says it is not so with "the supreme masters of the human heart" (*SEVL*, 133), who did not fall short of a true equipoise. Even so, in Thackeray's novels there are many scenes of tenderness and pathos, for he does not belong with Swift, Balzac, and Zola, even though he misses the human virtue and dignity we find in Shakespeare, Goethe, and Scott.

Although Harrison never met either Dickens or Thackeray, he knew Anthony Trollope very well, having dined with him, seen him in the act of writing at the Club, and often chatted with him there. He knows the world that Trollope lived in and finds rereading his works is like looking through a photographic album. He can almost hear Trollope telling the very anecdotes we find in the novels. The novelist is never bombastic, prurient, or grotesque, and he writes commendable, pure English. His danger is falling into the commonplace, for neither his plots nor his characters are new or remarkable (*SEVL*, 201–203, 206).

Perhaps Trollope's unique ability is to capture the very speech that people really do use, making it appear so easy that nearly anyone might seem able to do it, whereas virtually no one else has been able to. Also, his work has a unity of texture and a harmony of tone, without artificiality, but Trollope has none of Thackeray's greatness of style. In many respects, he most resembles Jane Austen, and in natural conversation he has no equal. Important for Harrison is Trollope's truth to nature in nearly every way. It is all the more remarkable that his characters, in worlds which he did not know very well, speak just as they do in real life. And his conception of characters is often as subtle and realistic as we can find (*SEVL*, 206–10). It would always perplex Harrison how such an earthy, vigorous, masculine character as Trollope could probe deep into the inner feelings of so many sensitive and delicate young maidens as he so successfully does. Unlike Dickens, he is free of caricature and distortion. He can describe courts of law, bishops' palaces, the House of Commons, and house parties of the nobility—places he knew little about—as accurately and vitally as he could the places he knew very well. But because he loved the vigor of field sports, he thought that he loved nature, but

Harrison says that he was really quite blind to the beauties of the countryside (*SEVL*, 222–23). Harrison accurately predicts that the day will come when some of Trollope's works will be revived, as indeed they have been since World War II. Again, Harrison marvels how this burly, boisterous, irrepressibly energetic "colossus of blood and bone" (*SEVL*, 223) could arise early in the morning before anyone else and, wherever he might happen to be, probe the conscience of a bishop or archdeacon or analyze the tender experiences of a delicate maiden's heart.

Harrison knew no novelist better than he did George Eliot, counting himself a close personal friend. He confirms that she was intellectually equal to the foremost minds of the day and considerably superior to anyone who attempted the imaginative prose of the novel. He read her *Felix Holt* in manuscript and advised her on points of law that arose in the context of the plot. When she embodied verbatim several of his lines in the novel as the lawyers' opinion of the case, Harrison told her that he would always be able to say that he had contributed several lines to English literature (*SEVL*, 240). He actually encouraged her to write her last novel, *Theophrastus Such* (1879), having written her that English literature was deficient in one form in which the French have excelled: *pensées*, or moral philosophical aphorisms. And he still thinks that she was the only one equipped to accomplish this literary form for English literature, which seemed especially suited to her abilities.

Harrison says that George Eliot was more than her books, for he doubts that she really reached the foremost rank of Victorian novelists (*AM*, 2:108–109). He thinks that although she ranks with Ruskin and Mill as a moralist and teacher, she labored too hard and seriously on her longer novels for them to emerge as spontaneous works of art. Her poems have everything but poetry. At the Sunday-afternoon receptions given by George Henry Lewes and George Eliot at the Priory, Regent's Park, where Harrison met many famous men and women of the worlds of art, literature, science, and politics, he observes that everyone listened to her thoughts on the burning moral and intellectual issues of the day with profound respect. As for George Henry Lewes, Harrison considers him the first English writer to understand the new era that began with Auguste Comte and the first to popularize Positivism in England. She learned much from Lewes, but Harrison wishes that he had "inspired her with a dose of the rattling devil within him" (AM, 109). In her, Harrison sees not so much poetic passion as a passionate yearning after it. She did not have the inevitable word or phrase but instead only the result of a highly calculated effort to reach the spontaneous. Nothing can make a poet but being a poet (SEVL, 242).

He finds *Middlemarch*, her most ethically involved novel and most complex in terms of plot, despite its wealth of subtle insight and intensive analysis, to be somewhat disagreeable and even interminable. *Adam Bede* is her freshest and most spontaneous novel, and her other earlier novels have the same quality in varying degree. But he thinks that she raised the art of romance, which is still in its infancy, to a higher plane, opening up a new vista of incalculable possibilities of subtlety, flexibility, and range for reaching both the heart and the mind of Humanity. It would be foolish to assert that she reached perfection here, but it may well prove to be true that she set the direction that the newest literary genre, the romance, will ultimately take (SEVL, 248).

Harrison is convinced that Eliot was in deep sympathy with the cardinal ideas of Positivism, with its rational religious sentiment toward the "collective wellbeing of mankind." Although she rejected all codes and systems of life, Harrison believes that she was the greatest supporter of the religious concept of Humanity that Victorian England produced, and throughout her novels and poems runs the faith that the future salvation of Humanity will lie in the sense of reverence and duty (CB, 225).

Other Victorian Prose Writers

Harrison knew rather well one of the greatest masters of English prose of the nineteenth century, Thomas Carlyle. He often passed Carlyle in the street and on several occasions talked with him in his home at Cheyne Row. Despite the picture of the Sage of Chelsea that emerges from the notorious biography by James Anthony Froude, Harrison found him, in old age, cheerful, generous, accessible, fatherly, and even patriarchal, although it was clear that the stately old gentleman had had his hours of darkness, his bewildered wrestlings. Harrison values him as a great literary artist rather than as a philosopher or a prophet. He powerfully rekindled the historical sense in men during his best years, which separated the eras of Bentham and of Darwin. At his zenith, somewhat reminding Harrison of Goethe, he powerfully and nobly influenced the religion, political thought, art, history, literary criticism, and poetry of his era. He was a combination of Puritan, Scottish peasant, and revolutionist, with a bright genius and wide culture through which his anarchic spirit violently erupted. We should learn to use his great work as we choose, but not to follow him, for his estimates too often are misleading and extravagant (*CB*, 190–92).

His poetic gifts, Harrison continues, were of the first order and his insight at times rivaled that of Tacitus, Bacon, and Goethe. But we have the tragedy of one of the genuine masters of the English language deteriorating into a purveyor of a tiresome technique of caricature. And, more tragic still, he really came to believe in nothing at all; every system and every doctrine was, at bottom, for him nothing more than cant, sham, and silliness. By nature unselfish, sincere, and desirous of goodness and truth, Harrison writes, he descended so deep into maniacal egoism that his single-minded credo became, "I believe in Thomas Carlyle; which faith, unless a man keep, without doubt he shall perish everlastingly." He adapted Descartes's *cogito ergo sum* to mean, "I think, therefore I am; no one else thinks, therefore all others are shams" (*CB*, 196). Harrison suspects that Carlyle's remarkable Jeremiads will not become permanent classics and that his rather too-obvious idiosyncrasies will keep him from the illustrious company of the wise and serene spirits of the ages (*SEVL*, 42–43).

Harrison admits that Carlyle's estimate of Cromwell reversed two hundred years of injustice to "England's greatest man," but the constant switching between the Puritan sermonizing of Cromwell and Carlyle's "Sartorian eccentricities" distort the artistic harmony of the book (*SEVL*, 46). *Sartor Resartus* is not only the most significant, most original, most lyrical, and deepest but also the most incoherent and sardonic of all his works. But nothing else could more effectively rouse men from their sensual, mechanical depravity than this ingenious resort to humor, pathos, poetry, and the sheer mystery of life.

The *French Revolution* is a prose poem with the essential character of an epic, full of unforgettable, powerfully dramatic movement of the action in endless contrasts of vivid scenes and ingenious tableaux. Although Harrison freely grants that large parts of the work are historically true and artistically brilliant, he contends that its principal misconception is that the Revolution was an anarchical rebellion against oppression rather than the systematic beginning of the foundation for a new order (*SEVL*, 50). (Comte dates his calendar from 1789.) Also, Carlyle treats the public men of France, other than Mirabeau and Napoleon, with ribaldry and caricature. Even so, Harrison admits that he rivals Aristophanes in imagination and insight and eclipses any other historian in the wondrous rapidity and variety he achieves in portraying the dynamic reality of the French Revolution.

Although Harrison disapproves of Carlyle's mistaking the whisperings of his own heart for scientific certainty, he has an affinity for two Carlylean prepossessions: an idealization of the Middle Ages and a reverence for the heroes of Humanity. He thinks that *Past and Present* (1843), in which Carlyle vividly contrasts the struggles of enlightened churchmen of the twelfth century in the early days of Western civilization with the weaknesses and vices of modern society, is electrifying. This volume, Harrison states unequivocally, has become the basis for intelligent opinion on the social and industrial problems of the latter nineteenth century (*SEVL*, 59—60).

In Heroes, Hero-Worship, and the Heroic in History (1840), Carlyle extended the idea of the hero beyond the military conqueror at a time when poets, preachers, and men of letters would not have been so characterized. No one in 1840, thinks Harrison, other than Carlyle, understood the heroic in Norse mythology, the true greatness of Oliver Cromwell, or the importance of the *Divine Comedy* as the essence of Catholic feudalism. Most of Carlyle's judgments in *Heroes* are accepted today, although he did omit reference to any great Catholic hero in his unfortunate partiality toward the Puritan religion. But he remains the supreme man of letters of his age and will long be read and remembered.

Harrison knew Ruskin very well over a period of forty years, having visited him in his own home both in London and in Coniston, and Ruskin visited Harrison's home, also. He taught with Ruskin at the Workingmen's College and associated with him at the Meta-physical Society, and they conducted an active correspondence, which at times became rather controversial. Ironically, it was the thought that there was a natural bond between many of Ruskin's ideas and Comte's that drew Harrison to Ruskin, yet it was Ruskin's adverse criticism of Comte that led to controversy between these friends. Further, Harrison knew the Alps, Italy, and France almost as well as Ruskin himself did, and he had traveled in parts of France, Italy, Germany, and Switzerland where Ruskin had never been. It was the essays in Ruskin's *Unto This Last* that prompted Harrison to secure an introduction to the author, who cordially invited him to Denmark Hill "for a chat" (*AM*, 1:229–31).

He found Ruskin always ready to talk, but he also quickly discovered that "John would take no ideas from the Angel Gabriel himself" (*AM*, 1, 231). He wanted no man's ideas or books but his own. Harrison was quite astonished at Ruskin's impracticality and even perverseness, although he always insisted on Ruskin's gifts of eloquence, which he thought had no equal at that time. In 1868, Harrison wrote him a long letter, in which he set forth the many ways Ruskin's ideas paralleled those of Comte, but Ruskin told him that he was not in the least interested whether his ideas agreed with Comte's or disagreed with them. When Harrison alluded to Comte's idea of subjective immortality, Ruskin became highly annoyed. And Harrison's articles on Positivism in the *Contemporary Review* in 1875 and 1876 led to a public exchange of views (published, respectively, in *Fors Clavigera* and in Harrison's *Choice of Books*).[5] Ruskin strongly attacked anyone, especially men of science, who defended evolution, democracy, or modern progress. He even misconstrued the word *positive* to mean strong-minded, with a sense of infallibility. Harrison replied that Comte never uses *positive* to mean absolute truth, for the basis of his thinking is that all our ideas are necessarily relative.

In June 1876, Ruskin printed in *Fors Clavigera* a letter addressed to Harrison, challenging him to defend his belief in Positivism and in the worthiness of the human race which it reveres (*CB*, 122). Ruskin wrote that the human race is utterly vile, and he asked Harrison whether he thinks that he, Ruskin, is as handsome as the Elgin Theseus, the renowned statue of the ancient Greek hero. Harrison

replies that Ruskin, taken all round—in body, mind, and soul—is a
nobler specimen of man than the wrestler who sat for the incomparable Greek sculptor Phidias. Men today are actually far larger and more
powerful than men in ancient days, anyway. And as for denigrating
the morality of the modern world, can Ruskin say much for the virtue
of Athens and Rome? And have not modern poets painted more
exemplary women than the ancients did? Is not Joan of Arc nobler
than Virgil's Camilla? Or how about the Victorian Florence Nightingale, the real, versus Camilla, the imaginary (CB, 125)?

But when Ruskin represents the Positivists as incapable of any
feeling for Gothic art or medieval life, Harrison reminds him that
Comte matches anyone else whomsoever (doubtless including Ruskin
himself) in his profound reverence for the medieval genius in religion,
poetry, art, and chivalry. So true is it, that Comte goes back to the
Middle Ages to discover his type and ideal for modern man's spiritual
future. Further, Comte was saying this before the Gothic mania
began to obsess England and while Ruskin was still an undergraduate
at Oxford. And Comte has much to say about medieval music as well
as art, a subject that Ruskin has been strangely silent on.

Harrison reminds Ruskin that Positivism dreams, not of a mob or
of a mere aggregate of men (as Ruskin terms Humanity), but of a
community of men living in a disciplined and organic way. If Ruskin
ever converts the entire world to live like his own St. George's
Society, he will then have come near to the Positivist idea of Humanity. Just as the name *England* means the nation in the full sense of its
history—its past, its present, and its future—so Humanity refers to
past and future as well as to present members of the human race.

But when Ruskin attacks the age of steam for its chaos and
brutality and excoriates progress as a mad scramble, he is right. But
then why should he also mock at the systematic philosophy that
might bring order to this chaos? He attacks a rational use of tradition
more violently than the most rabid Communist. He has nothing but
contempt for Auguste Comte, who actually works for the very goals
that Ruskin himself so frantically teaches. He falsely accuses Comte of
believing the origin of man was in primitive organisms, a doctrine
which Comte actually considers to be outside the realm of science and
philosophy. Instead of despising the past as Ruskin charges, Comte

exalts it more than any other thinker. And Comte, no more than Ruskin himself, thinks the modern world of steam and factories is perfect or ideal. After Ruskin has demolished all that men have achieved for centuries, he will find it unlikely that he can "birch them into sense" in the schools of the St. George's company (*CB*, 136–37).

Ruskin denounces the state of modern art, but he does not seem to realize that music in the eighteenth and nineteenth centuries by Bach, Handel, Mozart, and Beethoven rivals the art and sculpture of ancient Athens itself. And has not Ruskin himself spoken with fervor about the genius of Reynolds and Turner, of Scott and Wordsworth, and, above all, of Goethe? Harrison then assures Ruskin that he himself will not despair of the human race, even in the sphere of art. Of course, art will never regenerate life, but life and thought and society will ultimately regenerate art. If Ruskin believes in the Providential goodness of God, it is odd that he also thinks that the world is headed more and more to the dogs. Of all gospels, that of *Fors Clavigera* is most full of utter despair and anarchy, preached by the man who spoke as beautifully as anyone ever has done (*CB*, 142–44).

Harrison thinks that Ruskin's dilemma is that, in spirit, he is a thirteenth-century poet and mystic who wants to turn the nineteenth century back to the thirteenth. He regards Harrison as a lost soul for being so thoroughly a man of the nineteenth. But Harrison is quite impartial in his estimate of Ruskin's genius, accrediting him as the undisputed master of two styles of English prose. No writer of English has ever produced notes more strangely beautiful and inspiring or ever sustained so prolonged a "strain of limpid grace" (*TR & M*, 54). But it is far from being a perfect style, and it is one that one should never attempt to emulate. As Harrison says, "No man can bend the bow of Ulysses" (*TR & M*, 55). Luscious and gorgeous as this prose is in its wealth and sheer profusion of images, it is never the result of labored affectation, never euphuistic. Ruskin is also the master of a plain, simple English style which Swift, Defoe, and Goldsmith might well have envied. Ruskin is the absolute master of the subtle instrument of prose, which cannot be matched throughout the whole range of English literature. There is a fine modulation, a harmony of tone and ease of words, with the images melting naturally and effortlessly into each other. It is the first time that the eye of the landscape painter is matched with the voice of the lyric poet in the medium of prose (*TR & M*, 66). Harrison finds his *Unto This Last* the most original and creative prose since *Sartor* (*TR & M*, 74). Indeed, Ruskin has every essential faculty but reserve. Perhaps, adds Harrison, there is some possible extenuation for this fault in that all poets, prophets, and reformers are extravagant, including Comte himself.

Ruskin is unique in his ardent attempt to build a beautiful world as well as to write beautiful thoughts. Carlyle and Spencer talked much about regenerating society, but Ruskin, with his Guild of St. George, made it his personal task to accomplish it (*TR & M*, 95—96). Harrison wrote an article for the *Daily Chronicle* to commemorate Ruskin's eightieth birthday in 1899, which someone in the home read aloud to Ruskin and later wrote Harrison that Ruskin had shed tears over parts of it. Harrison was one of the group that placed the memorial to him in Poet's Corner in the Abbey where he was buried. In the commemoration, Harrison had written that Ruskin had begun by preaching to England a higher sense of art in order to lead its people to "a truer understanding of morality, industry, religion, and humanity" (*TR & M*, 110).

I have referred to Harrison's comments on Matthew Arnold as a poet and shall close my discussion of his views on Victorian literature with his consideration of Arnold as a master of prose. Harrison considers Arnold primarily as the preeminent critic of the silver age of Victorian literature. He can always picture Arnold writing in the library of the Athenaeum Club, tossing about, as Harrison once told him, "his sceptical epigrams and his risky *bons mots* like a free-thinking Abbé at Voltaire's supper-parties" (*AM*, 2:112). London society never had more splendid companion nor Oxford a more typical scholar. His religious views are a strange mixture of "intellectual audacity and social orthodoxy" (*AM*, 2:112). As a critic of literature, he has no superior, no rival, and it is unfortunate that he never was able to devote more of his time and energy, as did Sainte-Beuve, to this pursuit. His critical judgments are so sound that, for the most part, they are generally accepted. Arnold lived up to his own ideal of disinterestedness with his "serene sense of equity" and his "exquisite taste" (*TR & M*, 124).

Arnold thought, Harrison continues, that the role of critic is to lay down canons of judgment in order to sort the good from the bad and to maintain the purity of language and of style. He was seldom guided by any pet prejudice, favorable or unfavorable, of his own, relying confidently on his vast knowledge, excellent taste, and careful judgment. He has had a formative influence on all writing done in his own age. He can detect the weaknesses in his favorite writers as well as put his finger on their special strengths, as in his famous assessments of Wordsworth, Byron, Shelley, and Keats (*TR & M*, 125−27).

But this master, Harrison fears, who could so excellently adjudge literature, so soon as he passed into politics, theology, and philosophy, disclaimed any kind of fixed principles by which he might transform Culture into reality. In this world, we need some kind of specific guidance and not merely vague admonition on these crucial matters. What is the best? How are things to be seen as they really are? In what way are we to reach perfection? It would seem that Arnold's Culture approaches the problems of life, in general, not so much by logic or metaphysics as by *belles-lettres*. However, his mission of Culture sounds very much like that of Auguste Comte's. Harrison imagines the elegant Arnold, in his genial way, meeting Comte in some Elysian Fields and saying, "Ah, well! I see now that we are not so far apart, but I never had patience to read your rather dry French, you know!" (*TR & M*, 133).

Lionel Trilling says that Harrison, in the *Fortnightly Review* of November 1867, wrote "a brilliant satirical retort" to what was to become Arnold's first chapter of *Culture and Anarchy*.[6] Martha S. Vogeler considers this retort, "Culture: A Dialogue," "one of the most devastating satires produced by a Victorian."[7] Perhaps the polemical nature of the quasi-Platonic dialogues scattered throughout Harrison's voluminous writings calls forth a consummate, coruscant wit, so piquant and charming, that makes them sparkle like gems of pure delight. In this dialogue, Harrison has Arminius von Thunder-ten-Tronckh, a fictitious German aristocrat whom Arnold had used to criticize the English system, questioning Arnold's own idea of Culture. Arminius wonders whether Arnold's Culture is anything more than either "a preachment for aristocratic good taste or a pleasantly devitalized religion." He asks how this Gospel could aid suffering humanity, coming as it does from a preacher "passing his white hands through his perfumed curls and simpering thus about the fringes of a stole." Arnold was delighted with the satire, as he wrote Lady Rothschild, and had laughed over it so hard that he had actually cried.[8]

In this colloquy (reprinted in *CB*, 97−118), Harrison is obviously contrasting Arnold's theory of Culture with his own Positivist solution of modern man's problems. When Arminius asks how Sweetness and Light come to one, Harrison (who affects the defense of Arnold's Culture) refers to "a lofty state of the soul" that delights every "tunable spirit." This glow, this divine afflatus, has nothing to do with mechanical method, with systematic philosophy. "O that you had heard him [i.e., Arnold] dwell on it himself with that well-bred ardour and in that simple unsystematic way. . . ." Do not look for a system of philosophy: "'Tis ours but to cull the finer flowerets, to scent out the hidden perfumes, along the by-paths in the garden of truth. . . ." When Arminius grows more impatient, Harrison exclaims: "Train your soul, then, to feel sweetness and light. . . . Had you but heard the Olympian scorn with which he lashed our machinery, our wealth, our formalism, the hideous and grotesque illusions of our middle-class liberalism, and Protestantism, and industrialism!" Arminius asks Harrison how he describes the basis of Culture's social philosophy. Harrison, condescendingly amused, reminds the puzzled German that Culture knows nothing so finite as a system. "Do you ask of Culture what are its principles and ideas? The *best* principle, the *best* ideas, the *best* knowledge: the perfect! the ideal! the complete!" Harrison says he had to summon all his Sweetness and Light not to laugh right out loud at the naive German.

Finally, Arminius says, at least he honors the prophet of Culture for having consigned "to public odium" a sect of blood-thirsty fanatics out to undermine English society and led by the "sour French pedant" (i.e., Comte, of course). Arminius has nearly all of Comte's philosophy exactly backwards, for the Apostle of Culture has presented but an uninformed view of it. It is obvious that Harrison (out of his role as Arminius's interlocutor) believes that Culture lacks a methodology by which to implement the fine phrases it resorts to and that it lacks any precise definition of its terms. As with Theism and Neo-Christianity, its essence evaporates in thin air.

As for Arnold's writings on religion, Harrison parodies Huxley's famous characterization of Positivism by saying that Arnold's religion is no more than Anglicanism minus Christianity (*TR & M*, 133). It is not easy to remember that Arnold, the admirer of "the secret of Jesus," the unfathomable originality of St. Paul, and the beauty of the Psalmists, also doubted any reliable evidence for a personal God, for the heavenly immortality of the soul, for the reality of miracles, or for any rational foundation of dogmatic theology. Arnold's religion, continues Harrison, might more properly be called Anglicanism plus Pantheism. Arnold's philosophy is that of an enthusiastic student of Plato, Spinoza, and Goethe; and his theology is that of an English clergyman who has resigned from the Church on conscientious grounds. Let us remember, though, advises Harrison, the remarkable poet, the percipient literary critic, and the highly cultured gentleman "whose overambitious fancies are even now fading into oblivion," yet whose verse is yet to be sufficiently appreciated (*TR & M*, 134).

Harrison often protests that he is not a heavy reader or an avid scholar, but his generally well-informed and judicious observations on a vast range of literature and history would seem to somewhat belie his modesty. He writes with a confidence that can come only from vast reading and from research in considerable depth. As the reader becomes more familiar with Harrison's life and philosophy, he should more clearly perceive, even in his literary judgments, Harrison's intense Victorian morality and all-encompassing Positivism.

Harrison is gratified with the proportionate attention that Comte gave to the feelings and the imagination, or the affective function. It is coequal in the triunity of feeling, mind, and action. Even if the reader is unaware of Arnold's Culture and Harrison's Positivism, these underlying philosophies of the two critics should not significantly impair the validity of their critical judgments for him. But, of course, if he is familiar with their general theories, he should more adequately understand how their literary criticism is part and parcel, at nearly every point, of their respective philosophies of life.

Chapter Seven

Conclusion

Harrison's son Austin, writing in 1927, finds it strange that Western civilization, before the time of Comte, had not developed a religion of its own, an independent code of morality, divorced from the East. Wholly un-Eastern in his ingrained rationalism, Harrison was one of the leading pioneers in nineteenth-century England who sought to "establish a Western system of moral values on the basis of its own coherent and social spirituality" (*FH*, 131—32). A religion without a metaphysic, without belief in Absolutes, and without reliance on unverifiable evidence seemed to Harrison eminently suited to modern Western man.

In 1859, three startling works—*Essay on Liberty*, *Essays and Reviews*, and *The Origin of Species*—appeared on the English scene that would shake the Victorian world to its foundations. At this very time, Comte's Positivism was spreading across the Channel from France to capture the imagination and the zeal of a group of young Englishmen associated with Wadham College, Oxford, not least among whom was Harrison. Until the distraction of the Franco-Prussian War, the subject of Positivism fairly haunted the pages of the prestigious *Fortnightly Review*. And the public continued to associate the journal with the Comtists, as well as to view indiscriminately all rationalists and men of science as Positivists. [1] A satirical jingle of the time by one Mortimer Collins illustrates the popular view:

> Wise are their leaders beyond all comparison—
> Comte, Huxley, Tyndall, Mill, Morley, and Harrison.
> Who will adventure to enter the lists
> With such a squadron of Positivists?

Of the many articles published on the subject of Positivism in the *Fortnightly Review*, Harrison contributed nearly half. Small wonder that one might have concluded that the review was the house organ of the Positivists "with Harrison as its feature writer."[3]

In "Positivism: Its Position, Aims, and Ideals," an article Harrison contributed to *Great Religions of the World* in 1912, he concedes that, by its very nature, Positivism could not soon expect any considerable amount of conversion to its banner. It so covers the spectrum of human preoccupations that its very complexity prevents its early acceptance; nevertheless, he takes some comfort in believing that it is not dependent on a single issue that sweeps through a generation and then is forgotten. Some polities have no root in history and so wither away; other systems of thought are too otherworldly to withstand the vital passions and interests of mankind. In short, such one-sided philosophies pay the penalty for neglecting the totality of human nature. Only Positivism, he is convinced, provides a complete human synthesis, treating human nature as an organic whole (*GRW*, 167−69). To the end of his life in 1923, Harrison would never relinquish this conviction.

As W. M. Simon points out, it is surprising that organized Positivism and the Religion of Humanity should have lasted for two generations in France and "that it did so in England amounts to a *tour de force*." His answer is that its success was primarily due to the gifted and devoted men who led the movement. It is very likely, he supposes, that the membership at any given time probably never exceeded a few hundred and the grand total might have been no more than two thousand.[4] If this estimate be anywhere near the truth, Harrison's loyalty and persistence appears the more remarkable. Simon goes on to observe that the movement in England has become absorbed into more recent humanist organizations.

Christopher Kent quotes the *Spectator* as linking Harrison with Froude, Arnold, and Carlyle in that they were "always read, and never followed." Kent believes that Harrison increasingly came to fill the role, if not quite that of a "full eccentric," at least that of "a licensed irregular whose views were treated with the respect due to his sincerity, intelligence, and education, as well as his means and his numerous and important connections."[5] But Walter E. Houghton rightly explains that "the reconstruction of society on a scientific basis" was a frequent assumption of the time, when faith in science became very nearly "ecstatic." This optimism, in which Harrison was by no means unique, has been greatly diminished by two world wars and the continuing cold war, by the threat of atomic explosion, and by the alarming rate at which we are consuming our natural resources. With the loss of the Christian ethic, Harrison thought he had found a logical substitute in the home and the family as the source of those altruistic sentiments that might well broaden later into the entire human race and throughout our civilization of the future.[6]

Basil Willey notes that John (later Lord) Morley, an intimate friend of fifty years, refers to Harrison as "incomparable as controversialist, powerful in historical sense and knowledge."[7] Muriel Harris says of Harrison and Morley: "Much more perhaps than any of their contemporaries, they have influenced British thought, and their total influence has yet to be appraised."[8] Morton Luce, writing shortly after Harrison's death, asserts that Harrison probably wrote more pamphlets and occasional articles than had anyone else in his generation and that it would not perhaps be a mistake to speak of him "as an unofficial Prose Laureate of half a century. He is nearly the last of those great souls who were the glory of our Victorian literature."[9]

Of Harrison's personal style, S. Marandon believes that it is not possible to convey it through excerpts, for Harrison requires a vast architecture to develop the progression of his ideas and the articulation of his hypotheses. This French critic wonders why the present century has concerned itself so little with Harrison, so important in the preceding century, a writer so valued by Guizot and Michelet, to name but a few of a very long list of eminent admirers. Often a personality is so conspicuous in one age yet nearly forgotten in the next. Marandon then writes that although Harrison's posthumous fame has suffered because of his consuming interest in providing a guide to life in the great issues of his own day, he should be reevaluated for other merits. Because of his lucidity and his charm, his literary criticism places him in a rank we usually accord to some of his contemporaries as a matter of course.[10]

The prolific critic George Saintsbury knew Harrison at Bath, watching him pass under his window a thousand times. Since Harrison's work is so extensive and various, Saintsbury selects only *The Choice of Books* to comment on, saying that its first three sections are as sound as anything that he himself has ever read. Saintsbury adds that Harrison could arrange and employ his huge store of knowledge "in a style neither quaint nor gorgeous but forcible and in a manner faultless." But Saintsbury was astonished that so vigorous and variously gifted a mind should have been "addicted to the curiously intangible and unsucculent thing called Positivism, a fact which is itself curious enough."[11]

Saintsbury, like anyone else acquainted with the writings, was equally amazed that there was virtually no department of literature Harrison did not venture into, "and in all he exercised his vigorous and correct style, his independent and positive thought, and his very considerable experience of affairs, countries, times, and seasons." This critic refers to Harrison's work as "a remarkable representation of the nineteenth century as it really was." Prolific as the writing was, Saintsbury asserts that "At any rate, I never saw anything of his that was not worth reading, however little I might agree with the sentiments and opinions expressed in it." He thought Harrison a completely honest man, free from ostentation, and unusually good-natured. "He may not have been exactly a great man or a great writer: but a good man and a good writer he certainly was. And 'to be good is hard.' "[12]

Twentieth-century writers refer most often to Harrison's Positivism. However, A. Cochrane in the *Dictionary of National Biography* thinks that Harrison influenced the life and thought of his time less significantly as a leader of Positivism in England than as a leading spirit of reform, wherein his activity was distinguished by his vigor and intensely practical purpose.[13] His article "Neo-Christianity" continues to provoke discussion, as may be seen in Martha S. Vogeler's "More Light on *Essays and Reviews.*"[14]

However, in this century there has been an unfortunate dearth of extensive discussion of Harrison's many contributions on historical and literary subjects. Of course, it is not unusual to discover brief quotations from, or allusions to, his critical studies on Gibbon, George Eliot, Trollope, Tennyson, Arnold, and Ruskin, for example. His memories of persons and events of the nineteenth century are fairly often cited, especially his personal relationship with the novelist George Gissing.[15] But there is no complete published study of

Harrison's extensive literary criticism or historical writings and scarcely any detailed reference to his own creative literary efforts.

Like Arnold and Ruskin, Harrison thinks it is of the utmost importance to ascertain and to perpetuate the works of mankind's highest genius. Comte had devised his calendar of great men to replace the Catholic calendar of saints, including the most famous names of science, literature, religion, philosophy, and politics. Actually, the Religion of Humanity essentially means a veneration of and gratitude for human genius throughout history—past, present, and future. And Harrison sought no more than to be a humble instrument in the furtherance of its influence. As he himself said, the best part of one continues to live so long as Humanity itself does, merged with the great, endless stream that flows from the past through the present into the future. This is his subjective immortality.

Notes and References

Please see List of Abbreviations for key to Harrison's works.

Chapter One

1. *Memories and Thoughts* (New York and London, 1906), p. 12.
2. See below, chapter 5.
3. John Stuart Mill, *Autobiography* (New York: Columbia University Press, 1924), p. 93.
4. Austin Harrison, *Frederic Harrison* (New York and London, 1927). This work is not actually a biography but a collection of valuable impressions the son retains of his father.
5. Gertrude Himmelfarb, *Victorian Minds* (New York: Alfred A. Knopf, 1968), pp. 303–4.
6. *Autobiographic Memoirs*, 2 vols. (New York, London, and Toronto, 1911), 1:14. The biographical material in the remainder of this chapter, unless otherwise indicated, will be drawn from this work. Quoted passages will be individually noted.
7. The father, Frederick Harrison, although originally trained to be an architect, went into the firm of R. and W. Hichens, stock-brokers, at the age of seventeen. He ultimately became senior partner in this eminent firm and retired with a very considerable fortune. He was the son of John Harrison, an important builder and contractor in London, coming from a large family of yeoman farmers near Leicester. The only interest Frederic would have in tracing his ancestry through the innumerable Harrisons strewn throughout the northern counties would be to establish descent from the brave Ironside who died for the Commonwealth at Charing Cross; but a professor at Oxford has proved that Gen. Thomas Harrison left no descendants. This same professor also scotched all attempts to link the two American Presidents named Harrison with the same great Puritan (*AM*, 1:71–72).
8. The mother, Jane, was the only daughter of Alexander and Elizabeth Brice, the latter a daughter of an Irishman named Johnson (*AM*, 1:66).
9. Bertrand Russell, "What I Believe," in *Why I Am Not a Christian*, ed. Paul Edwards, an Essandess paperback (New York: Simon and Schuster, 1957), p. 79.

10. He includes in those changes such things as steam, steel plates, shells, low decks, enormous cannon, torpedoes, the entire absence of lofty masts and yards, electric lights and signals, and wireless telegraphy—all during the sixty years within his memory.

11. Henry Salt writes that in 1900 he edited a quarterly, the *Humane Review*, which lasted for ten years, "thanks chiefly to the occasional friendly assistance it received from such writers as Bernard Shaw, Edward Carpenter, . . . Frederic Harrison, . . . Ouida, . . . and W. H. Hudson himself." Henry Stephens Salt, *Company I Have Known* (London: G. Allen and Unwin, 1930), p. 122. "Humanitarian topics brought me letters from many quarters, as from Tolstoy, Thomas Hardy, Goldwin Smith . . . and not least from Frederic Harrison, who also corresponded with me on the subject of translation from the Classics" (p. 182).

12. John Henry Newman, an early leader of the Oxford Movement in the Church of England, later was converted to Roman Catholicism, ultimately attaining the rank of cardinal. His younger brother, Francis William Newman, renounced belief in supernatural religion and adopted a vague kind of theism. Both brothers were highly learned and very active in the intellectual life of England. Both wrote autobiographies, telling of their respective spiritual development. In their beliefs, they were complete opposites. Only in their intellectual flair were they alike.

13. It is ironic that Harrison would later attack these two examiners in one of the most controversial articles of the nineteenth century. See below, chapter 3.

14. Richard Cobden was director of the Anti-Corn Law League, perhaps the first highly organized agitational movement in the modern sense, a movement that was instrumental in overthrowing the old aristocratic landed interests. John Bright was closely associated with Cobden in the Free Trade movement. He was a powerful advocate of the Second Reform Bill. Harrison considered him the most moving orator of the era. Latitudinarianism refers to a belief in greater freedom of thought on religious matters.

15. See below, chapter 4.

16. Sir John Seeley supported the empire building Great Britain was involved in, and in his *Expansion of England* (1883) he espoused the idea of the White Man's Burden.

17. Harrison observes that the College continued to thrive on the basis of Maurice's Christian Socialism and Thomas Hughes's Muscular Christianity, with their strange mixture of Christianity, a little armchair socialism, and a "mild infusion of real working men."

18. See below, chapter 3.

19. Sidney and Beatrice Webb, *The History of Trade-Unionism* (First published in 1894; reprint New York: Augustus M. Kelley-Publisher, 1965). In 1920, however, Harrison comments on the revised edition of the Webbs' *History* (1920), noting that he now differs widely with the views of the authors. The character of unionism has changed, he observes. "It had begun with the intention to equalize the resources of Labour in dealing with Capital; now it is a vast social war to eliminate Capital. Today the movement has become Socialist, urging catastrophic revolution. . . . It has become class war in the name of 'direct action.' . . . 'Direct action' is aiming at what all history proves to have been the worst of all forms of government, when, as at Athens, on the death of Pericles, noisy bands of some thousands of mob orators dragged down their state to ruin." *Novissima Verba: Last Words—1920* (London, 1921), pp. 122, 125, 126, 130.

20. Ibid., p. 270.

21. Ibid., p. 271.

22. The Harrison family, though not wealthy, was comfortable financially. Never extravagant, Harrison lived sensibly within his means and never encountered straitened circumstances.

23. *Times Literary Supplement*, November 1909, p. 434.

24. *My Alpine Jubilee* (London, 1908).

25. F. Martin in his introduction to *De Senectute: More Last Words* (London, 1923). He thinks that Harrison was one of the most characteristic figures of the Victorian Age and that he summed up many of its best qualities.

Chapter Two

1. *The Positive Evolution of Religion* (New York, 1913).

2. *The Creed of a Layman* (New York and London, 1907).

3. *De Senectute* (London, 1923). Published posthumously.

4. *The Philosophy of Common Sense* (London, 1907).

5. This passage is taken from a speech which Harrison delivered on September 5, 1907, to commemorate the fiftieth anniversary of Comte's death.

6. "Evolution," *Encyclopaedia Britannica* (13th ed.), 10:29.

7. Wilhelm Windelband, *A History of Philosophy*, 2 vols., trans. James H. Tufts (New York, 1958), 2:650.

8. Actually, Caroline seems to have been a penniless prostitute whom Comte had picked up at the Palais-Royal. Poverty and her adulterous conduct caused their seventeen years of unhappiness. See Richmond Laurin

Hawkins, *Positivism in the United States (1853–1861)* (Cambridge, Mass.: Harvard University Press, 1938), pp. 55–56n.

9. Harrison translated the second volume during the early 1870s.

10. Hawkins, pp. 54–55n.

11. See below, pp. 41–42.

12. "The Calendar," *Information Please Almanac*, 19th ed. (New York: Simon and Schuster, 1965), pp. 300–301.

13. "Comte, Auguste," *Encyclopaedia Britannica*, 13th ed., 6:821–22. In July 1876, Morley writes Harrison that he is just beginning this article for the *Britannica*, saying that he has pondered the whole topic of Positivism day and night. He wonders how *"you* of all men on this bright planet have gone over to such an idol. . . ." "'And how does Harrison, he moans during the night, find a key to this stuff—this dreary'—No more—or we quarrel." Quoted in Edwin M. Everett, *The Party of Humanity* (Chapel Hill, N.C., 1939), p. 102.

14. Harrison's son Austin thinks Marx, who contributed socialism to the world, and Comte, who founded sociology, were the two dominant creative thinkers of the nineteenth century. "Marx," he says, "advocated revolution without religion; Comte, religion without revolution. Both men were children of the revolutionary era. The one based his socialism on materialism; the other, his sociology on what Austin terms 'temporal' spiritualism" (*FH*, 211).

15. Mill writes that the ideas of Positivism have "manifested themselves on the surface of the philosophy of the age. . . . They are symbols of a recognized mode of thought, and one of sufficient importance to induce almost all who now discuss the great problems of philosophy, or survey from any elevated point of view the opinions of the age, to take what is termed the Positivist view of things into serious consideration, and define their own position, more or less friendly or hostile, in regard to it. . . . The time, therefore, seems to have come, when every philosophic thinker not only ought to form, but many usefully express, a judgment respecting this intellectual movement. . . ." John Stuart Mill, *Auguste Comte and Positivism* (London, 1865), pp. 1–3.

16. In this section and the next one, I have drawn considerably from Harriet Martineau's translation and condensation of Auguste Comte's *Positive Philosophy*, 2 vols., 3rd ed. (London, 1893), one of the first works on Positivism that Harrison read; and L. Lévy-Bruhl's *The Philosophy of Auguste Comte*, authorized translation by Kathleen de Beaumont-Klein (London, 1903), a work that Harrison, in an introduction to the translation, says is the best interpretation of Comte in existence.

17. Kenneth Thompson, *Auguste Comte: The Foundations of Sociology*, in The Making of Sociology Series, a Halsted Press book, ed. Ronald Fletcher (New York: Wiley, 1975), pp. 39–40.

18. *Filiation* is an important word in Positivist writings, indicating the formation of branches and offshoots, derived from a parent or source, The supreme example of filiation is the unending organic relationships that exist throughout the historical development of Humanity. See below, p. 87.

19. This argument for the Absolute sounds not unlike ontological arguments by the Scholastics of the Middle Ages. The following remarks by Harrison come from his response to a talk previously given by an Hegelian. He handles technical polemics with obvious accomplishment.

20. *Novissima Verba* (London, 1921). Harrison dedicated this volume to the Earl of Rosebery, K.G., in 1921. He writes that it includes notes on events and books of the day and that its chapters appeared month by month in the *Fortnightly Review* during the year 1920.

21. Philip Appleman, "Darwin and Pater's Critical Dilemma," in *Darwin*, a Norton Critical Edition, ed. Philip Appleman (New York: W. W. Norton and Co., 1970), p. 612.

22. Richard Hofstadter, "The Vogue of Spencer," in *Darwin*, ed. Philip Appleman, p. 489.

23. In the following discussion, I have drawn much of my material from Harrison's *The Philosophy of Common Sense*, especially from the introduction and chapters 1–5 and 11–12 (pp. ix–xxxvii, 1–101, 164–88). I have also drawn from relevant portions of his *De Senectute*. Harrison concurs with any idea I have drawn directly from Comte.

Chapter Three

1. Frederic Harrison, "Positivism: Its Position, Aims, and Ideals," in *Great Religions of the World* (New York and London, 1912). Harrison's article on Positivism appeared along with others on Confucianism, Buddhism, Mohammedanism, Brahminism, Zoroastrianism, Sikhism, Babism, Judaism, and Christianity (Protestant and Roman Catholic). It is interesting that, as late as 1912, Positivism was counted, in this collection, among the eleven great religions of the world. Its prestige at so late a date is probably due to the reputation of several of its English devotees, especially Harrison. Today such an inclusion would be unthinkable.

2. Gertrude Himmelfarb, *Victorian Minds* (New York: Alfred A. Knopf, 1968), p. 303. H. L. Mencken wonders why the men of the Reformation did not complete their revolution rather than developing a new theology "quite

as silly as the old." He concludes they were courageous, but not very intelligent. See Henry L. Mencken, *Treatise on the Gods*, Vintage Books (New York: Alfred A. Knopf, 1963), pp. 222–23.

3. Leslie Stephen, "Shaftesbury's Characteristics," in *Essays on Free-thinking and Plainspeaking* (New York and London: G. P. Putnam's Sons, 1908), p. 272.

4. Leslie Stephen, "Are We Christians?" in *Essays on Freethinking and Plainspeaking*, pp. 176, 167, 169, 163–64.

5. Noel Gilroy Annan, *Leslie Stephens: His Thought and Character in Relation to His Time* (Cambridge, Mass.: Harvard University Press, 1952), p. 217.

6. The Broad Church movement in the Anglican Church adopted a more liberal attitude toward biblical criticism from Germany, reduced the content of Christian belief, and was more favorable to social improvement. It minimized the miraculous and sacramental emphasis.

7. The Higher Criticism, originating in objective study of Homer and extending later to the Bible, studied the Scriptures critically and scientifically as though they were not different from other works of literature.

Tractarianism, or the Oxford Movement, attempted to revive the spirit and form of the early Church of Christendom, with more emphasis on the corporate, Catholic side of the Church.

8. Alfred William Benn, *The History of English Rationalism*, 2 vols. (London, New York, and Bombay, 1906), 2:114.

9. Ibid., p. 129.

10. See Harrison's discussion of his activities in his *Autobiographic Memoirs*, 1:205–9. Most of my discussion of *Essays and Reviews* relates to Harrison's article "Neo-Christianity," *Westminster Review* 36 (October 1860):293–332, reprinted in his *The Creed of a Layman*, pp. 81–151.

11. Dr. Francis A. Schaeffer, *Escape from Reason* (Downers Grove, Ill.: Inter-Varsity Press, 1965), chapter 4.

12. Huxley's phrase for Positivism in his essay "The Physical Basis of Life."

13. Desmond Bowen, *The Idea of the Victorian Church* (Montreal: McGill University Press, 1968), p. 169.

14. Ibid., p. 166.

15. Ibid., pp. 173–75, 162.

16. Much of the material in the remainder of this section is drawn from this work, *The Positive Evolution of Religion*.

17. *Erastian* refers to the influence of the state on church affairs.

18. The English philosopher Herbert Spencer agrees with Comte and

Harrison that thought, by its very nature, excludes the idea of an Absolute, for it conditions that which is unconditional. Yet we may well assume a reality lying beyond thought and experience. Spencer calls this Reality the "Unknowable" (Benn, 2:224).

19. Bertrand Russell, "Has Religion Made Useful Contributions to Civilization?" in *Why I Am Not a Christian*, p. 45.

20. Benn, 2:287.

21. There are undoubtedly reflections of "the noble and fascinating theories" (as he termed them) of Auguste Comte in Bellamy's Religion of Solidarity. His principle of brotherly love resembles Comte's creed that we should live for others, which should be the foundation of society. He, too, believed that a positive religion is necessary for any civilization that is based on the happiness and welfare of Humanity (Sylvia Bowman, *The Year 2000: A Critical Biography of Edward Bellamy* [New York: Bookman Associates, 1958], pp. 21, 36, 49, 255−68).

22. Thomas Whitaker, *Comte and Mill*, in *Philosophers Ancient and Modern* (New York, n.d.), pp. 55−56.

23. Alfred North Whitehead, *Adventures of Ideas*, A Free Press Paperback (New York: Macmillan Co., 1967), pp. 36−37.

Chapter Four

1. *Order and Progress* (London, 1875).

2. *The Meaning of History* (New York and London, 1896).

3. *On Society* (London, 1918).

4. *Realities and Ideals* (London, 1908).

5. *George Washington* (New York, 1901).

6. Vera Wheatley, *The Life and Work of Harriet Martineau* (London: Secker and Warburg, 1957), pp. 332−33. Comte was still little known when Martineau published this translation. He thanked her for improving on his too-often redundant and ornate prose and for her speaking out in his defense. Her translation was reprinted many times, and Frederic Harrison wrote a preface for the 1896 edition, in which he said that even such severe critics as Mill and Morley conceded that Comte had made a profound contribution to modern thought. And Carlyle believed that since Comte had given a new religion to the world, he might justly be considered the central figure of the century (p. 334).

7. Oswald Spengler, *The Decline of the West*, trans. Charles Francis Atkinson, 2 vols. Vol. 1: *Form and Actuality* (New York: Alfred A. Knopf, 1926). Vol. 2: *Perspectives of World History* (New York: Alfred A. Knopf, 1928).

8. See above, on p. 46, a reference to the Positivist use of the word *filiation*. It is a favorite term of the Positivists, illustrating the growth of society in the same organic way that branches grow from the trunk of a tree.

9. Auguste Comte, *A General View of Positivism* (Paris, 1848), trans. J. H. Bridges (Stanford, Calif.: Academic Reprints, n.d.), p. 390.

10. Ibid., pp. 392–95.

11. Ibid., pp. 411–12.

12. Auguste Comte, *The Catechism of Positivism, or Summary Exposition of the Universal Religion in Thirteen Systematic Conversations Between a Woman and Priest of Humanity*, 2d ed., trans. Richard Congreve (London, 1883), p. 230.

13. Comte, *A General View of Positivism*, pp. 227–29, 234.

14. "Comte, Auguste," *Encyclopaedia Britannica*, 13th ed., 6:821, 822.

15. Comte, *A General View of Positivism*, pp. 366–68.

16. Adriano Tilgher, *Work: What It Has Meant Through the Ages*, trans. from the Italian by Dorothy Canfield Fisher (New York: Harcourt, Brace and Co., 1930), pp. 76, 90–99, 110, 114.

17. John Stuart Mill, *Auguste Comte and Positivism* (London, 1865), pp. 132–80. Reprinted from the *Westminster Review*. My discussion of Mill's opinions has been based on these pages. I refer the reader to Herbert Spencer, *Reasons for Dissenting from the Philosophy of M. Comte and Other Essays*, in which Spencer contrasts points in his own doctrine with those of Comte. But since the discussion is of a technical scientific nature, I have not included it here. I have alluded to Harrison's controversy with Spencer elsewhere, and I have discussed Ruskin's criticism in chapter 6.

18. Someone in Harrison's group had selected one hundred books from the *Positivist Library* as core reading for students of Positivism.

19. Henry Thomas Buckle (1821–1862), in his unfinished *History of Civilization* (1857), argues that the process of history depends on impersonal laws derived from man's physical environment.

20. Harrison draws most of his reply to Mill from the *Letter* of 1864, which Dr. John Bridges published in reply to Mill's *Auguste Comte and Positivism*, a response that Harrison terms a "model of controversial method" (*OS*, 212).

21. Huxley had been especially caustic in his *Essays upon Some Controverted Questions* (London and New York: Macmillan, 1892).

22. Ernest Heinrich Haeckel (1834–1919) was a German biologist who applied the doctrine of evolution not only to zoology but also to philosophy and religion. An uncompromising monist, he asserted the essential unity of organic and inorganic nature. He thought that the higher faculties in man

have evolved from the brute beast. He also denied the immortality of the soul, the freedom of the will, and the existence of a personal God.

Chapter Five

1. *Theophano* (London, 1904).
2. *Nicephorus* (London, 1906).
3. These pages include from the *Fortnightly Review* "Constantinople as an Historic City" 55 (April 1894) and "The Problem of Constantinople" 55 (May 1894).
4. *Among My Books* (London, 1912), pp. 232−48.
5. *Choice of Books* (London and New York, 1888).
6. The picture of the scheming and conscienceless Joseph Bringas, the Eunuch, brings to mind the picture of Eusebius, the Eunuch, in Gore Vidal's historical novel *Julian* (Boston and Toronto: Little, Brown, 1964). Note especially the picture of Eusebius on p. 44.
7. This passage reflects overtones of Henry IV's being humbled before Pope Gregory VII at Canossa as he had no choice but to comply with the Pope's Investiture Decrees.
8. Translated and edited by Harrison; reprinted in New York, 1971.
9. Ibid., pp. 3−6.

Chapter Six

1. *Tennyson, Ruskin, and Mill* (London, 1899).
2. *Studies in Early Victorian Literature* (London, 1895).
3. Christopher Kent, *Brains and Numbers: Elitism, Comtism, and Democracy in Mid-Victorian England* (Toronto, 1978), p. 23.
4. An especially strong opposing view may be found in F. E. L. Priestley's recent study, *Language and Structure in Tennyson's Poetry*, in *The Language Library*, eds. Eric Partridge and Simeon Potter (London: André Deutsch, 1973), pp. 125−36. Priestley credits Tennyson with having created new genres rather than having attempted, but failed, to manage the too-formidable task of preserving the traditional forms. Further, he insists that Tennyson was not simply making a blank-verse paraphrase of Malory or remodeling models.
5. Ruskin writes in *Fors Clavigera*, letter 66, June 1876, "Well, I can't get that paper of Mr. Frederic Harrison's out of my head; chiefly because I know and like its writer; and I *don't* like his wasting his time on writing that kind of stuff. What I have got to say to him, anent it, may better be said

publicly, because I must write it carefully, and with some fulness, and if he won't attend to me, perhaps some of his readers may." The material pertaining to Harrison runs from paragraphs 9 to 15, pp. 618—25, in *The Works of John Ruskin*, ed. E. T. Cook and Alexander Wedderburn (London and New York, 1903—1912), vol. 28.

6. Lionel Trilling, *Matthew Arnold*, Meridian Books (Cleveland and New York: The World Publishing Co., 1963), p. 250.

7. Martha S. Vogeler, "Matthew Arnold and Frederic Harrison: the Prophet of Culture and the Prophet of Positivism," *Studies in English Literature: 1500—1900* 2 (1962):450.

8. Trilling, p. 251.

Chapter Seven

1. Edwin M. Everett, *The Party of Humanity* (Chapel Hill, N.C., 1939), p. 101.

2. Ibid.

3. Ibid.

4. W. M. Simon, *European Positivism in the Nineteenth Century* (Ithaca, N.Y., 1963), p. 69.

5. Christopher Kent, *Brains and Numbers: Elitism, Comtism, and Democracy in Mid-Victorian England* (Toronto, 1978), pp. 157—58.

6. Walter E. Houghton, *The Victorian Frame of Mind: 1830—1870* (New Haven: Yale University Press, 1957), pp. 35—36, 347.

7. Basil Willey, *More Nineteenth Century Studies: A Group of Honest Doubters* (London: Chatto and Windus, 1956), p. 255.

8. Muriel Harris, "Two Victorian Portraits," *North American Review* 212 (September 1920):404. Harris corroborates what others have said about Harrison's health and sanity in his latest years: "His is the secret of eternal youth" (p. 407).

9. Morton Luce, "Harrison," *Nineteenth Century* 93 (March 1923):435.

10. S. Marandon, "Harrison," *Études Anglaises* 13 (1960):424—26.

11. George Saintsbury, "Harrison," *Fortnightly Review* 113 (March 1923):374—77.

12. Ibid., pp. 375—81.

13. A. Cochrane, "Harrison, Frederic," *Dictionary of National Biography, 1922—1930*, (London: Oxford University Press), pp. 406—8.

14. Martha S. Vogeler, "More Light on *Essays and Reviews*," *Victorian Periodicals Review* 12 (Fall 1979):105—16.

15. When George Gissing was down and out early in his career, Harrison

brought him into his home as tutor for his boys. It was this kindness that saved Gissing's life, thereby enabling the unfortunate young man to proceed with his career onto later success, although his pessimism was in strange contrast with Harrison's exuberance and optimism.

Selected Bibliography

PRIMARY SOURCES

1. Books

Among My Books: Centenaries, Reviews, Memoirs. London: Macmillan and Co., 1912.

Annals Of an Old Manor House. London: Macmillan and Co., 1893.

Autobiographic Memoirs. 2 vols. Vol. 1: 1832–1870. Vol. 2: 1870–1910. New York, London, and Toronto: Macmillan and Co., 1911.

Choice of Books and Other Literary Pieces. London and New York: Macmillan Co., 1907.

The Creed of a Layman: Apologia pro Fide Mea. New York and London: Macmillan Co., 1907.

De Senectute: More Last Words. London: T. F. Unwin, 1923.

George Washington and Other American Addresses. New York: Macmillan and Co., 1901.

The Meaning of History and Other Historical Pieces. New York and London: Macmillan and Co., 1896.

Memories and Thoughts: Men—Books—Cities—Art. New York and London: Macmillan Co., 1906.

My Alpine Jubilee—with Portrait. London: Smith and Elder, 1908.

National and Social Problems. New York and London: Macmillan and Co., 1908.

The New Calendar of Great Men. Edited and partly written by F. H. London and New York: Macmillan and Co., 1892.

Nicephorus—A Tragedy of New Rome. London: Chapman and Hall, 1906.

Novissima Verba: Last Words—1920. London: T. Fisher Unwin, 1921.

On Society. London: Macmillan and Co., 1918.

Order and Progress. London: Longmans and Co., 1875.

The Philosophy of Common Sense. London: Macmillan and Co., Limited, 1907.

The Positive Evolution of Religion: Its Moral and Social Reaction. New York: G. P. Putnam's Sons, 1913.

Realities and Ideals. New York: Macmillan and Co., 1908.

Social Statics. Translation of Comte's *Positive Polity.* Vol. 2. London: Longmans & Co., 1875.

Studies in Early Victorian Literature. London and New York: Edward Arnold, 1895.

Tennyson, Ruskin, Mill and Other Literary Estimates. London and New York: Macmillan and Co., 1899.

Theophano: The Crusade of the Tenth Century. A Romantic Monograph. London: Chapman and Hall, 1904.

2. Selected Articles

"Among My Books." *English Review* 10 (1911):10−23, 210−24, 425−41, 568−83; 11 (1912):19−36, 177−88. Reprinted in *Among My Books*, pp. 3−123.

"Byzantine History in the Early Middle Ages." The Rede Lecture, Cambridge, 1900. Reprinted in *Among My Books*, pp. 180−231.

"Constantinople as an Historic City." *Fortnightly Review* 55 (April 1894): 438−58. Reprinted in *The Meaning of History*, pp. 309−40.

"The Creed of a Layman." *Nineteenth Century* 9 (March 1881):455−77. Reprinted in *The Creed of a Layman*, pp. 208−42.

"Culture: a Dialogue." *Fortnightly Review* 2 (November 1867):603−14. Reprinted in *Choice of Books*, pp. 97−118.

"A Few Words About the Eighteenth Century." *Nineteenth Century* 13 (March 1883):385−403. Reprinted in *Choice of Books*, pp. 351−87.

"A Few Words About the Nineteenth Century." *Fortnightly Review* 31 (April 1882):411−26. Reprinted in *Choice of Books*, pp. 417−47.

"Formative Influences." *Forum* (New York) 10 (October 1890):152−64. Reprinted as "My Memories" in *Memories and Thoughts*, pp. 1−19.

Introduction to L. Levy-Bruhl's *The Philosophy of Auguste Comte*. Authorized translation by Kathleen de Beaumont-Klein. London: Swan Sonnenschein and Co., Lim., 1903.

"The London Library Subject Index." *Times Literary Supplement*, November 1909, p. 434.

"Mr. Huxley's Controversies." *Fortnightly Review* 52 (October 1892):417−37. Reprinted in *The Philosophy of Common Sense*, pp. 275−307.

"Neo-Christianity." *Westminster Review* 36 (October 1860):293−332. Reprinted as "Septem Contra Fidem" in *The Creed of a Layman*, pp. 92−151.

"On the Choice of Books." *Fortnightly Review* 25 (April 1879):491−512. Reprinted in *The Choice of Books*, pp. 1−93.

"Positivism." In *Great Religions of the World*. A new edition with introductions. New York and London: Harper and Brothers Publishers, 1912.

"Positivism: Aims and Ideals." *North American Review* (one of a series on the aims and ideals of various religions) 172 (March 1901):456-67. Reprinted as "Aims and Ideals" in *The Creed of a Layman*, pp. 243-60.

"The Problem of Constantinople." *Fortnightly Review* 55 (May 1894): 614—33. Reprinted in *The Meaning of History*, pp. 341—67.

"The Royal Road to History: an Oxford Dialogue." *Fortnightly Review* 54 (October 1893):478—91. Reprinted as "The History Schools: an Oxford Dialogue" in *The Meaning of History*, pp. 118—38.

"Ruskin, John." *Encyclopaedia Britannica*, 13th ed., 23: 858—61.

SECONDARY SOURCES

Benn, Alfred William. *The History of English Rationalism*. 2 vols. London, New York, and Bombay: Longmans, Green, and Co., 1906. A classic in its field and well known to Harrison.

Cochrane, Alfred. "Harrison, Frederic." *Dictionary of National Biography, 1922—1930*, pp. 406—408. A brief survey of Harrison's life and contributions.

Comte, Auguste. *The Catechism of Positivism, or Summary Exposition of the Universal Religion in Thirteen Systematic Conversations Between a Woman and Priest of Humanity*. 2d ed. Translated by Richard Congreve. London: Trubner and Co., 1883. Perhaps Comte's clearest exposition of the Religion of Humanity that the Wadham Positivists adopted.

———. *A General View of Positivism*. Translated by J. H. Bridges. Paris, 1848; Stanford, Calif.: Academic Reprints, n.d. Comte's attempt, in summary form, to combine the Positivist philosophy and polity for a program of action, designed especially for implementation in Western Europe.

———. *Positive Philosophy*. 2 vols. 3rd ed. Freely translated and condensed by Harriet Martineau. London: Kegan Paul, Trench, Trubner and Co., Ltd., 1893. One French scholar wrote Martineau that her work was so well done that he wished that it could be retranslated back into French, for it would popularize the Positivist doctrines more effectively than Comte's own works in the original. This work by Comte found favor with some English Rationalists, whereas the later *Positive Polity* pleased very few.

———. *The Positivist Library of Auguste Comte*. Translated and edited by Frederic Harrison. A preface by Harrison. Burt Franklin: Bibliography and Reference Series 419. Philosophy Monograph Series 61. New York: Burt Franklin, n.d. The library selected by Comte to educate the Positivist in the culture and wisdom of Humanity.

"Comte, Auguste." *Encyclopaedia Britannica*. 13th ed., 6: 814–22. This article contributed by John Morley, a close friend of Harrison's and longtime editor of the *Fortnightly Review*. Not written as a follower of Comte, though fair. Viewpoint more like that of John Stuart Mill.

Everett, Edwin Mallard. *The Party of Humanity: The Fortnightly Review and Its Contributors, 1865–1874*. Chapel Hill: The University of North Carolina Press, 1939. Full account of Harrison's relations with John Morley and the *Fortnightly Review*.

Harris, Muriel. "Two Victorian Portraits." *North American Review* 212 (September 1920):404–11. A personal recollection of Morley and Harrison that is extremely favorable to both men.

Harrison, Austin. *Frederic Harrison*. New York and London: G. P. Putnam's Sons, 1927. Personal memories and impressions of Harrison by his son Austin. The best and fullest account of Harrison's personality and character.

Kent, Christopher. *Brains and Numbers: Elitism, Comtism, and Democracy in Mid-Victorian England*. Toronto: University of Toronto Press, 1978. Concentrates on Morley and Harrison. Contends that Harrison used Comte's philosophy to reconcile intellectual and political activity within a mass society.

Lévy-Bruhl, L. *The Philosophy of Auguste Comte*. Authorized translation by Kathleen de Beaumont-Klein. Introduced by Frederic Harrison. London: Swan Sonnenschein and Co., Lim., 1903. Harrison considered this the best informed discussion of Positivism by anyone, Positivist or non-Positivist. It is a model of objectivity and clarity on a controversial and difficult subject.

Luce, Morton. "Harrison." *Nineteenth Century* 93 (March 1923):427–36. Tells of conversation during a week's visit Harrison paid when he was ill. Highly laudatory of Harrison both as man and writer, whom it is not a misfortune to know personally as is usually the case with literary authors.

Marandon, S. "Frederic Harrison: 1831–1923." *Études Anglaises* 13 (October-December 1960):415–26. Has much to say about Harrison's style as a writer. Marvels how a man can be so prominent in one era and virtually forgotten in the next.

Mill, John Stuart. *Auguste Comte and Positivism*. London: N. Trubner and Co., 1865. Reprinted from the *Westminster Review*. Thought by

Harrison to be the most important attack on Comte, upon which other critics largely based their own objections.

Ricks, C. B. "Harrison and Bergson." *Notes and Queries*, May 1959, pp. 175−78. Owns a copy of Bergson's *Introduction to Metaphysics*, which had once belonged to Harrison. Finds the marginalia a testimony to Harrison's emphatic rationalism in his reaction against Bergson's philosophical ideas. He reproduces many of Harrison's notes verbatim.

Ruskin, John. *Fors Clavigera*. In *The Works of John Ruskin*. Library ed. 37 vols. Edited by E. T. Cook and Alexander Wedderburn. 27:618−25. London: G. Allen; New York: Longmans, Green, and Co., 1903−1912. In these pages Ruskin takes Harrison publicly to task for his glorification of Humanity and challenges him to a reply, with which Harrison promptly obliged. See above, chapter 6.

Saintsbury, George. "Harrison." *Fortnightly Review* 113 (March 1923): 374−81. Knew Harrison personally during the latter's last years at Bath. Interesting for personal memorabilia. Also for assessment of Harrison as a writer. Comments favorably on Harrison's critical powers in *Choice of Books*.

Simon, Walter Michael. *European Positivism in the Nineteenth Century: an Essay in Intellectual History*. Ithaca, N.Y.: Cornell University Press, 1963. A full discussion of the progress of Positivism in several countries and of what finally happened to organized Positivism in them.

Vogeler, Martha Salmon. "Frederic Harrison and John Ruskin: The Limits of Positivist Biography." *Texas Quarterly* 18 (Summer 1975): 91−98. Discusses Harrison's contribution of the life of Ruskin to the new *English Men of Letters Series*. Harrison tactful about Ruskin's mental condition; praises the writer and his art, not his theories.

————. "Matthew Arnold and Harrison: The Prophet of Culture and the Prophet of Positivism." *Studies in English Literature: 1500−1900* 2 (1962):441−62. Stresses the similarity between Arnold's Culture and Harrison's Positivism. Notes the irony that Harrison should be remembered in the pages of a book that he had attacked.

————. "More Light on *Essays and Reviews*: The Role of Frederic Harrison." *Victorian Periodicals Review* 12 (Fall 1979):105−16. A well-documented exploration of Harrison's motives in writing "Neo-Christianity" and the circumstances surrounding the intricate affair of the publication of *Essays and Reviews* and its aftermath.

Webb, Sydney and Beatrice. *The History of Trade Unionism* (1894). Reprint New York: Augustus M. Kelley, Publisher, 1965. In this monumental work on the history of English Trade Unionism, the Webbs have much to say about the role of Harrison in the successful efforts to pass legislation to legalize unions and to protect the rights of working people in England. Harrison had much to do with the legal problems involved.

Whitaker, Thomas. *Comte and Mill.* In *Philosophers Ancient and Modern.* New York: Dodge Publishing Company, n.d. Perhaps the best study of the relationship between these two philosophers, as well as a good exposition of their respective theories.

Windelband, Wilhelm. *A History of Philosophy.* Translated by James H. Tufts. Harper Torchbooks. New York: Harper & Brothers, Publishers, 1958. Includes a survey of Comte's leading ideas and their relation to the thought of the nineteenth century. One of the most authoritative histories of philosophy.

Index

(The works of Harrison used in this volume are listed under his name.)

192
H319

115 471